D0513373

England in the Age of CHAUCER

Already published

ENGLAND IN THE AGE OF HOGARTH by Derek Jarrett

William Woods

England in the Age of CHAUCER

BOOK CLUB ASSOCIATES
LONDON

This edition published 1976 by Book Club Associates
By arrangement with Granada Publishing Ltd
Frogmore, St Albans, Hertfordshire AL2 2NF and
3 Upper James Street, London W1R 4BP

Copyright © 1976 by William Woods

All rights reserved. No part of this publication may be reproduced, stored in a retrieval system, or transmitted, in any form or by any means, electronic, mechanical, photocopying, recording or otherwise, without the prior permission of the publisher.

Printed in Great Britain by
Butler & Tanner Ltd, Frome and London

To the memory of Professor W. F. Thrall
of Chapel Hill, who many years ago first
taught me to love Chaucer

CONTENTS

CHAPTER ONE

A FAIRE FELDE FUL OF FOLKE

It is unlikely, one would think, but nevertheless a fact, that fourteenth-century England, though it differed in almost every superficial respect from the England we know, was in many essentials remarkably the same.

Its problems were notably similar. It witnessed the decline of empire, and became aware of a circumscription in the practical powers of government. It suffered an almost unparalleled monetary inflation, a terrible increase in lawlessness, and a rise in the influence of certain mercantile groups as powerful in fourteenth-century terms as today's multinational corporations. It witnessed the gradual breaking up of great estates, an enormous increase in taxes, the birth of a sense of power in the working classes, an improvement in the standard of living and the gradual turning of workers–the primary producers–into consumers.

It became aware that the church which, like the science we have worshipped, had once seemed to be pregnant with answers to every perplexity under the sun, could not actually solve the really important questions any more than modern science can. As the century progressed, although material wealth and individual comfort increased, so–as with us–did expectations. Higher pay for what was often diminished effort meant that the quality of workmanship declined. And all these things bred a fear in many quarters that the good and noble days were past, the problems too diverse to be overcome, the future uncertain in the extreme.

More important than any of this, the Englishman had by then evolved and become a type that has not changed in the six hundred years intervening. His dislike of rhetoric and flourishes, his seemingly phlegmatic reaction to circumstance, his manner of reasoning, his pride in nationality, his sense almost in the blood since the days of the Saxon folk-moot

A*

that he possessed certain inalienable rights under what Langland calls 'the might of the commons', these were already recognizably English. And for reasons which will gradually become apparent, he already had in his bones a stubborn conviction which he has not yet lost, that in spite of much evidence to the contrary, he was in some indefinable way a bolder and a juster man, and lived a better life than did his neighbours across the water.

It was only three hundred years since the great invasions had ended. They had culminated in the gutting of the country by a clique of powerful Norman marauders and the division of England into two classes, one a strong, centralized governing body determined to squeeze every penny of profit it could out of the conquest, and the other subjects powerless to do anything except mutinously to start the long process of assimilation.

Whereas in the early centuries after Hastings, the lord spoke Norman-French and the vassal an early English after the manner of Harold and his thanes, whereas in the late eleventh century the power lay in the hands of an Anglo-Norman elite under the leadership of a stubborn king and a shrewd and ubiquitous oligarchy, by the fourteenth century, not only could a great poet write in a tongue which had become an amalgam of both languages, possessing many of the virtues of each, but the very state had changed. Edward III might levy taxes to pursue his interminable war with France, but his anglicized henchmen had become able to control both policy and expenditure in a manner which their predecessors would have found all but impossible.

How this came about, how the indigenous tradition gradually absorbed men and women who thought it had been swept aside is beyond the scope of this book. It may have been the very rapacity of the Normans that kept the memory of Englishness alive.

Edmer, the twelfth-century monk of Canterbury, sets down many a story to make plain what fear and loathing the conquerors inspired. He tells, for example, how people fled into the woods whenever the king and his entourage travelled into a district, how the knights plundered whatever they found, devoured the provisions in people's houses, washed their horses' hooves in the drink, or forced owners to carry their goods to market so that money could be seized instead of property. Wives were ravished in front of their husbands, barelegged peasant daughters in the sight of their fathers. And the king's court was perpetually on the move.

If a Norman was murdered, says Richard of Ely (who died in 1194), and the murderer not known, the entire district had to be fined.

But if the victim was English the law ought to be more lenient, for an Englishman might very well be a serf, and no Hundred could be punished *en masse* for the death of a villein. In 1132 there had been rumours of a plot to kill every Norman in the kingdom, all on a single day, and whether or not such a plan existed, the talk of it expressed the almost universal wish. We forget that the now faceless dead were as intense and bloody-minded as we, the living. And as a result of that bloody-mindedness, 'How many have had their eyes plucked out', writes Goscelin, the French monk of Canterbury, 'so that the light of the world is a prison to them!'

In a word, for perhaps two hundred and fifty years after the Conquest England remained two nations, and in a thousand rustic hamlets tales were handed down from father to son of beautiful, half-forgotten days when English kings like the great Alfred had wandered amongst common folk, as unpretentious and forgetful as any simple rustic who might have let his wife's cakes burn in the oven. Edward, Earl Godwin and a good many other heroes were suddenly found to have been of peasant origin, and legends began to be believed of dead and long-buried English lords who were not dead in fact, but would rise at some desperate time to scatter the invader.

Arthur was one of these—Geoffrey of Monmouth first gave the legends wide currency about 1136—and even in the twentieth century I have met an old Welshman whose grandfather had stumbled into Arthur's cave where the king and his warriors lay sleeping. Havelok, the Dane, was another. Harold was said actually not to have been killed at Hastings. Robin Hood roamed Sherwood forest and robbed rich prelates. Hereward the Wake had led a rising against the Conqueror, and he too passed into folklore, so that the stubborn but impoverished peasant kept alive in his imagination well into the Middle Ages—like the Welsh, the Basques or the twentieth-century Poles—a sense of his own integrity and of his membership in a defeated, but potentially resurgent nation.

By the time Geoffrey Chaucer came to be born, probably about 1340, the population of England was, as nearly as we can judge, a little over four million. For nearly three hundred years the mortality had been so heavy that numbers had grown by only about one and a half per cent a year. Even at the end of the nineteenth century infant mortality in agricultural communities was 138·8 per 1,000 males. What it had been in the fourteenth we can only imagine.

Thus in the countless hamlets of which the country was largely composed, growth had been all but imperceptible. According to the poll tax records of 1377, the adult population of Hereford was only 1,403, of Leicester, 2,101, of Lincoln, 3,412, of Southampton, 1,152, and of the great city of York, only 7,248, though these figures of course relate to a time after the plague. London itself seems to have had a population of only about 40,000. Most people, however, were isolated in rustic settlements, in groups of anything from twenty to a hundred souls.

As late as 1340 there was, practically speaking, no property other than landed property, no work other than rural work. So the economic basis of the state—at least at the start of our period—was not the merchant or the man of money or the owner of what we know as capital goods, but the landed proprietor.

The virgin forests that covered almost a third of the country, the deeply rutted roads, knee-deep in winter snow and spring mud, dusty cart tracks in summer, the unbridged streams that often flooded into low-lying fields, the need to beware of outlaws and marauders, all these made travel dangerous and not to be undertaken lightly. So the vast majority spent their lives in whatever hamlet they happened to have been born in, and well over half were *adscripti glebae*, serfs, villeins, *nativi*, bound by birth and by the possession of Saxon blood to the lord of some particular manor. To that lord who owned the land they lived on they owed both obedience and, at least in theory, all that they earned or ever possessed. Not only this. On many specified days of the year they were required to work for him without wages, as though in part settlement of a debt for having been born into an inferior status in the first place.

And this was most emphatically not a mere form of words, for, according to law, serfdom was in the blood. There had been a time in England when a girl could be bought for as little as 2s. 10d., or perhaps £30 in modern money, the price of eight sucking pigs. Indeed, the parallel is not unapt, for a villein was neither more nor less valuable than the beast he worked with. 'A bond serving wench is bought and sold like an animal', writes Bartholomew, the twelfth-century Bishop of Exeter. '[She] is beaten with rods, tied down and held there with many and contrary fines.'

One Thomas Cusin of Sherborne was charged in 1244 with having dragged a certain Gunilda de Stokes out into a field by force, and then seized all her goods. So Gunilda had her assailant brought before the justices (and it was only old Saxon folk custom that enabled her to do so). There Cusin admitted the truth of her accusation. He did not even claim that he had thrown her out because she was a bad tenant or in arrears with her rent. He simply said that she was his villein, her property was his, and that by right of lordship he had evicted her from a holding. The jury agreed that he had acted within his rights, and Gunilda's complaint was dismissed.

Or there was Henry de Vere (note that both these attackers have Norman names) who stormed into the house of a villein of his one night 'with a torch of wax lighted, being carried before him', and demanded physical possession of the man's daughter, who had been promised him. But the girl's mother had managed to get her out and away through a window, and when de Vere discovered this, he set his torch to the barn and burned it as well as the corn that had been stored there to the ground. At the court hearing it came to light that the daughter had just married, and that de Vere knew it. But she had married without his consent, and this she had no legal right to do.[1] In burning down the barn, he had simply been imposing salutary discipline. 'Like a willow,' said the proverb, 'the villein sprouts the better for being cropped.'

The laws and indeed the customs having to do with villeinage were not only complex, but various in the extreme. They had their origins in Saxon and Roman slavery, and also in the vassalage under which the lords and the great landowners had in past ages lent what was known as 'war gear' to their dependents for use in whatever struggles the lord might be engaged. If most serfs were of Saxon origin, that was only natural. They were descendants of a subject nation. William had given the landed estates to his Norman adherents, and with these had gone whatever tenants were attached to them. He had decreed, furthermore, that any man who had fought against him at Hastings should be a serf, he and his children for ever. Even today the language bears witness to the fact that the Saxon Englishman herded the *cows*, the *calves*, the *pigs*, the *sheep*, but that the Norman landlord ate them and in so doing translated them into *beef, veal, pork* and *mutton.*

Indeed, most things the peasant handled or worked with are known today by words Saxon in origin. He tilled the Saxon ground, used Saxon ploughs. He sowed, he reaped, handled fork, spade, harrow, hook. His crop came home out of the earth at harvest time, and was made up out of the six Germanically named products, corn, oats, rye, barley, wheat and hay.

The colours of his world, too, had Saxon names–blue, red, yellow, green, brown, and of course black and white. His chickens laid Saxon eggs containing Saxon yolks. The leaf, the bark, the sap, the wood and root of a tree were all Saxon in nomenclature. It was the Normans, on the other hand, who dressed in subtler colours, in violet, orange, cherry and crimson. It was the Norman who talked in generic terms, of vegetables, of forests, of cultivation, of the peasant himself–as opposed to the workman–and to do so he used words Latin in origin.

As we have seen, a serf might not marry off his daughter without the lord's consent, and for that consent he would be required to 'buy his blood', i.e. to pay what was called *merchet*, which might amount to eight or ten shillings, almost half a ploughman's annual wage. He might not grind his own corn except at the lord's mill. If he could not or would not do so, he paid a sixpenny fine for going elsewhere. If the lord's miller was busy, or the water low, he might have to wait two or three days. One abbot of St Albans went further. Whenever he found handmills in his serfs' possession, he confiscated them to pave his private parlour. If a man did go to the lord's mill, the grinding generally cost a sixteenth of the crop, and millers were notorious thieves. 'What is the bravest thing on earth?' ran a riddle. And the answer: 'A miller's shirt, for it clasps a rogue by the throat daily.' A free man, on the other hand, was required to pay only a twenty-fourth, and in time of shortage the fractions were obviously more valuable than when the crop was a good one.

A villein might not cut wood for his fire except 'by hook or by crook' after he had paid his wood penny. In other words, he might not use an axe to collect firewood. He might not fatten his pigs on the lord's acorns without paying his 'mast penny', or bake bread in any but the lord's oven after paying for that privilege too. And how valuable his pig was to him we can gather from the fact that we still store food in what is called a larder.

He might not kill pigeons, even if they devastated his crops. Pigeons were too valuable. In 1339 the dovecote of the monks of Pontoise produced four cartloads of dung for the abbey farm, and in 1491 the monks sold more than 4,500 birds for the table. In 1379 a dovecote at Blyth priory was estimated as being worth 10*s.*, or half the price of a water-mill.

A villein might not kill hares, even if they fed in his garden. The parishioners of West Wittering in Sussex complained that their wheat had been overrun year after year by the Bishop of Chichester's rabbits (rabbits had been imported from France in the thirteenth century), and that the damage had amounted to £7 6s. 8d. A hundred acres had been annihilated by the rabbits of Earl Warrenne. It made no difference; it was proper for 'lewede men to laborie, and lordes to honte', says

Langland, and it was clearly normal for wild beasts to feed on the peasants' flocks, for 'the wolf shiteth woolle'.[2] The Prior of Durham commanded that no tenants should keep dogs that might chase game on pain of a fine of 6s. 8d.

The serf must fold cattle on the lord's land, at least for a certain part of the year, to manure it; indeed, even manure in the road belonged to the lord. If the serf wanted to keep poultry he had to pay for the privilege in chickens or eggs. If his son went to be taught by the priest, he had to pay a fee to the lord who permitted it, and in time even that was prohibited, for according to a statute of Richard II it was 'ordained and assented that he or she which used to labour at the Plough or Cart, or other Labour or Service of Husbandry till they be of the Age of Twelve years, that from henceforth they shall abide at the same Labour, without being put to any Mystery or Handicraft; and if any Covenant or Bond of Apprentie be from henceforward made to the contrary, the same shall be holden for none'.[3] And the point to bear in mind is that almost all we know about the serf, about his supposed ugliness or idleness, about his incompetence and ignorance, comes out of the mouth of his oppressor. The villein is mute, and in the rare instances when a literate serf escaped into freedom, even into power or affluence (and there were bishops and archdeacons among them), he remained silent about his past.

But the age could not be made to stand still. The ferment was already working, and by 1406, according to the Statute of Artificers, 'Every man or woman, no matter of what state or condition, shall be free to set son or daughter to take learning at any school that pleaseth him within the realm.'

These various fines and prohibitions were not all, however. At the year's end the serf had to pay a tenth of his harvest to the priest in tithes, and since this tithe was actually collected in bundles off the fields, and was thus a gross yield, it cost him about twenty per cent of his net earnings. Then there were the 'ales' he was required to attend (and pay for), the Whitsun ale, the scot ale, the hock ale, the play ale, all of them profitable either to priest or landlord, to bailiff or forester who held them.

And when at last he died, the heirs paid his best beast to the lord as heriot, what had originally been the *hergeat*, the 'war gear' which he had presumably been lent when he came of age. But since war gear no longer existed, the lord took his best beast instead, or, if he owned no beast, a sum of money to take its place. Sometimes the heriot was defined as a third of all movable property.

On one manor in 1414, not only was the best beast led away. The lord took all copper vessels too, all carts, hives, sides of bacon, porkers and uncut woollen cloth. There is a record dated 1347 of a widow who lost her horse and cart, a sheep, two pigs, and had to buy them back for 12s., which would have amounted to about a year's wages. Even then the poor creature was not done. For after the lord was satisfied, the priest made charges too. He not only demanded a penny for the mass, but the second best beast as well–for mortuary, a tax levied in lieu of tithes which a dead man had presumably withheld from the church while he was alive.

We have understood [wrote Bishop Quivel in the *Decrees* of Exeter (1287)] that the rendering of mortuaries arose from this healthy source, that...tithes, when they have through ignorance remained unpaid, should be handed over to the churches thus defrauded, so that forgetfulness... might at least be excused before the face of the ultimate judge. Yet some, careless of their salvation, have withheld them, and thus handed on their spiritual wretchedness to their posterity. What a miserable excuse for those who do not admit the debt! It is an excuse bred in sin, and it leads the excuser only to destruction.

Of course, conditions were not everywhere the same. The varieties of soil, the yields, the crops themselves, the sizes of holdings, the very nature of the villeinage, what was called 'the custom of the manor' differed from place to place, from county to county, and so far as conditions of service were concerned, from decade to decade.

There were impecunious lords, for example, eager to exchange services for a money rent, and they gradually established precedents that tended to erode the whole manorial system. There were peasants able to buy manumission, though this cost about £8 or, in the early years of the century, something like seven years' income. A woman might escape bondage by marrying a freeman, but this was not secure, for she reverted to bondage on the death of her husband. A man could become free by proving himself a bastard, for, as I have said, serfdom ran in the blood. A man might simply run away as though out of an open prison–to the woods or to one of the royal boroughs. Indeed, customs were so various, circumstances on the many hundreds of manors so different that it is all but impossible to lay down hard and fast rules.

In cases of dispute–and the thousands of court records have not all been examined even now–in cases, for example, where the peasant denied villeinage because one of his parents had been free, or when he argued that he was not in fact attached to a particular manor (for he could

Above Harrowing. The peasant leads his horse – short-legged and heavily built like all northern horses that had not yet been interbred with the long-legged Arabs. His wife carries stones and a sling to scatter the rooks. From the Luttrell Psalter. (The Mansell Collection)

Below Ploughing with oxen. The wife walks ahead with a goad, and except for some differences in detail, the drawing reminds one strongly of a scene in *Piers the Plowman's Crede*. (The Mansell Collection)

Above The harvest, cut and tied, being piled for carting away. The peasants' faces look haggard and almost brutalized. (The Mansell Collection)

Below The harvest, roped into a cart, being pulled up a steep hill. No sense of perspective, but a great eye for detail. Metal studs on wheels and horses' hooves help them along the muddy roads. (The Mansell Collection)

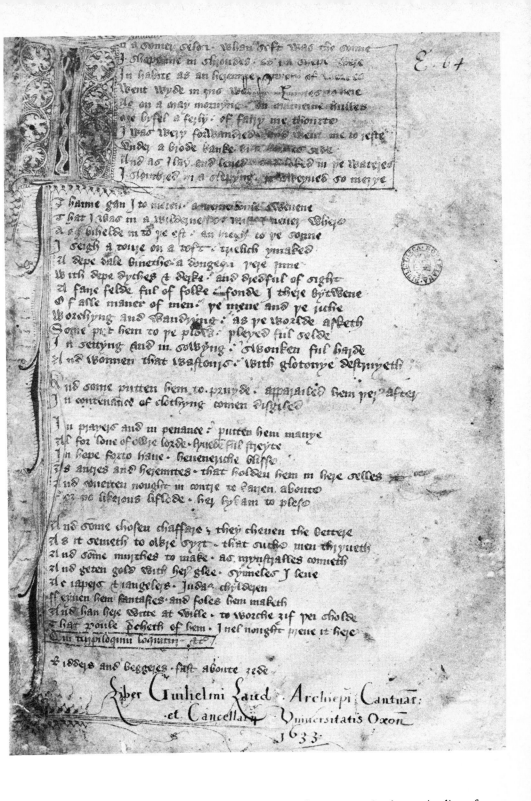

First page of the famous MS Laud Misc. 581 in the Bodleian Library. It contains the opening lines of *Piers Plowman,* and Skeat, who knew whereof he wrote, was of the opinion that the corrections were so meticulous that this was very likely Langland's own manuscript. (Bodleian Library, Oxford)

Above The peasant at work, reaping, sowing, digging and scything hay. (The Master and Fellows of Trinity College, Cambridge)

be the serf only of a specified owner or his heirs), or when he claimed to have lived the statutory year and a day in a chartered town or Royal Demesne and thereby gained his freedom–in most such cases English courts found on the side of individual liberty. William of Wykeham's need for ready cash to found New College freed many a serf. The Black Death of 1349 and its subsequent visitations all during the rest of the century created such a shortage of labour that landlords became willing to pay almost any price to gather harvests which, without payment, would not have been gathered at all.

So conditions varied enormously. Nevertheless, if only to make the bare bones come alive, we must look at some not untypical village and see what it was like to be alive there.

We have to imagine a little cluster of rickety, thatched cottages huddled round a church that looks fairly new, or else perhaps in reasonably close proximity to the manor house itself. Round each cottage lies a small patch of garden. There the peasant grows his cabbages and leeks, his onions, garlic, shallots, his bit of mustard and parsley. He may have an apple or a pear tree, or a cherry. In summer he will grow peas and beans, but no root vegetables, no carrots or potatoes, no turnips or beet, because these have not yet been imported.

The cottage (he will often have built it himself) will be of wattle and daub, hardly ever of stone, and indeed we read of 'decrepit hovels with rotten beams and half ruined walls'. In 1426 a certain William Found was charged with having run away and actually carried his cottage with him. Geoffrey Whitring's cottage in Littleport is described in 1325 as being 24 ft long and 11 ft wide. Whitring lived there with his wife, his son and whatever animals he happened to own.[4] In 1293 three cottages belonging to the Priory of Bridlington were valued at twenty shillings, or £200 in modern money, all three. A few years later a sheep house was valued by the same priory at £3 6s. 4d., and a dovecote at £6 13s. 4d. And yet, strangely enough, in spite of their fragility, many of these cottages survived and were inhabited well into the nineteenth century.

Whatever the building's size or value, it never had a chimney, and there was no glass in the windows. But if the peasant had been a careful workman he would have made wooden shutters to be fitted into the window apertures when it rained and taken away in dry weather or when the smoke from the fire indoors had become unbearable.

According to Bromyard, the fourteenth-century lecturer at Cambridge, the cat sat in front of the hearth and 'often burned her hips'. And no sooner had the housewife sprinkled and swept the earthen floor than in came the barnyard fowl and scratched it up until it was as filthy as before.

The cottage would be divided into two rooms, one generally a stable, the other for human habitation. And we may catch a hint what it was like in practical terms to live one's life, to go courting, to do business, to find even enough privacy for quarrelling when Hardy writes of such cottages that 'it was the custom...to discuss matters of pleasure and ordinary business inside the house, and to reserve the garden for very important affairs which, as is supposed, originated in the desirability of getting away at such times from the other members of the family when there was only one room for living in'.[5] As long as two hundred and fifty years after Chaucer, Bishop Hall describes such a place:

> *Of one baye's breadth, God wot! a silly cote,*
> *Whose thatched sparres are furr'd with sluttish soote*
> *A whole inch thick, shining like black-moor's brows...*
> *At his bed's head, feeding his stalled teme,*
> *His swine beneath, his pullen ore the beame,*
> *A starved tenement, such as I gesse*
> *Stands stragling in the wasts of Holdernesse.*[6]

Soot an inch thick on the head-high ceiling! 'Our fathers,' Harrison wrote two hundred years afterwards, 'yea, and we ourselves also have lien full oft upon straw pallets covered onelie with a sheet, under coverlets made of dogswain [a coarse and shaggy fabric] or hopharlots [like harlots, they kept one warm, but were of no permanent value] (I use their owne terms), and a good round log under their heads in stead of a bolster...Pillowes (said they) were thought meet onelie for women in childbed. As for servants, if they had anie sheet above them, it was well, for seldome had they anie under their bodies, to keepe them from the pricking straws that ran oft through the canvas and rased their hardened hides.'[7]

'In times past,' he says elsewhere, 'men were contented to dwell in houses builded of sallow, willow, plumtree, hardbeame and elme, so that the use of oke was in maner dedicated wholie unto churches, religious houses, princes palaces, noblemens lodgings and navigation: but now all these are rejected, and nothing but oke anie whit regarded. And yet see the change, for when our houses were builded of willow, then had we oken men; but now that our houses are come to be made of oke, our men are not onlie become willow, but a great manie (through Persian deli-

cacie crept in among us) altogither of straw, which is a sore alteration...
Now have we manie chimnies; and yet our tenderlings complaine of
rheumes, catarhs and poses. Then had we none but reredosses; and our
heads did never ake.'[8]

Perhaps not, for Harrison prided himself on being tough as old leather.
But Master Rypon of Durham draws a vivid picture in one of his fourteenth-century sermons of the sick who lie awake in the straw, listening
hour after hour for cockcrow, and who, when it comes, feel easier, for
they know that daylight is near.

At meal time, bread and ale for breakfast; in the middle of the day,
bread again, perhaps cheese, an onion and a mug of ale, and at night a
pottage, a sort of vegetable broth served with more cheese–and bread to
be used as a spoon. Trenchers and bowls had been carved out of wood
on winter nights, along with the handles to scythes, rakes and shovels,
and flails made out of holly or blackthorn. The peasant had plaited his
baskets during the winter too, and stitched away at leather jugs and bot-
tles, or plugged them if they leaked.

In an inventory dated 1301 a peasant's tools are listed as a hoe, a
spade, an axe, a billhook, two yokes for buckets and a barrel, total
value 10*d*. One peasant's will has been recorded wherein the widow
received three shillings, three farthings in cash and a cow worth five
shillings more. The funeral expenses, including food and drink,
wiped out the entire inheritance.[9]

Yet, as Coulton so charmingly points out, it was not all darkness.[10]
Robust and homely he calls the 'moist and corny aile' of Chaucer's
England–though without hops (for they had none) it must have been
rather sweet. And who would not like to have hobnobbed with
Walter Mustard, he asks, with John Stoutlook and Gilbert Uncouth
of Durham, or danced on the green with Agnes Redhead or Alice
Dobinsdoughter, or–if I might add another good name–to have held
Maud Malkynsmaydin's sweaty little hand at twilight along some sun-
warmed road? Who would not willingly have bobbed for apples with
Watsdoughter at Christmas, so simple, so undistinguished a wench,
Coulton remarks, that not even her Christian name has come down to
us?

But–peace to Coulton's shade–Watsdoughter, with her lovely hair,
bright as a new penny, was a little girl of eleven or twelve. In the normal,
animal way she would have married and turned herself into a drudge
by the time she was thirteen and had breasts, and a year, or perhaps only
a few months later have started the long, sad sickness, the bearing and

burying of children that would probably last for the rest of her short life. Maud Malkynsmaydin or Watsdoughter or Agnes Redhead–call her what you please–was haggard in her twenties and in her grave by what we should think of as middle age.

Coulton chose a few names that delight us with their vividness, but all we need if we want to be teased is to read Hardy again, who knew almost the selfsame villagers five hundred years later, a little better off, to be sure, a little longer lived, just quaint enough to make us sigh with nostalgia, and just simple enough to make us envious.

But even in Hardy's more modern world, Tess was hanged for murdering her lover, Marty South sold her hair to get money, Jude was sickened by poverty and the hopelessness of his aspirations, young Henchard sold his wife in a fairground, and over and over again the innocent and enviable people were twisted by ignorance, a sense of their own limitations and a world too complicated for them to understand.

Of course, there was joy in the fourteenth century too. We have to imagine the children sent out in troops to pick fruit in the orchard, the cries, the quarrels, the laughter, the ten-year-old girl perched bare-legged in the boughs and tossing apples down to whoever is holding the basket. We have to imagine the children, brother and sister perhaps, herding a half-dozen goats, who when they hear some traveller perhaps a mile away on the road, come pelting as hard as their legs will go to stand and gape and give hesitant little waves at the stranger going by out of the wide world.

We have to imagine the housewife, all lean muscle and watchful eyes, coming slowly up from the well with water in two buckets yoked over her shoulders, or the barefooted, dusty girl with a pitcher on her hip, who stops to talk to someone driving a flock of hissing geese in the lane. We have to think of autumn mornings heavy with mist, the gulping noise of greedy sows, the peasant calling to his sons across the dawn-dark garden to remember mattock or hoe, the wife, face pale as cheese and heavy with sleep, but yoked and clanking with those same buckets on her way out to milk the cow, its tail already flapping against the flies.

In summertime she rose at three. Work was what hands were made for; legs were for walking, bodies for bearing loads. Nothing in the world ought ever to be wasted. And not ten minutes ago, daughter Joan had still been lying beside her young man, naked as a nail in the straw, muscular, but still supple, smiling at promises.

On spring mornings the warm earth steams behind the plough, and deep in the woods there are cobwebs shining with dew. On summer twilights the dry-witted forester stops to look back at the trees he has felled and lopped, work done, never to be undone, and reaches down for the leather bottle of ale he has left stowed in the bracken. On his walk homeward he will hear the frightened flapping of wings at his approach, where birds had already gone to roost along the path.

No, it is not all darkness, though death came earlier. The countryman knew trees by their touch, and St John's Wort was not only a flower, but medicine. He and the badger, the hart, the polecat watched each other and knew each other's habits. He knew by the sound when an invisible, careless fox in the forest had stepped on a dry twig. Our urban generation that cannot even tell south from north in the dark by the smell of the wind would have seemed to him mightily ignorant. Birdsong was louder, for it had less to compete with, and the ridiculous mole left a hill indoors in front of the very hearth. Not all darkness, but little help for toothache or tiredness, less for fevers that carried off children and grown men.

What none of the historians ever quite says–and some of them have loved the Middle Ages deeply, and known about them in great detail–is how people were shaped by their environments, that these men and women had better eyes and ears than we because they needed them, that a man's work, his very station in society showed in his hands, and that the slow turn of the seasons was not only necessary, but, because it was necessary, looked to him more vivid than we can easily imagine.

The wind blew and made a sound in the trees like a hundred neighbours threshing. Sometimes the winter rain came down day after day. One heard it pelting into the thatch at night, and at work it crept into every crack in one's clothing. Yet after the months of salted meat, after the bitter cold,

Sumer is icumen in,
Lhude sing cuccu!
Groweth sed and bloweth med,
And springeth the wud nu.

The Prologue to *The Canterbury Tales* begins with the sweet showers of April that have made the first sap rise, with the time when the small birds chirrup that sleep with one eye open all night long. To start his *Piers Plowman*, Langland goes wandering on a May morning. In *The Book of the Duchess* we read of the little birds in May that sing, some high, some low, their positively festive service, the cloudless air all bright and blue and clear, the thick, sweet grass tangible underfoot. The anonymous author of *Sir Gawain* tells us how in autumn,

> *The leaves loosen from the lime tree and light on the ground.*
> *Then all grays the grass that green was ere;*
> *And all ripeth and rotteth that rose up at first,*
> *And the year yearns away with its yesterdays many,*
> *Till winter winds again...*

The author of *Pearl* loses his daughter in a green garden in the August high season when men are cutting corn, when the clove-scented pinks, the ginger and peonies are 'powdered all between'. And whoever wrote *The Parlement of the Thre Ages* about 1350 begins by telling how he went out to hunt the deer on a hot May morning, and the green grass was overgrown with primroses, periwinkles and wild thyme. Dew dripped from the daisies. Cuckoos and wood pigeons called, and throstles jangled in the brakes. For a hundred lines he sings almost effortlessly like one of his own birds, about the fox and the polecat fleeing to earth at his approach, the hare hastening to its burrow while he, preparing a hide, covers himself and his bow with leaves, his eyes perpetually on the watch as the mild mist rises, for the hart he will eventually carry home.

April, May, high summer, but rarely, except in a few lyrics, a poem about the cold. Only now and then do we hear the sound of the cruel intruding on celebrations of the delightful. 'Costly the fire in hardest of the year', wrote the old priest Barclay in the fifth of his eclogues. And that was a hundred and more years later. 'When men have moste nede, then everything is dere.'

> *The winter snowes, all couered is the grounde,*
> *The north wind blowes sharpe & with ferefull sound,*
> *The longe ise sicles at the ewes hang,*
> *The streame is frosen, the night is cold & long,*
> *Where botes [boats] rowed nowe cartes haue passage,*
> *From yoke the oxen be losed and bondage*
> *The ploweman resteth auoyde of businesse,*
> *Saue when he tendeth his harnes for to dresse,*
> *Mably his wife sitteth before the fyre*
> *All blacke and smoky clothed in rude attire,*
> *Sething some grewell...*[11]

But the poets rarely sit or stir gruel in front of the fire. Mostly they sing love, the sweet torment of the unobtainable. They sing the Virgin,

Jesus on the cross, the ale house, the street cries in town, the fighting, the herbs piled in a student's chamber, the greed of millers, the song on the rebeck or guitar, the ladies' hats, the carpenter's young wife, straight as a pear tree, her body sleek as a weasel, soft as wool, with a fillet in her hair. Her eye is lecherous, her mouth tastes of apples, and it is a splendid thought to lie between her legs.

Women, wine, music and the May morning, an English broader, richer-vowelled, more rhythmical, more pungent than our own. Summer, good ale, the love of age for youth, bawdy humour, all universals. Yet so isolated were these little clusters of people that except for merchants or the royal entourage endlessly travelling in rich coats and hoods, or the thousands of itinerant friars whose arrival was announced with a barking of dogs, few Englishmen and certainly no peasant ever in his life knew by sight more than two or three hundred souls. And since the peasant could not read (it has been estimated that only ten or fifteen per cent of the population was literate), not only was his vocabulary limited to about six hundred words, but without schools, without books, without experience of any wider world, he had to learn whatever he knew by word of mouth. In fact, over a hundred years afterwards Caxton set down a story that illustrates perhaps more clearly than any other how linguistically isolated each section of the country was.

Common English, [he writes in his preface to *Eneydos*] that is spoken in one shire varies from that in another. So much so that in my day it happened that certain merchants took ship in the Thames to have sailed over the sea to Zeeland. But for lack of wind they tarried at the foreland and went on land to refresh themselves. One of them, a mercer named Sheffield, went into a house and asked for food. And especially he asked for some eggs. But the good wife answered that she could speak no French.

At this the merchant was angry, for he could speak no French either. But he wanted eggs [egges] and she understood him not. Then at last another asked to be given 'eyren' and the good wife understood him well. Lo, what ought a man write in these days, egges or eyren? Certainly it is hard to please every man by reason of the diversity and change in the language.

And if this was true in 1490 when Caxton wrote, when after the long turmoils men had been crisscrossing the country for a century, how much more true a hundred or a hundred and fifty years earlier? London, for all the peasant knew, might have been as far as Jerusalem, and his own market town, whatever it was, the only metropolis in the world.

We have to understand how the very face of England has been altered during the six hundred years since these people were alive. Today we travel past copses and hedged fields, past gardens, woodland, stretches of pasture. But Chaucer's England would have looked to us as wild and vast as parts of the African veldt, for of course the tiny population cultivated only what it needed. Between settlements there lay nothing except huge tracts of fenland, moor and forest, and the settlements themselves must have looked like nothing so much as clusters of hayricks perched round the newly built churches, glowing with freshly chiselled stone.

How did they spend their year, those villeins? The main crops (as I have already mentioned) were wheat, oats, rye and barley, and to these we must add vetches, peas and beans. A man carried his seed out to the narrow, furrow-long strips in a sack, and then poured a certain amount of it into a basket hung round his neck.

From this he sowed broadcast with long sweeps of the arm to right and left as he walked. After that came the harrowing—for those who could afford it, with a toothed, wooden frame, for those who could not, with a bush harrow pulled by a horse or an ox, and a boy walking alongside to throw stones at the birds. After that came ditching and draining, the ploughing of fallow land and, in June, the haymaking. Each man was in duty bound to go first to the lord's fields, to seize the best weather for these. His own had to wait. And the hay had not only to be cut (an acre a day with the little scythes they used); it had to be turned as well, perhaps two or three times, then loaded and carted home.

After that came hoeing of thistles and docks, the second ploughing of the fallow, gathering hemp and flax, rotting it, cleaning and hanging it on strikes to dry. Then followed what were known as the 'boon days'. From the end of July until Michaelmas the villein not only had to spend two days more a week in his lord's fields than at other times, but if these were not enough, he gave up extra days of his own free will as a boon. During the harvest his whole family would go out to work with him. It was four to reap and one to bind, and every such team was expected to clear two acres a day.

When winter came there was work to do on the manor house or barns. Fences had to be repaired, ditches cleared and manure carried to the fields. There were stakes and hurdles to be made and hedges to be layered, most often not on his own land, but on his master's.

We can do no more than conjecture about the intangibles. At best we extrapolate from other evidence or from our grandparents' memories. For not only the daily round, but the very cast of rural thought did not actually change until the turn of the present century. So a man unused to using words expressed himself with his body instead. If we cannot hear what our city neighbour says we have little idea what he thinks. The fourteenth-century peasant expressed a canny watchfulness by narrowing his eyes into chinks. He gaped at the unexpected. His face widened when he was satisfied, narrowed when he was angry. He puffed out his lips when he called up a philosophy too deep for words, his cheeks when something struck him as funny. Indeed, the word buffoon, from the French *bouffer*, means one who puffs out his cheeks. He decapitated flowers with his stick as he strode along the lane, and by the arc of the casual blows a knowledgeable observer could have told almost to a 'T' what he had in his mind. Everything about him was broader, just as today, humour in the country turns to irony in the town. And the words used even now to describe this rustic are pejorative words–yokel, lout, churl, oaf, clod (or clot, which is earlier), servant (or serf), even villain, to indicate the contempt in which his contemporaries held him.

Corn, cattle, sickness, the minutiae of work, these were the stand-bys of ordinary talk, for corn, cattle and work were what made the hamlet move. They were the machinery of existence. The sun was his clock, the season his calendar, and nothing existed that did not have a venerable history. The metaphors he used, the similes through which he saw things, were none of them invented. They were derived out of the world he knew, that of animals and the things he made with his hands.

Thus, one is dead as a doornail, sly as a fox, quick as a cat, proud as a cock on a dunghill, has a voice like a crow, eats like a horse, is fat as a pig. And of course, even after six hundred years such phrases are still part of the language, for they were invented just at the time the English language was being formed, not by men in towns, but by the rustic to whom they were a kind of verbal shorthand.

The countryman was a cautious man. In field and furrow he had seen too many a slip betwixt cup and lip, and he knew by experience that a pitcher was in danger if it went too often to the well. More important, a man's work gave him many of his individual characteristics. Indeed, his work, or where he lived were often the only things that identified him, and the modern Welsh 'Jones, the milk' or 'Griffiths, the bread' are precisely the same as the medieval John Atwood or John Richardson, or indeed, Gilbert Uncouth. Conversely, Watsdoughter or sweaty, barefooted

Malkynsmaydin had brown arms and cheeks because she worked in the fields, and it has taken six hundred years for a healthy tan to come back into fashion. When the girl who pitched hay had a ruddy face, one had to indicate one's higher social standing by being elegantly pale.

The manure on a peasant's holding was never enough for his fields, and the technique of rotation was imperfectly understood, so yields decreased steadily during the thirteenth and fourteenth centuries. Wheat might bring back 8 bushels an acre, oats 10 and barley about 13. As Bennett has computed,[12] after the peasant had deducted the quantity of seed he would require for the following spring, after he had paid his tithe and the miller's charges, he was left with a total average grain harvest of a little over 7 bushels–or about 370 lbs–per acre.

To the modern urban Englishman this will not mean very much. But on a Welsh hill farm today–very poor land compared to some down in England–a man will grow about nine times as much. And this has nothing to do with modern harvesting machinery, but with better seed, better manuring and better protection against disease.

Then, as now, a farmer was vulnerable more than most to misfortune. Even a healthy harvest could be a mixed blessing; good years made for glut and low prices. A bad harvest, on the other hand, could reduce him to penury. So, as a dozen adages make clear, the medieval peasant had to have a keen eye, not only for the look of the weather, but for the state of his neighbour's crops.

But taking good years with bad, according to Thorold Rogers the average price of wheat during the fourteenth century was £1 3s. 7d. per hundredweight.[13] So a peasant on an average holding could expect to be paid about £1 15s. 4d. for his wheat. Barley and oats he would probably not sell at all, but store to make his own beer, bread and pottage. And these, apart from a few vegetables, were the total of what he grew. Out of that total he paid a first charge of ten per cent to the priest in tithes.

We can take it that a shilling (at least during the first half of the century) had about two hundred times its present value, so the peasant must even in good years have been continually on the brink of serious want. Even though cows and bulls cost only about 10s. a head, oxen a little more, he could rarely afford to buy one. Even though chickens cost about a penny and sheep about 1s. 5d., they too were often out of reach. The saleable part of his harvest simply left him with too little money.

The difficulty was compounded by the fact that with yields far lower than they are today, with murrains and diseases of crops far more damaging, with innumerable manorial fines and taxes to be paid, he had perforce to give up a goodly proportion of days to work on the manor that brought him no money at all. So he never had time to turn his hand to anything else. Indeed, we can appreciate his problem all the more acutely when we learn that before the time of the Black Death a ploughman–and ploughmen were paid comparatively good wages–earned a penny a day. A good dairyman, on the other hand, rarely got more than 5s. a year. A carter might see as little as 6s. 8d., or about £67 annually in modern money.

It has often been remarked that, but for the accident of language, Chaucer might very well be taken for a Frenchman. He speaks with the voice of a man of the world, of a man with experience of cities, of travel, of commerce and politics. He knew how to express subtle shades of opinion and express them both simply and poignantly. There is nothing of the old Saxon rawness in him. But his almost exact contemporary, Langland, could never have been anything but an Englishman.

Allan Bright conjectured with some degree of probability that Langland was the bastard son of some peasant girl near Ledbury, just west of the Malvern hills.[14] He was what we should today called a loner, an outsider. Almost six hundred years after his death he still sounds big with a clumsily articulated torment, and with the sort of pity that shakes one's body for the suffering he has watched. Perhaps it was his simple conservatism that made him the peasant's voice if ever there was one. He sat in the ale house with Wat and John. He worked with them dourly in the fields, argued with them sententiously and lived in the same raw poverty. But in spite of his having thumbed many books, there is a good deal of evidence that he wrote in a language that tasted like iron in their mouths.

In the perspective of old age, and during the last revision of his poem *Piers Plowman*, he set down a good deal that had disturbed, indeed, plagued him, and that he had not dared, or perhaps even been able to express when he was younger–not only about people he had known, wild and racketting characters, but about his own misspent youth, his idleness, his lusts of the flesh, his physical and spiritual hunger, his enormous expectations, quite unrealized, and the fact that in almost every respect he exemplified a way of life which he utterly abhorred.

It would be too gross a simplification to say that he felt the world had treated him unjustly. He, too, had been at fault. But now, instead of owning land or having procured advancement in the church, he lives with his wife, Kytte (he even confesses his sexual inadequacy), and a daughter, Calotte (Nicolette), in a cottage in Cornhill. He who calls himself Long Will, too tall to stoop, supports himself quite literally by singing for his supper, the *paternoster*, the *placebo* and the *dirige*, going from house to house where he is known and expected, to each perhaps once a month, and being allowed to take his proper place and eat in return for performing such offices as were permitted to one in minor orders. At night he sits with the noises of Cornhill below him in the alleys, reads, turns over innumerable authors and works at his interminable, and indeed never-to-be-finished, poem.

Now in old age he remembers with pain the hot harvest times when he had been young and his father and friends had sent him to school. 'And never, in faith, since my friends died,' he says, 'have I found a life that I liked, save in these long clothes.'[15] 'If there is heaven on earth,' he adds elsewhere, 'and ease to any soul, it is in the cloister or the school, for no man comes to a cloister to quarrel. But everything is books and obedience, reading and learning.'[16]

But he had lost time, 'tynt tyme', banged time in the face, he says. The friends have died, and so has the hope of advancement. His father seems to have forbidden him to take his name, and he can only pray that at the end God will give him a 'gobet' of his grace, and somehow turn the long misfortune to profit after all.

I shall have a good deal to say about Langland later, but I mention him here because I have to introduce him, so to speak, before I can quote some of what he has to say about the reality of life in such poor cottages as he had known.

The most needy aren oure neighebores . and we nyme good hede,
As prisones in puttes . and poure folke in cotes,
Charged with children . and chef lordes rente,
That thei with spynnynge may spare . spenen hit in hous-hyre,
Bothe in mylk and in mele . to make with papelotes,
To a-glotye with here gurles . that greden after fode.
Al-so hemselue . suffren muche hunger,
And wo in winter-tyme . with wakynge a nyghtes
To ryse to the ruel . to rocke the cradel,
Bothe to karde and to kembe . to clouten and to wasche,
To rubbe and to rely . russhes to pilie,
That reuthe is to rede . othere in ryme shewe
The wo of these women . that wonyeth in cotes;
And of meny other men . that muche wo suffren,

Bothe a-fyngrede and a-furst . to turne the fayre outwarde,
And beth abasshed for to begge . and wolle nat be aknowe
What hem nedeth at here neihebores . at non and at euen.
This ich wot witerly . as the worlde techeth,
What other by-houeth . that hath meny children,
And hath no catel bote hus crafte . to clothy hem and to fede,
And fele to fonge ther-to . and fewe pans taketh.
Ther is payn and peny-ale . as for a pytaunce y-take,
Colde flessh and cold fyssh . for veneson ybake;
Frydayes and fastyng-dayes . a ferthyng-worth of muscles
Were a feste for suche folke . other so fele cockes.
These were almes, to helpe . that han suche charges,
*And to comfortie such cotyers . and crokede men and blynde.**

As we might have expected, the manor courts were loud with complaints about these people, about their idleness, their drunkenness, their shoddy workmanship, their theft and violence. The ale house opened before the church did, and Langland himself writes about the beggars who roamed about to fill their bags and their bellies, who tricked men to get food, fought at the tavern, dropped off gluttonous to bed, God knows, and rose again only for ribaldry.[17]

Years afterwards, Skelton wrote about one Elynour Rummynge who

---

* Passages such as this may at first glance seem difficult for the modern reader, but I want to quote them in the original, first because they possess a wonderful richness and vigour as they stand, and second, because they are not actually as difficult as we may at first imagine. They were written to be read aloud, and Langland's long, alliterative line, if we pronounce every syllable and give the vowels their modern continental values, will swing along like a ripple of thunder. When, as now, his vocabulary presents difficulties, I append a literal translation in a footnote.

If we but look, the neediest are our neighbours, such as prisoners in dungeons and poor folk in cottages, burdened with children and the landlord's rent. What they scrimp by spinning, they pay out in house hire, in milk or meal for porridge to satisfy their young ones that groan aloud for food. They, themselves, suffer much hunger and woe in wintertime, what with waking at night, rising to rock the cradle, with carding and combing, patching and washing, rubbing and reeling and peeling the rushes, that a pity 'tis to read about or try to show in rhyme the misery of these women that live in little cottages, and of many other men that suffer much evil. For they are both ahungered and athirst, yet they keep up appearances. They are too abashed to beg, and will not have the neighbours know, noontime and even-time, how much they are in need. I know inside myself what the world teaches, what the fate is of him that has many children, who has nothing but his labour to clothe them with and feed them, and many to clutch at the few pence taken. There are bread and small beer in place of any charity. Cold meat and cold fish are to them like venison. On Fridays and fasting-days a farthing's worth of mussels or so many cockles would be a feast for such folk. It were alms indeed to help them that are so heavily burdened, to comfort such cottagers, and crooked men and blind. *Piers Plowman*, C. X. 71ff.

kept such an ale house near Leatherhead. We have to make allowances for a certain jocular exaggeration, but there is nevertheless a good, sound basis of truth in his picture.

That alewife and the devil were kin, he says. She had a hooked and perpetually dripping nose, and her skin was as rough as a sack. Her eyes were bleared, she munched her gums and her fingers were greasy to the knuckles. Her cloak was of Lincoln green (the best green dyes came out of Lincoln). Her kirtle was Bristol red (but then, most kirtles were red), and with her tallow-smeared shoes and greasy skirt, her wide hips, her grey hair, her face wrinkled as a pig's ear, she was as blowsy and pretentious an old harridan as could be found anywhere on earth. Incidentally, some of her descendants were to be found in the Leatherhead parish registers as late as the seventeenth century.

> *Come who so wyll* [*says Skelton*],
> *To Elynour on the hyll...*
> *Thyther cometh Kate,*
> *Cysly, and Sare,*
> *With theyr legges bare,*
> *And also theyr fete*
> *Hardely full vnswete;*
> *Wyth theyr heles dagged* [*their heels bemired*]
> *Theyr kyrtelles all to-iagged,*
> *Theyr smockes all to-ragged,*
> *Wyth tytters and tatters,*
> *Brynge dysshes and platters,*
> *Wyth all theyr myght runnynge*
> *To Elynour Rummynge,*
> *To haue of her tunnynge...*
> *Some wenches come vnlased,*
> *Some huswyues come vnbrased,*
> *Wyth theyr naked pappes,*
> *That flyppes and flappes;*
> *It wygges and it wagges,*
> *Lyke tawny saffron bagges;*
> *A sort of foule drabbes*
> *All scuruy with scabbes:*
> *Some be flybytten,*
> *Some skewed as a kytten...* [*walking obliquely*][18]

Some come without money and she sets the dogs on them. Hens roost over the open ale tubs and their droppings fall in the drink, but never mind, for Elynour strains out the dung. Sometimes she leaves it, for it makes the ale thicker. Others bring her a rabbit or a pot of honey, a spoon, a skillet in lieu of money. Some come boldly along the highway. Others unwilling to be seen, climb over the paling at the back.

Here are Malkynsmaydins with a vengeance. Here are Watsdoughters with breath no longer sweet as apples, but sour as boiled beer. Come to old age, they are sunk to pledging reaping hooks and hatchets, husbands' hoods and caps, wedding rings, spinning wheels, needles, thimbles. 'They ask never for meat, but drink, still drink.' They weep; they piss where they stand. One cuts a bit of leather off the sole of her shoe to stop a hole in the jug she has brought.

The court records tell us that people fought even in church. With intense poverty and the dissatisfaction brewing that had not yet found a positive way to express itself, the obligatory work days no longer produced any work, and it was said that a man accomplished only half as much in a given time for his lord as he did for himself. He cut only half an acre of corn, mowed only a single acre of hay, and yet a 'day' at harvest time was supposed to amount to fourteen hours, from well before sunrise until well after dark, from five in the morning until seven or eight at night.

It is pertinent to remember that in every period in history capital has demanded as much work from a man as it could successfully get away with, and almost always it has done so on the grounds of immediate necessity. In 1831 up in Newcastle the factory bells rang at a quarter to six in the morning before a man could reasonably be expected to see his tools, and work went on until nine at night when it was generally impossible to see them again. Here, too, there were fines for indiscipline, fines for swearing, fines for profaning the Sabbath by indulging in strong drink. Little had changed.

At least during the fourteenth century the peasant rarely suffered from war on his own ground. In Flanders, according to van Houtte, 'When the lords attacked one another they took pains to lay waste each other's lands.'[19] In Italy, according to St Peter Damiani, when two lords quarrelled, the poor man's thatch went up in flames.[20] In Tours the États Généraux, according to their *Recueil*, stated in 1483 that 'A number beyond all calculation are dead of hunger. Others who had no livelihood have killed their wives and children. Many who own no animals, among them even women and children, plough by dragging the yokes on their shoulders.'

Barclay makes plain the contempt in which the peasants were held.

Ye smell all smoky, of stubble and o chaffe,
Ye smell of the grounde, of wedes and of draffe... [hogwash]
Ye shall be plowmen and tillers of the grounde,
To payne and labour shall ye alway be bounde,
Some shall kepe oxen, and some shall hogges kepe,
Some shall be threshers, some other shall kepe shepe,
To digge and to delue, to hedge and to dike,
Take this for your lot and other labour like,
To drudge and to driuell in workes vile and rude,
This wise shall ye liue in endlesse seruitude.[21]

God gave them, he writes, the cart and the harrow, the gad and the whip, and they may groan at these gifts, but groan in vain.

'Crooked men and blind', Langland had written. If one broke an arm or a leg it was a matter of pure good luck if it was properly set. Wounds suppurated and left scars. Diseases of malnutrition were endemic. The lame and the halt, the crooked and the blind were more numerous than we can readily imagine. Indeed, one has only to travel to some North African city today to see beggars in every street, men with sores on their bodies, adolescents crippled with rickets, children with white eyes, blinded by glaucoma. Here comes a peasant woman, pregnant, an infant swaddled into a bundle at her back and two or three others clinging to her skirts as she walks. As for the French families in Tours that yoked themselves into the plough, it could happen in England too, or as near as makes no odds.

And as I went on my way, weeping for sorrow,
I saw a simple man nearby, hanging on the plough.
His coat was all in rags of a cloth called cary,
His hood full of holes and his hair came through.
His knobbled shoes were just the same, patched thick and broken,
And his toes stuck out as he trod along the ground.
His hose hung down on every side, round about his heels,
All beslobbered in mud as he walked behind the plough.
Two mittens he wore, made all of rags,
From which his fingers protruded, heavy with mud.
This poor wight was wading almost to the ankles,
Four heifers in front of him, all skin and bones.
You could have counted every rib in the sorry looking beasts.
His wife walked beside him with a long goad,
In a coat cut short, riding high off the ground,
Wrapped in a winnowing sheet to shield her from the weather,

Barefoot on the bare ice so the blood followed.
And at the furrow's end lay a little crumb bowl,
And therein a small child, wrapped all in clouts,
With two more of two years old, one upon each side.
They all sang one song that sorrow was to hear.
They all cried one cry, a miserable note.
The simple man sighed sore and said, 'Children, be still.'[22]

These figures were not invented, the crooked men and blind, the cottager too proud to admit he is starving, the fingers clutching at the few pence taken. They are parts of a broad spectrum which I hope will grow more distinct, become sharper and merge with others until we are able to see the whole of that remarkable time of which they are only fragments. As long as English is read or spoken, however, that miserable, not untypical ploughman will stand at the end of his furrow, about to turn his cold beasts, perhaps, sighing with the whole, hopeless world on his back as he says, 'Children, be still!'

B

CHAPTER TWO

IN JUSTICE IS GREAT PROFIT

Look for contemporary pictures that show the peasant in a happier light, and mostly you look in vain. There were saints' days, of course, red-letter days in the calendar when the villein did no work, but on some manors the master insisted that these be made up afterwards. There were feasts; there were dances. But the preachers complained that people gambled and played games even on holy days. 'One hour a week with God A'mighty,' says Hardy in *Two on a Tower*, 'and the rest with the devil.'

Strangely enough, it was ball that the authorities chiefly condemned, and not, as we might suppose, because it interfered with the practice of archery. No, at East Merrington near Durham, there was no reason given when in 1382 it was ordered that 'none shall play at ball under penalty of 40s'. At Acley, probably modern Acle on the road between Norwich and Great Yarmouth, games of ball were likewise forbidden. At South-wick three men were fined 20s. for getting into a fracas at a ball game (a terrifyingly high penalty). And Philip Stubbes, the great Puritan pamphleteer and antagonist of Nashe, offered what is probably the explanation when he wrote that football 'was rather a friendlie kind of fyght than a play or recreation'.[1]

Sir Thomas Elyot was more specific.

Football [he wrote] is a game in which young men...propel a huge ball, not by throwing it into the air, but by striking and rolling it along the ground, and that not with their hands, but with their feet. A game, I say, abominable enough and, in my judgment at least, more common, undignified and worthless than any other kind of game, rarely ending but with some loss, accident or disadvantage to the players themselves.[2]

In the streets of London football was so popular that merchants had to petition the king to have it put down, for ball and players often went flying into stalls and barrows. So in 1314 Edward II issued a proclamation forbidding the game on the grounds that it often led to a breach of the peace. And Richard II forbade 'all playing at tennis, football and other games called corts [possibly quoits, though this is doubtful], dice, casting of the stone [and] kailes [a kind of skittles]'.

As for archery, it was of course widely practised. Targets were set up at about 220 yards, or an eighth of a mile. William Cloudesle was said to have been able to split a hazel rod 400 paces off. Cornish archers could penetrate armour at 480 yards. According to Giraldus Cambrensis, a Welshman could pierce a four-inch oaken door, and one Robert Arundell could hit a target at 240 yards, shooting with either hand, or even with the bow behind his head.

In winter, blocks of ice were turned into sledges, and as early as the twelfth century, according to FitzStephen, people went ice-skating on the shin bones of animals, and propelled themselves along the ice with long, iron-tipped poles. Then there was a game which survived into the nineteenth century, wherein two opposing teams of indeterminate numbers of country lads tried to drive a ball into their opposing villages, sometimes three or four miles apart. 'The hurlers take their next way,' says Strutt, 'over hilles, dales, hedges, ditches; yea, and thorow bushes, briars, mires, plashes and rivers whatsoever, so you shall sometimes see twenty or thirty lie tugging together in the water, scrambling and scratching for the ball.'[3]

There seems even to have been a form of cricket (they called it club ball) played with a straight bat. In a word, gambling, ball games, drinking, gossip, fighting and fornication, these were the countryman's recreations, and for pursuing them he was dragged up before the justices. The court records look remarkably similar to those of today.

John Jentilman is fined 6*d.* for attacking Agnes Ingleton. Agnes pays 6*d.* for cursing John Jentilman. John Lollis draws a knife against Robert Swan and is fined 3*s.* 4*d.* John Smith threatens the curate with a dagger. In 1375 the women of Hazeldean are ordered to restrain their tongues and not curse any man. The only difference between us and them –as we shall see in a moment–is that we are rarely put into the dock for unchastity.

Peasant marriages were often difficult things to arrange. Until the Lateran council of 1215 they had been prohibited within seven degrees of consanguinity, but even afterwards the prohibition included any couple that had a common great-great-grandfather. So in little hamlets with no access to the outer world, hamlets wherein one knew everybody and was related to most, it was not easy to find an individual one might legally marry in the first place.

To marry a girl from the next village, on the other hand, could sometimes be altogether impossible, for the prospective bride's landlord was her owner. If she married and moved away, he stood to lose the fruit of her womb, and he might not be willing to accept a merchet for the loss. Even if he were, it might be difficult for the bride's father to raise the money.

It cannot too often be repeated that the bondwoman was the landowner's chattel, as much a piece of property as a cow or an ox. A century earlier he had even claimed the right to choose a husband for her, just as he chose a ram, a bull or a stallion with which to mate any of his animals. In Halesowen in 1274, John of Romsley and Nicholas Sewal were permitted time until the next sitting of the court 'to decide about the widows that have been offered them'. In 1279 Thomas Robins of Oldbury was summoned and ordered to take Agatha of Halesowen as his wife.

In a word, the serf's body and blood belonged to his lord, and could never be disposed of in marriage without the lord's consent. Sometimes consent was simply not granted. Sometimes it was given only after complicated arrangements had been made to divide the children of such a marriage between the respective owners of its parents.

In time, payment was generally accepted in lieu of a right difficult to enforce, but that payment rankled more than any other all during the Middle Ages, for it was held, morally and indeed legally, to be an irrefutable token of one's villein status. It could also be a considerable burden, for the price was normally about 8s. 6d., or more than three months' income.

In practice, of course, matters were rarely as difficult or custom as cut and dried as the law allowed. But the principle remained valid. If the landlord was owner of a chattel, then, in plain terms, whoever alienated that chattel by marrying it, carrying it off or using it for his own pleasure was guilty of embezzlement. It had nothing to do with morality, for that would have been taken care of by confession and penance. It was a civil offence, a tort. It had to do with property, and the taking of another man's property was theft.

So whenever marriage was difficult or too expensive, many a couple took the next best course and tumbled in the hay, for that could often be done without anyone being the wiser. But of course the landlord objected even to this, for a girl ought not to allow herself to be possessed by a man. The loss of her maidenhead depreciated her value. The Abbot of Bardsley imposed a fine of 2s. on any of his bondwomen convicted of fornication. One abbot of Glastonbury set down the reasons for this quite clearly. Whenever a bondgirl was unchaste of her body, he wrote, the lord must be paid, for he might very well have lost the sale of her. And we have to remember that the bondgirl was probably twelve or thirteen years old.

The same was true all over the country. In Wilsend, one Christiania is fined 2s. 'leyrwite'. In 1366, Margaret Calvert pays a shilling for leyrwite with the Chaplain of Hazeldean. In 1368 she pays it again. On one Durham manor the vicar's daughter pays leyrwite for copulation with we know not whom. At St Albans the abbot demands twelve-pence from one Hugh, the clerk, because Hugh's daughter has been made pregnant to the damage of her lord. Thomas of Bradley confesses to having committed fornication with Agnes, daughter of Gilbert, the smith. He is flogged. But Agnes is stubborn in maintaining her inno-cence, so she is excommunicated instead. At last she confesses, the excommunication is revoked and she is given her flogging after all. Henry of Frankly is accused of fornication with Matilda of Honderwode. The girl admits her crime and is publicly whipped in the market-place.

At Easter, at Whitsun and at Christmas the bondman's very world turned upside down. In an age when everything else seemed either to be dying or undergoing a new birth he could turn back to feasts as old as agriculture. No matter that the church had taken them over and made them holy days in a superficially Christian year. He and his ancestors had celebrated midwinter, sowing time and the first greening of the crops long before the church was ever heard of.

During the Roman Saturnalia, master and man had been equal. In Saxon England they had burned the *yole-stok*, or yule log, for *yole* was the Saxon December, the darkest month of the year, when demons roamed forest and field to snatch up careless souls. So the forebears of our feudal peasant had burned fires to keep them away, and feasted to celebrate not only the successful consummation of the year, but also the imminent return of the sun.

At Christmas the tenants cut and carried logs for the fire. Every man brought his faggot of brushwood so that the cook might not serve his portion raw. Every man had a trencher, a mug and a napkin of some sort. He was allowed to eat off a cloth. There were broth and ale, spices, two kinds of meat, apples and various cheeses. At East Pennard near Shepton Mallet the lord was precise in the ordering of his own particular custom. A tenant had the right to four places at table for members of his family. He was entitled to a white loaf (white bread was an expensive luxury) and after dinner he was permitted to sit drinking in the manorial hall.[4]

Boughs, flowers, hangings, garlands, writes Polydore Vergil, were heathen emblems all, and ever since the sixth century the church had never ceased speaking out against them. But it made no difference. Fresh rushes would have been scattered in the hall. There would be music, perhaps, practical joking, very likely a dance by one or two of the girls. In his *Fifteenth Century Verse and Prose* A. W. Pollard sets down one of their carols modernized, and no doubt something like it was thumped out at many a medieval board.

> *Make we merry, both more and less,*
> *For now is the time of Christmas!*
> *Let no man come into this hall,*
> *Groom, page, nor yet marshall,*
> *But that some sport he bring withal,*
> *For now is the time of Christmas!*
> *If he say he can nought do,*
> *Then for my love ask him no mo!*
> *But to the stocks then let him go,*
> *For now is the time of Christmas!*

Sometimes on grander occasions there would be mummers brought in, maskers, men and women who exchanged clothes and visited each other's houses to do tomfoolery in disguise. Stow tells of a mumming in 1377 in honour of the boy king, Richard, when 'one hundred and thirty citizens disguised and well horsed in a mummerie with sound of Trumpets, Shackbuts, Cornets, Shalmes [a wind instrument like an oboe] and other Minstrels and innumerable torch lights of Waxe, rode from Newgate through Cheape over the bridge, through Southwarke, and so to Kennington besides Lambhith, where the young Prince [he had actually been king five months] remayned with his mother and the Duke of Lancaster, his uncle, the Earls of Cambridge, Hertford, Warwicke and Suffolke, with divers other Lordes'.[5]

According to Brand, writing in his *Popular Antiquities*, the boar's head was traditionally the first course served at the feast, stuck with branches of rosemary and carried up to the principal table with great state and solemnity. In Chaucer's *Frankeleyn's Tale*, we read that:

Ianus sit by the fyr, with double berd,
And drinketh of his bugle-horn the wyn.
Biforn him stant braun of the tusked swyn,
And "Nowel" cryeth every lusty man.[6]

But of course our rustic villein never saw anything so grand. We have to think of his Christmas feast as simply an older and perhaps more splendid version of the rent-day dinners served by local squires well within living memory.

There was the Christmas game, but what it was, I think nobody knows. In any case, celebrations came to an end at Twelfth Night, and the long, wet misery of ditching, dyking and carting dung began again, the cold, the snow (deeper then than now), the meagre rations, the winter nights by rushlight, the smoky fires, the sickness, the time when a man walked in the fields, 'al beslombred in fen'.

From time to time throughout the year, [Bennett writes] the great religious festivals gave the peasant a few hours of pleasure making: the ceremonies connected with Easter would enthral him with such dramatic incidents as crawling to the Cross on Good Friday, or the rending of the veil which had hidden the Sanctuary during Lent; or perhaps, if he were near some great Abbey church, he might behold the elaborate miming which portrayed to the congregation the rising of Christ and His absence from the tomb. Then again at the Corpus Christi feast he would take part in the processions, and enjoy such rough dramatic representations of the events of the Scriptures as the wandering players or the nearby town guilds could perform. Less closely associated with the Church were the great popular festivals of May Day, or of Midsummer Day, when the whole village gave itself up to mirth and dance.[7]

Listen to *The Seasons* of Vivaldi, or look at the vigorous peasants of a Breughel and you will hear and see at once the loud, animal strength, the unsubtle romping, smell the sweat of the dancers and be able to taste the speech dangerous as knives, the quick tempers, the emotion just under the skin, the laughter, the willingness to give and take bloody mouths. No allegory here, no courtly love, but blunt words. 'An old black ram,' says Iago, 'is tupping your white ewe,' and that is precisely how the peasant would have expressed it.

Funerals were just as festive as marriages and christenings, for the peasant's awful need to be compensated turned even death into what a church council of 1342 called an excuse for copulation and theft. The mourners would troop into some house to talk and drink, and if we can take the many complaints at face value, there must have been as much conviviality at such gatherings as on Sundays when, as a friar writes, 'there reigneth more lechery, gluttony, manslaughter, robbery, back-biting, perjury and other sins than reigned all the week before'.[8]

As for marriages Richard Poore, the thirteenth-century Bishop (successively) of Chichester, Salisbury and Durham, ordered that they 'be celebrated reverently and with honour, not with laughter or sport, or in taverns, or in public drinking bouts and feasts'.[9] The drinking he refers to was done at what they called the bride ale (we have shortened it to bridal), and the profits went to the bride.

May was considered an unfortunate month to be married in, and even today we think of a June bride as luckier than others. The ceremony itself was almost invariably performed in the church porch, and so were those of baptism and funeral. That is why the font is still generally to be found near the door. Edward I was married at the entrance to Canterbury Cathedral, and of course Chaucer's Wyf of Bath said of herself that 'Housbondes at chirch-dore I have had fyve'.

There is an interesting form of words that has survived in a missal of the late fourteenth century, and it seems to me a good deal more vivid than that in use today. 'Ich,' says the groom, 'take the to my weddid wyf, to haven and to holden, for fayrer, for fouler, for bettur, for wors, for richer, for porer, in seknesse and in helthe, fro thys tyme forward, til dethe us departe, if holichurche will it orden; and therto I pliht the my treuthe.' When giving the ring, he says, 'With this ring I the wedde, and this gold and selver I the yeve, and with my bodi I the worschepe, and with all my worldly catel I the honoure.'

Even more amiably, the bride must say, 'Iche take the to my weddid husbond, to haven and to holden, for fayrer, for fouler, for better, for wors, for richer, for porer, in seknesse and in helthe, to be bonlich and buxum [blithe and obedient] in bed and at burde, tyl dethe us departe...' And it is worth noting that in the simple phrases, with only one or two excep-tions–porer, bonlich–every word is of Saxon origin.

Of course there were love matches, and many a fine bastard begot in the hedge (our village registers are full of them), but a large proportion of marriages, like those of the masters and betters, was based on purely practical considerations. One needed hands on the land, a cook in the kitchen, a woman to milk the cows.

We have seen men being offered widows in order that the widow's fields be properly tilled. There were in fact manors on which the lord took every chattel a woman owned if her husband died and left her childless. She was no longer a unit of value. She could be discarded.

So now and then a man who had not managed to make his wife pregnant would lend her to a neighbour, just as one puts a cow to a different bull. In Germany a man who could not find–or was perhaps embarrassed at the thought of looking for–such a friend, might take his wife to market and offer her to a stranger. *The Mayor of Casterbridge* makes plain that the selling of wives in markets was not unheard of even a hundred years ago. In *The Woodlanders* we discover how even in the nineteenth century the ending of a certain number of 'lives' could automatically end a tenancy as well. So one had to be practical, and anyway, the author of *The Owl and the Nightingale* assumed early in the thirteenth century that no peasant married for love in the first place, but only out of a lust for copulation.

Often true, of course, but more to the point, the peasant antagonized his intellectual superiors because unlike them he observed what men felt to be the important sacraments, baptisms, marriages and funerals, only superficially in Christian terms. As I have said, he was a practical man. He acted in public as he had been taught to act. The innumerable sermons and teachings he had absorbed, the wall paintings in churches had built a patina in his mind of accepted forms. The incantatory prayers he repeated, the genuflections and endless *Aves*, these were the compliment he paid to what seemed unquestionably virtues. And in his conscious mind he accepted and was sometimes delighted by those virtues.

What moved him, however, what really stirred in him at times of stress were the folk beliefs older than Christianity, the magic that worked in practical terms, the primitive concept of sympathy in all animate things, the world of demons gentle as Queen Mab or fierce as the direst hobgoblin. Scratch the villein, and in a quite unpejorative sense you found an animal whom it was beyond even the vast powers of the medieval church to control. And the evidence for that fact is all but overwhelming.

He was not only dirty, he not only stank; he was perverse and immoral. Preachers and poets expressed themselves about him almost invariably with horror and disgust. He was what they said he was, an animal.

To be sure, John Gower, who was nothing if not respectable, looked at him with a certain sympathy, with the emotionalism, perhaps, of a theoretical Socialist who happened to be a poet. We are all Adam's

children, he says while he sits in his comfortable Kentish study. High
and low are born equally naked. Injustice is visible everywhere, and
orphans cry out against the power of their lords.

But not even he had been aware how strong, how unpredictable in
his fury the animal could be, how irrational and lacking in Christianity.
As soon as he himself suffered the terrors of the peasant's revolt, his tone
changed almost out of all recognition. In his *Vox Clamantis* the peasants
became four-legged beasts. They were oxen that refused to be yoked, he
cried, and would eat straw no longer. They breathed fire and smoke; they
devastated the fields. They were metamorphosed into swine possessed of
the devil. They became wild dogs that barked, not at horses, but at
men's heels.

'The peasant shall drive out the lord', they shouted.

If their leader tells them to strike, Gower complains, they strike. If he
orders them to kill, they kill. There they are, the once humble and familiar
figures, Wat and Tom and Sim, Bet and Gib and Hik, armed with old
bows and rusty sickles, with spades, mattocks, stakes, rusty swords,
some only with stones.

Gower tells how he fled out of his house and wandered the fields. He
crept into caves, trembling for his life at every sound. He lay hidden all
during the daylight hours, but death walked everywhere, and spared
not even the women and children. And he himself felt such terror, such
gross disillusionment, that he wanted only to die. He had not even an
inkling that the dogs let loose were quite unconsciously creating English
institutions, carrying in their illiterate heads a sense of justice and liberty
that was to be the envy even of their enemies.

We shall see later what so terrified him. We are not there yet. We are
still in the early days, before the Black Death, before the Statute of
Labourers and the terrible increase in wages, before these simple peasants
–like Chekhov's peasants in his story of the same name–had taken to
wandering the roads as criminals and fugitives, 'wolf's heads' that anyone
might cut down. Edward I had had the edges of highways cleared for
200 ft on each side, and men had been hanged, drunk, for thefts amounting to no more than twelvepence. That had only been the beginning.
There came a time when labour was simply not to be had and crops
rotted in the fields, when oxen wandered untended in the streets and few
men were safe in their beds.

Gower's wild peasant was an Englishman, however, and our delight
lies in the fact that if we listen–as we shall–to those heterogeneous and
illiterate multitudes, grimy and barelegged, those confused and hooded

animals scattered here and there in angry isolation, we can recognize their voices. The iron of English rings on their tongues. Their half-formulated ideas about justice, about freedom, about equality and the need for a limitation to the rights of powerful men and of the church, all these had already begun to take shape.

I have here and there referred to manorial courts, and before we go any further it would be as well to describe how they worked and how those many manors were organized. But first let us look at the lie of the land.

Around the village or the abbey with its big house stood what was known as the common, a large arable field that stretched out unhedged as far as the eye could see in every direction. And this common–not common property, but used in common–was divided and almost endlessly subdivided, first into a number of large blocks called furlongs or shots or dells, and then every furlong into a number of strips or selions, each parallel to the others and separated from its neighbours by raised ridges of unploughed land. At the top of each series of strips lay the headlands, unploughed sections built into low embankments, both separating and offering access to the adjoining sections.

But the peasant did not hold his rented strips all in one block. They were scattered here and there round the various fields, so it was almost impossible for an individual to cultivate and harvest by himself. The growing of barley or oats in adjoining strips had to be done communally. If a man wished to sow a particular crop he had to do it by agreement with his neighbour in the adjoining strip, who would do the same. He ploughed when his neighbour ploughed, harrowed when he harrowed, and since boundaries were ill-defined he had to be perpetually on the watch both against shoddy work that let weeds or thistles blow from one strip to another, and against encroachment from his neighbours on either side.

In his *Medieval Village,* Coulton quotes a monograph on the monastery of Leubus, where the medieval field system was not abolished until early in the nineteenth century.

Of some 1,200 patches into which the domain was parcelled out, a very large number did not even measure half an acre. The smallest were from twenty square rods to thirty. They went sometimes lengthwise, sometimes across at every conceivable angle. No man could conveniently arrange his patches for sowing because they were often too small to plough. Those who had ill-drained land, if the autumn were wet, could not leave it unsown in winter and sow it in the spring with some quick growing crop...partly because in spring they could not get at their unsown land by reason of the other strips. The plots were so inextricably confused that nobody, even among the interested parties, could tell exactly who owned this or that parcel of land. So that one interested party had often happened to dung a piece belonging to his neighbour, while another had sown and reaped it.

As one might have expected, the intrusion was often deliberate, and Langland admits as much.

Yif I yede to the plow . I pynched so narwe,
That a fote-londe or a forwe . fecchen I wolde,
Of my nexte neighbore . nymen of his erthe;
And if I rope, ouer-reche . or yaf hem red that ropen,
*To seise to me with her sykel . that I sewe neure.**

Even with the best will in the world, the strips shifted as the ridges between them were trampled to one side. Sometimes a holding was actually 'lost', and could never again be identified. And of course the waste was enormous, because paths and baulks had to be left, over which men moved ploughs and oxen between strips. When, as frequently happened, heirs divided the strips into still smaller sections, the confusion became so great that the only cure would have been to redistribute every man's holdings into blocks. But this was almost never done.

On one Norfolk manor, what had been 68 tenants in the eleventh century increased to 107 by 1291. Their holdings had been split up into 935 separate sections divided into 2,000 strips. One six-acre block was shared by ten different tenants so that some of them had only a few square yards that they could call their own.

Sometimes a man would come to a private arrangement with his lord, and for a few pence would be allowed to break up certain acres of virgin land on the outskirts of the property, and this was called an 'assart'. But if he had not done this, his work had to be integrated with that of his neighbours, and since on several days of the week he could not even spend the odd hour on his holding because he had to work on that of his lord, it becomes even clearer why his crops were generally poor and his income pitiable.

---

* If I walked behind the plough, I pinched so tightly that I could fetch a foot or a furrow of my nearest neighbour's, take it of his earth. If I reaped I would over-reach, or advise whoever reaped to seize with their sickles what I had never sown. *Piers Plowman*, B. XIII, 371ff.

Near the village lay the meadows, either fenced or protected by a ditch, and these, like the arable fields, were owned by the lord, but used in common by his tenants, each man being allowed to graze a certain number of animals there, the number being in proportion to the amount of arable land that he had the use of.

From the common pasture or the virgin wastes he cut his turf for roofing, picked up dead wood for his fire, dug clay for his dykes, carted bracken for litter and gathered such wild fruit and berries as he or his family could find. But uniformity there was none, so any description of life on the medieval manor has to be set down with the warning that the situation could vary enormously in different parts of the country, and—even more important—that particularly in the fourteenth century it was undergoing a continual process of change.

There were categories of peasants too, and they ranged from the comparatively rich man who might be renting as much as thirty acres to the 'pytel-holders' who could work no more than an acre round their cottages. Yet in the manor court they were equals, for rich or poor, they were villeins, and thus members of an inferior society.

Not only did payments and services vary according to the size of one's holding. A complicated organization was required to run a manor successfully in the first place. So there were large numbers of officers responsible either to their immediate superiors or to the land-owner himself. According to Vinogradoff,

> On every single manor we find two persons of authority. The bailiff, or beadle, was an outsider appointed by the lord, and had to look after the interests of his employer, to collect rents and enforce duties, to manage the home farm, to take care of the demesnial cattle, of the buildings, agricultural implements, etc....By his side appears the reeve...nominated from among the peasants...and mostly chosen by them. [He] acts as the representative of the village community and...has more especially to superintend the performance of the labour imposed on the peasantry.[10]

Who, having read *The Canterbury Tales*, can ever forget Chaucer's reve,

> *a sclendre colerik man,*
> *His berd was shave as ny as ever he can.*
> *His heer was by his eres round y-shorn.*
> *His top was dokked lyk a preest biforn.*
> *Ful longe were his legges, and ful lene*
> *Y-lyk a staf, ther was no calf y-sene.*[11]

He dwelt on a heath with green trees round his cottage, and over a period of years had managed to steal so successfully that he could lend his master the man's own property, and get not only a 'thank you', but a coat and hood into the bargain.

On his rounds a reve would carry a white wand of office tucked in his belt, and although he was generally illiterate like his fellow peasants and could not even do multiplication, many such an overseer was able to carry complicated sums in his head and not only present true accounts, but remember to a fraction the debts and the entitlements of several hundred men. He knew what a horse or a heifer would fetch (or should have fetched), what each field would bear, and the villeins lived in perpetual dread of him.

Being a serf, he knew his fellows better than any other of the officers. He knew if William Atwood was ill, or only trying to get out of his work day, or if there was any use in punishing John Watson to make him mend his plough (it was never in the fields), or indeed if John's sister, Cicely, was on her back in the neighbour's byre and ought to be made to pay leyrwite. Free tenants always insisted that they be exempt from service as reve, and in fact to have been a reve was clear legal evidence that one was not a free man.

Over bailiff, reve, beadle (or constable), messor, or hayward (whose task it was to keep cattle from straying) stood the lord's steward, and he was generally not only well born, but well paid and a man of very high standing in the district. In 1300 the steward of Berkhamsted was paid a salary of £15 6s. 8d. a year, as well as two fur-lined robes and all the hay, litter and firewood he needed. The reve was paid only 5s., with the addition of such perquisites as he could arrange for himself.

The steward was manager, planner, organizer, and as Bennett so aptly sums it up, he had to know

how many acres could be ploughed and how much seed will be needed. He must know all his bailiffs and reves, how they conduct the lord's business and how they treat the peasants. He must know exactly how many halfpenny loaves can be made from a quarter of corn, or how many cattle each pasture could support. He must forever be on the alert lest any of his lord's franchises lapse or are usurped by others. He must think of his lord's needs both of money and of kind, and see that they are constantly supplied.[12]

The steward was not only in charge of the records, legal and financial; he conducted the manorial court when the lord was not able to be there. And at these courts all contractual arrangements were made, all 'customs of the manor' redefined, for it was 'custom' that regulated almost the whole of the relationship between landowner and peasant. It was a body of legal precedents that both limited and defined rights and duties and by which everyone on the manor was bound.

At court sittings–which a villein was bound to attend–transfers were made of holdings if a man had died or disappeared. There the reve reported what repairs needed to be done. Such or such a roof had fallen in. The tenant had petitioned for wood and straw to rebuild it. On the other hand, this tenant or that had been idle or rebellious. He owed a certain number of work days. John, the hayward, petitioned for leave to marry his daughter to a man from the next village. Suitable arrangements had to be made, suitable fines imposed. Another villein requested the right to send his son to school. The priest recommended the boy. Still another had broken the ordinance about the lord's mill and had ground his corn at home. A sixth had baked bread, and on Shrove Tuesday had snared two rabbits. A seventh had stolen three feet of land from a neighbour.

Sometimes a peasant would dispute a point, and not only the court but 'custom of the manor' would decide it, for custom had been moulded generation after generation as either a strong steward or a strong body of villeins had had the upper hand.

Very early, peasants had begun to demand that the steward's word not be considered all-powerful, that they be tried and judged by their peers. Thus gradually in many courts it became the whole body of petitioners that rendered verdicts, and the steward who then delivered the court's decision about what ought to be done.

So far as we can see, when the lord's interests were not being actively asserted, the serf who sued or was sued in the manorial court got the same justice as that which the free man got; he got in theory the judgement, not of the lord, but of a body of doomsmen [or judges] who were at least his peers. We say that such a judgement he got in theory; in practice the question became of less and less moment, for trial by jury gradually forced its way into the manorial courts. In strictness of law the lord could not compel his free men to serve as jurors in civil causes; but the lord could force his bondmen to serve, and many a small freeholder would serve rather than quarrel with his lord. At any rate, trial by jury made its way into these courts, and it hardly leaves a place for the doomsman.[13]

At one time there had been juries of free men to hear cases involving the free, and juries of bondmen to hear cases involving serfs. But gradually the categories were combined, and since in time jurymen became a select class, chosen on the basis of their standing in the community, a sort of manorial bureaucracy arose. More and more often these jurymen insisted that they deliberate on manorial rights that had never previously been in question. And whether because they had been slack or because they had been partial, there were even juries fined for what looks remarkably like subversion of justice on behalf of fellow tenants.

In general, however, the business of the court was to ensure that manorial law and agreements between landlord and tenant were not only regulated, but enforced. In course of time, as various factors combined to loosen the ties between tenants and owners, the functions of the courts changed too. Services were remitted in return for rent. Bondmen fled and could not be found, or they pleaded successfully that they had not been rightfully bond in the first place. As early as 1349 serfdom was showing symptoms of decay, and although no law was ever passed to destroy it, within a hundred and fifty years it had all but disappeared. It is a measure of England's primacy in the establishment of equal rights under the law that serfdom was not destroyed in France until 1789, and in Russia and America until just over a hundred years ago.

There were many causes in England for the death of the Middle Ages, and not the least of these was foreign war and the increasing royal demands for manpower. For a hundred and fifty years after the Conquest the English peasant had seen little of the conflict that so often devastated parts of the Continent. But with wars in the Welsh marches, then war in Scotland, and at last with Edward III's long-drawn-out forays into France, all England became liable for service. What was more, the king paid 2*d.* or 3*d.* a day instead of the penny a man could earn at home on the land. So during campaigns abroad the peasant began at last to catch a glimpse of the outer world. He learned on many a field to take and to give hard knocks, and just as the Crusades had been the herald of renaissance, so war began teaching the peasant how in his own smaller cause he might begin to fend for himself.

War broke out against the Welsh in 1276, and writs were issued 'authorizing special officers to raise a specified number of men; such writs became more common from the war of 1282 onwards, and the system was in full force in 1294'.[14]

But the king was constantly calling for fresh levies, and it became more and more difficult to find even half the men he required. The peasant

It is hard to imagine that in the Middle Ages they not only played handball and a game in which the ball was hit with the fist – but golf as well. From Strutt's *Sports and Pastimes of the English People*, 1876. The costumes date from approximately 1340. (Radio Times Hulton Picture Library)

Above Preparing the feast in the great hall. (Radio Times Hulton Picture Library)

Left A bronze cooking pot of the fourteenth century. (London Museum)

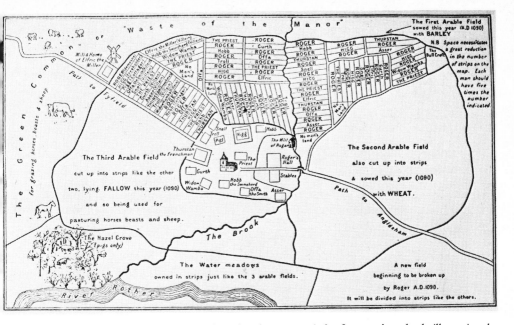

The map shows the following labels:

"Waste of the Manor"

The First Arable Field sowed this year (A.D 1090) with BARLEY

N.B Space necessitates a great reduction in the number of strips on the map. Each man should have five times the number indicated

Mill & Home of Elfric the Miller

The Green Common or Waste for grazing horses, beasts & sheep

Path to Tyfield

The Second Arable Field also cut up into strips & sowed this year (1090) with WHEAT.

The Third Arable Field cut up into strips like the other two, lying FALLOW this year (1090) and so being used for pasturing horses beasts and sheep.

The Hazel Grove (pigs only)

The Brook

Thurstan the Frenchman

Gurth

Widow Wamba

Hobb the Swineherd

Offa the Smith

Asser

The Priest

Roger's Hall

Stables

The Mill of Roger

No men's land

Path to Anglesham

The Water meadows owned in strips just like the 3 arable fields.

A new field beginning to be broken up by Roger A.D.1090. It will be divided into strips like the others.

River Rother

Above The Manor of Tubney, 1090 A.D.: far earlier than our period, of course, but clearly illustrating the method of strip farming that was used for many centuries thereafter. (Radio Times Hulton Picture Library)

Below Chaucer's Sergeant of the Law, from the Ellesmere manuscript of the *Canterbury Tales*. 'Nowhere so busy a man there was, and yet he seemed busier than he was.' (The Mansell Collection)

Above The reve, horn at his belt and carrying his wand of office, superintends the reapers. (The British Library Board)

Left Chaucer's reve, 'a slender choleric man' (Ellesmere MS). (The Mansell Collection)

was too fearful of the unknown, and at heart too conservative to be moved even by the huge increases in pay he was being offered. In 1300, sixteen thousand men were ordered to be in Carlisle by 4 June. By 1 July–four weeks late–only 3,000 had been assembled, and by the middle of the month, 7,500. Then men began deserting, and by early August there were hardly 3,000 still available in camp.

From then on, however, the story is loud with trumpets, and a great potential change began to be brought about in the villein's way of life. In 1307 the serfs of Pentirik were ordered out *en masse* to follow their lord to the wars, even though in 1300 it had been noted that in spite of levies, threats and even imprisonment, there were some commanders in camp without any men to command.

Here and there a hayward or a bailiff was convicted of taking bribes to release men from service. Still–two steps forward and one back–the armies grew. By the time of the French wars of Edward III the king often went so far as to muster all able-bodied men between the ages of sixteen and sixty, and the echoes of that order must have been heard in every village in England. Indeed, the women of Painswick in Gloucestershire once petitioned their lord, Sir John Talbot, for mercy. Sixteen men, they said, had gone overseas, but eleven had died, and their widows had lost not only their husbands, but their holdings as well. Now they were destitute.

Many of course drifted home again–deserters or discharged–but many were left forever in France as Shakespeare's Henry V foresaw at Agincourt, for the time would come 'when all those legs and arms and heads, chopped off in a battle, shall join together at the latter day and cry all, "We died at such a place", some swearing, some crying for a surgeon, some upon their wives left poor behind them, some upon the debts they owe, some upon their children rawly left'.[15]

Or we can look at them as Langland saw them, coming home quite unlike their former simple selves to brag and tell huge lies.

Pore of possessioun . in purse and in coffre,
And as a lyon on to loke . and lordeliche of speche.
Baldest of beggeres . a bostour that nouht hath,
In towne and in tauernes . tales to telle,
And segge thinge that he neuere seigh . and for soth sweren it;
Of dedes that he neuere dyd . demen and bosten,
And of werkes that he wel dyd . witnesse and seggen–
'Lo! if ye leue me nouht . or that I lye wenen,
Axeth at hym or at hym . and he yow can telle,

What I suffred and seighe . and some tymes hadde,
And what I couth and knewe . and what kynne I come of.

The important thing, as I have already pointed out, is that the peasant who had never in his life handled anything more dangerous than a stout stick learned to handle a pike. He looked down over the lip of the hill above Poitiers and saw the French cavalry in all their glory. He fought at the siege of Calais and stood in the ice before Paris during that terrible April when horsemen froze to death in their saddles. On a hundred village greens he practised the art of the longbow, the peculiarly English weapon that time after time routed far superior forces of armoured knights and crossbowmen.

All that he lacked when he got home again was leaders, but his sense of strength in community grew, and it grew in many subtle ways. Now and then the lords allowed more assarts, and these gave a man more money. Freemen, or men who had successfully acquired freedom rented little plots and tilled the ground for themselves. Craftsmen of one sort or another joined the isolated but slowly growing communities and set up small independent businesses.

Such people were not involved in the seasonal ploughing or in work days. So they had more time, both to talk, to listen to the itinerant tellers of strange news and to look with a certain perspective at what was happening around them. As craftsmen they went more often to market. There they met men of their own kind from distant and different manors, and so in time they became a means of passing ideas, or indeed facts, from mouth to mouth. In the Sussex manorial rolls, in addition to the old names denoting purely farming occupations, now we find Robert the Mill, Adam Baker or Alexander Carpenter. Elsewhere we begin to see records of men called Weaver, or Dyer, Taylor or Mason, Smith, Tanner or Cooper.

Eventually men like these, men able to earn more than the pittance their neighbours earned, began emigrating to the towns in search of opportunity. And as these Saxon peasants became able to climb the first rung or two of the economic ladder, one of the first things they did was

---

* Poor in possessions, in purse and in coffer, with a look like a lion and lordly of speech, boldest of beggars, a boaster that hath nought, telling his tales in towns and in taverns, boasting and swearing to deeds he never did, swearing to works we well did, saying, 'Lo, if you believe me not, or think I am a liar, ask of him or of him. And he can bear witness to what I suffered and saw and what I once had, what I knew and could do and of what kin I come.' *Piers Plowman*, B. XIII, 301ff.

to abandon their Saxon names, for it became elegant, it became the mark of a successful man to seem Norman in origin.

In the London rolls of the thirteenth and fourteenth centuries, names like Alfred, Egbert, Harold, Edward, Oswald and Edwin almost never appeared. In their places we find John, William, Robert, Richard, Lawrence, Thomas, Simon. And although Christian names like these were very often followed by surnames denoting either a trade, a place of origin, a characteristic, or even a quality positively ridiculous, at least, being Norman by praenomen, their owners had acquired some pretensions to gentility.

Thus we meet William Milksop and Reyner Piggesflesshe or, among women, Alice Strumpet, Letice Uggele and Matilda Strokelady. Some, Riley says in the introduction to his *Memorials,* are positively unprintable, but unless one followed his example and searched the thousands of appropriate London records, it would be impossible to say just what they were.

There was a contemporary fashion in feminine names, as indeed there always is. Mary was distinctly upper-class. But Mary's commoner sisters were Joan and Isabel, Peronel and Desiderata, Alice, Margery, Cicely and Clarice. The only Saxon feminine name I have found among Londoners is Godiyeva, or Godiva.

Sussex, being a rural area, was more old-fashioned. There, in the tax rolls for 1381, among the masses of Margerys I found an Etheldreda, a certain Hawota Brigg, and even a good Saxon Gundreda. But there was also an unhappy Alicia Shitte, and I suppose hers was the sort of name Riley found it impossible to print.

Even in the twentieth century there is a certain cachet in Norman origin. Hardy's D'Urberville was thought preferable to plain English Derbyfield. Simple Bewley is still spelled Beaulieu, and in my own small corner of the country there exists a landowning family that found it desirable a few generations ago to change its name from Wilkins to De Winton.

The towns suffered an almost insatiable need for manual labourers, and the peasant who fled to some such place in the hope of bettering his lot could generally find work—as a porter, a waiter, a streetsweeper or with some ostler at an inn. But there, although he might dress more warmly, wear shoes and now and then, eat fresh fish, he often found himself unhappier than before. Temptations were more immediate. The luxury in which his betters lived was more clearly apparent. His own opportunities for advancement, on the other hand, were rarely greater than they had been before.

The trouble was that medieval society was still inelastic, for by the thirteenth century men were certain that the world in which they lived had reached a stage of political and economic equilibrium (and indeed it had). In a world where no property existed except landed property, and as I have already pointed out, no work other than rural work, where the economic basis of the state was the landed proprietor, they were probably right. Today it is the rural workers who are individuals, the urban workers who are a class. In the thirteenth and fourteenth centuries it was the other way round.

No man of any consequence questioned the validity of Christian teaching, though I hope it is already plain that many a simple peasant paid it no more than lip service. Few questioned the divine sanction that upheld hereditary kingship, though Saxon kings had never been thought in any way divine. No one questioned the inalienable right of the powerful to enrich themselves, indeed, to prop themselves, albeit paternalistically, on the backs of their dependents. Wycliffe (we shall come to him in a moment) was the only notable medieval thinker who ever questioned the inherent justice of the feudal system.

Men might have an uneasy sense that all was not well, that the times were beginning to show signs of disequilibrium. But they also felt an almost righteous horror of any change, any word that threatened the scheme of things with which they were familiar. If anything new were to be born it would require the death of the only practical world they could imagine.

We have to remember that notions of scientific method or of political science simply did not exist, that the only ideas they had of economics were based on pragmatic experience hundreds of years in the making. As for concepts of social justice, while they might have existed in embryo in the Sermon on the Mount, Christian teaching had been so drastically reinterpreted in the millennium and more since it had first been preached that, except in the minds of a few impractical and emotional mystics, the concepts no longer existed. Change would have had to be so disruptive that it could have been achieved only by revolutionary means. It would have had to be the result of a positive explosion in the simple, suffering people who needed it, of a sense of injustice so profound that it could simply no longer be tolerated.

As early as 821 there had been a conspiracy of serfs in Italy. In the eleventh and twelfth centuries there had been sporadic revolts in Normandy. Henry I of England had dreamed one night that he was set upon by rustics, and he awoke in such horror at what he had seen that even his attendants were frightened.

In 1323 there was a rebellion in Flanders when the peasants actually plundered an abbey to get at the bread the monks had stored in its barns. In 1358 the Jacquerie rose in France and perpetrated horrors of incendiarism, rape and murder that were not to be repeated (at least in France) for over four hundred years.

But the English peasant was still quiet. He had not yet found his leaders. When he did eventually rise, it was to be not only for bread. Nor would he plunder and rape. He would rise in the name of half-formulated ideas about social justice, some of which look revolutionary even today.

CHAPTER THREE

SITh The PESTILENCE TYME

In the early years of the century the sense, not so much of grievance as of a need to invent new balances was no more than a rumour in the wind. But the clockwork had started, the villein's status was gradually and almost imperceptibly being changed.

As I have said, landlords had begun more and more often to commute services in return for rents, for unpaid labour had often been scamped or even avoided. So to be able to accept money in lieu of that labour and thus be able to hire workmen when they were needed made it possible for the reve or the bailiff to organize whatever had to be done with a great deal more assurance.

Change, once started, moved with an inertia of its own. Men who could buy themselves free of work days did so. When they could not, they sometimes disappeared. The manorial system began to look like a ship parting at the seams. There were other difficulties–we shall come to them anon–that worried thinking men. But then, quite without warning, a blow was struck, but from an entirely different quarter, and England was shaken by the most frightening catastrophe that has befallen it in the whole of its two thousand years.

It began in the late summer of 1348 when, at first in Bristol and Weymouth, people started falling ill in an awful and quite unusual way. Malnutrition was common, so mortality in the crowded towns had always been heavy. Infectious fevers had been endemic all through recorded history. But now, quite suddenly and in ever-growing numbers, people of all ages and of both sexes began to take to their pallets with abrupt and violent pains in their chests. No one knew why. There were no physicians to examine, no pathologists to identify an organism. They vomited blood; they developed what looked like a gangrenous infection of the throat, and in the few hours before they died they gave off such a stench that the very odour betrayed even a man trying to hide the fact that he was ill.

A certain Gabriel de Mussis, an Italian lawyer, records that in 1347 he had been in Caffa, a Genoese commercial port in the Crimea when an unusual sickness broke out among people living near the harbour. Contemporary Russian chroniclers report that the infection first sprang up in China, where thirteen million were reported to have died of it. Already India was said to have been all but depopulated. De Mussis travelled with the disease to Genoa, and landed there with only a handful of surviving companions.

At once the sickness spread west and south and north like a tide. Ten or fifteen thousand a day were reported to have died in Cairo, though this is surely an exaggeration. Armenia, Syria and Mesopotamia were foetid with dead bodies. Five hundred died every day in Aleppo. In Gaza there were 22,000 dead in the space of six weeks. Sailors in the Mediterranean came upon cargo ships drifting with not a man of their crews left alive.

Those who vomited blood died in about twelve hours, or even less. Others, who seemed to have a different variety of the sickness, developed hard, dry swellings in neck or groin, or in the armpits. They lived a little longer, generally about three days. Some were all at once covered with boils. They became feverish and delirious.

What, of course, no contemporary knew was that the disease was carried by a flea, *Pulex cheopis*, which moved on to men's bodies from those of diseased rats. Once transmitted from the animal, the infection passed more and more rapidly from man to man–in sputum, in faeces and in vomit. Chiefly it attacked the poor, the crowded, the perpetually half-hungry who lived in rat-infested houses. Mice, rabbits and squirrels became infected too, and helped spread the sickness into the countryside. Horses, cattle, sheep, goats and pigs seem to have been more or less immune, but even here, as we shall see in a moment, there were exceptions.

From North Africa and the Middle East the sickness travelled with terrible speed into Europe. Two out of every three people in Florence fell ill and suddenly died. Sixty-two thousand died at Avignon in the course of three months. The pope's physician, Guy de Chauliac, a surgeon and anatomist far ahead of his contemporaries, moved about for a while in one of the worst centres of contamination. People, he wrote, were so stunned with terror and with a sense of the hopelessness of their situation that 'a son did not visit his father, or a father his son'.

It was said–though it seems doubtful–that 50,000 fell ill and died in Paris. But there, instead of going into isolation as Boccaccio's tellers of tales had done, the rich gave banquets and danced half the nights away. In taverns the poor began drinking to get drunk. Instead of flocking into the churches, they crowded the law courts in pursuit of those who owed them money. People actually became avaricious for worldly goods.

It was two years since the wonderful victory against huge odds of the English archers at Crécy, where Edward of Woodstock, the Black Prince, the sixteen-year-old heir to the throne, had first proved himself a soldier. Then in 1347 there had been the siege of Calais, and when on 14 October 1347 Edward III landed back in Sandwich, Walsingham reported that 'a new sun had risen over the people, in the peace, in the plenty of all things and in the glory of such victories'. There was hardly a woman of any consequence who did not possess spoils that had been brought home from Caen or Calais or any one of a number of French towns.

As for the victory at St-Lô, 'there is no man living,' wrote Froissart, 'who could believe or imagine the huge riches that were seized and plundered there, nor the great abundance of cloth that they found'. At Caen they had loaded their barges 'with cloth, jewels, vessels of gold and silver, and many other treasures of which they had great plenty'. After Crécy they had positively danced and rejoiced, Froissart says, 'so great were the spoils'. At the sack of Barfleur even the *garçons* had spurned furred robes. 'The English were transformed from rags to riches', says another chronicler, and Walsingham remarks that, by 1348, furs, quilts, clothing and utensils were seen everywhere. 'Scattered throughout England in every [well-to-do] house were to be seen table cloths and jewels, bowls of murra [porcelain] and silver, linen and linen cloths.'

In 1348 when these things had so recently happened, the population of England was somewhere between four and five million.[1] Thirty years afterwards, according to the Subsidy Rolls of 1377, that number had sunk to 2,350,000.

The summer and autumn of 1348 were abnormally wet. From 24 June until Christmas the rain poured down almost every day and night. Oats, wheat, hay and straw rotted in the fields, so that, whatever happened, it promised to be a dear and hungry winter. People stayed indoors as much as they were able. Then, late that summer, reports arrived in London that fishing taxes were not being collected in Guernsey and Jersey because too many fishermen had fallen ill and the boats had not gone out.

The monk, Galfridus de Baker, wrote that the plague first came ashore in Dorsetshire. One chronicler mentioned the sickness as having first appeared on 25 July. Two others became aware of it on the 1st and 4th of August. But whatever the date, as soon as it arrived its progress was extraordinarily rapid. Robert of Avesbury, chronicler of the court at Canterbury, wrote that 'It passed very swiftly from place to place, quickly killing ere midday many who in the morning had seemed well.'

It was among the clergy that the most—indeed, the only—meticulous records were kept, and where the devastation can thus be most accurately seen. Between January and May 1348, the king had presented men to 42 livings that had fallen vacant. From June to September the number had been 36. In other words, these were the normal figures for a four-month period. But between September and December the presentations had risen to 81, and then in the next year, 1349, they leapt enormously. In the first four months of the year the number was 249. During the summer this grew to 440, and in the autumn ebbed away again to 205.

It has been estimated that in Somerset half the beneficed clergymen died. Bathampton had four parsons in a matter of months. Between the middle of December 1348 and 4 February 1349, three priests successively held the living at Yeovil. In Bristol it was said that the survivors were hardly enough to bury the dead, and grass grew inches high in Broad Street. In the diocese of Hereford there had been an average of 15 benefices that had fallen vacant every year. In 1349 there were 175. In the register of the Cistercian abbey of Newenham it was recorded that 'at the time of this mortality or pestilence there died in the house twenty monks and three lay brothers. Walter, the Abbot, and two monks only were left alive'. In Exeter some incumbents lasted only a few weeks.

Bodmin had fifteen hundred dead, and Gloucester, anxious to save itself, tried to cut off all the intercourse with the people of Bristol. In the *Eulogium Historicarum*,[2] we read that 'there was not a city, not a town, not a hamlet, nor even except in rare instances any house in which this pestilence did not carry off the whole, or a greater proportion of the inhabitants'.

For lack of transport, and indeed of customers, the price of barley fell at first to 9*d.* a quarter, of wheat to a shilling, of beans to 8*d.* and of oats to 6*d.* One could buy a good ox for forty pence, or about a quarter of its price the year before. A horse costing £2 was suddenly worth no more than 6*s.* Cows were going for 2*s.* and even 18*d.* a head. And yet by the autumn of 1349 travellers became aware that women and even children had had to be yoked into the plough.

On 1 November the plague reached London, which means that since it had first come ashore it had travelled about a mile a day. Parliament was prorogued, for the pestilence 'daily increased in severity, so that grave fears were entertained for the safety of those coming in at the time'.[3] We can imagine what sanitary conditions in London must have been like when we look at a document issued by the king to the mayor and sheriffs thirteen years afterwards.

Because of the killing of great beasts, from whose putrid blood running down the streets, and the bowels cast into the Thames, the air in the city is very much corrupted and infected, whence abominable and most filthy stench proceeds, and because sickness and many other evils have happened to such as have abode in the said city or have resorted to it... bulls, oxen, pigs and other gross creatures are to be killed henceforward either at Stratford or at Knightsbridge.[4]

In 1346–8 wills proved in the Court of Husting averaged 22 a year. In 1349 alone there were 222. At Westminster 22 monks were buried together in a common grave. Altogether, the death toll in London seems to have amounted to something like 20,000. Stow more than doubles that number in his *Survey*, but his figure is surely an overestimate.

The sickness spread northwards, but its virulence remained undiminished. Jews were said to be going about, poisoning wells. In Norfolk the diocesan registers list several parishes that had three or four vicars in the space of eighteen months. In Norwich itself, one of the most flourishing cities in England, with a population estimated at 70,000, there were at that time sixteen parish churches and seven conventual establishments. According to the Guildhall records, 57,374 people died, and by 1368 ten of the parishes had simply disappeared.

William of Worcester says that 7,000 died in Yarmouth. In the Yorkshire Abbey of Meaux, only 10 of the 50 monks in residence survived. In Ely it was 28 out of 43, but in Hickling only 1 out of 10 lived to see the end of it, and at Havingham no one survived. St Albans lost 49, but in Canterbury, on the other hand, only 4 monks died out of 80. The best available estimates have it that 5,000 beneficed clergymen died in a single year, two-thirds of those in all England.

On country manors the story was much the same. Thus at Cornard Parva in Suffolk, where there were fifty separate holdings, 51 peasants died and 29 families were entirely obliterated. Even the handwritings of those who kept records tell a story, for in almost every contemporary document they change abruptly, sometimes several times, in the course of the year. At Hunstanton in Norfolk 172 peasants died in the space of eight months. Seventy-four of these left no male heirs, 19 no heirs at all. It was an omen of what was to come. Dead villeins cannot be revived. The number of men bound to the land was reduced, once and for all.

On the manor of Sladen in Buckinghamshire, a jury in August 1349 declared under oath that the mill was of no value, for not only was the miller dead, but there were no tenants left who wanted any corn ground. The total rents of freemen and serfs had in the previous year amounted to £12. This year nothing had been collected, and the land was untilled.

A cloth mill on the manor of Storington in Bedfordshire 'stands empty through the mortality of the pestilence, and there is no one who wishes either to use it or to rent it'. Woodlands were unable to be sold. In several places in Berkshire it was reported that no court fees had been collected, no manorial services performed, no mills used, because no one on the land had been left alive. As William Rees remarks, and it was true almost as often as not, 'The manor was fast becoming but a bundle of legal rights'.[5]

Sometimes the records allow us to look into the fate of a single family. Thus on 18 May 1349, a Monday, Sir Thomas Dene of Ospring, near Faversham, died. Four young daughters survived him–Benedicta, aged 5, Margaret, who was 4 and two others, Martha and Joan, who were younger still. On Wednesday, 8 July, Sir Thomas's wife died. By 3 August two of the children had died as well. And it is impossible not to be made aware of the tears, the horror, the confusion and the acute sense among survivors that the rest of their lives had been twisted beyond repair.

In Rochester it was reported that 'men and women carried their children on their shoulders to the church and cast their bodies into the common pit. From thence there proceeded so great a stench that hardly anyone dared walk across the churchyard.' The result was that many chaplains and other clerics refused to serve except at exorbitant salaries. The Bishop of Rochester took note that 'Some priests refuse livings that are now vacant. Some with poor livings will no longer keep them because their stipends are now so reduced by reason of the numbers dead.'

Persones and parisch prestes . pleyned hem to the bischop,
That here parisshes were pore . sith the pestilence tyme,
To haue a lycence and a leue . at London to dwelle,
And syngen there for symonye . for siluer is swete.[6]

All over England the picture was the same. In ten Lancashire parishes for which the records survive there were 13,180 dead between September 1349 and January 1350. There were 3,000 dead in Preston, another 3,000 in Lancaster, 2,000 in Garstang and 3,000 again in Kirkham. According to William Dene, a monk of Rochester, more than a third of the land in the kingdom lay untilled. He says that the terror turned ordinary men and women to every kind of depravity, and that 'the people no longer spared a thought for salvation'.

It was the friars who suffered perhaps most of all, for they lived, preached and begged in the most crowded sections of cities. In 1346–8 the Austin friars of Winchester had sent four men to be ordained as priests. During the next ten years they sent not one. Of the Franciscans in Winchester and Southampton, three men had been ordained in 1347 and 1348. During the next ten years there were only two.

Winchelsea was a far more important harbour then than now. But in 1349 it was reported that ninety-four houses in the town were 'deserted and uninhabited'. According to Archbishop FitzRalph, Chancellor of the University at Oxford, there had been 30,000 students at the university in 1347. In 1357 there was only a third of that number.

Manorial rents could not be collected, and thus the landed gentry suffered not only a terrible loss in crops, but almost the total loss of their incomes. On many a manor there must have been long talk about whether corn should be used to feed the starving or saved for the spring sowing. 'In these daies,' writes a monastic chronicler, 'was burying withoute sorrowe and wedding without frendschippe and fleeing without refuge or socourse, for many fled from place to place because of the pestilence; but yet they were [without] effecte and myghte not skape the dethe.'

The pope announced a full remission of sins for those in danger, *plenam remissionem de cunctis peccatis cuilibet in periculo mortis*, says Knighton, and it was Knighton too who reported a huge mortality, even among animals. He had counted 5,000 dead sheep in the pastures, stinking and so putrid that not even the carrion crows were willing to go near them. He had seen sheep and cattle wandering in the fields and even amidst the corn, and no one available to go after them and collect them. Many farms had not a single soul left alive on them, and it was, he says, just as in the time of Vortigern when, according to the Venerable Bede, the living were not numerous enough to bury the dead.[7]

In the autumn that followed, that is, in 1350, a man would charge at least 8*d.* a day for reaping, and he expected to be given his food too.

North of the border, the Scots, who had so far escaped, hoped it would be 'the foul deth of Engelond'.

According to Knighton again, whose account is one of the most vivid that has survived,

Many villages and hamlets have become quite desolate. No one is left in the houses, for the people are dead that once inhabited them. And truly, many of these hamlets will now be forever empty. That winter there was a terrible lack of men to do any work. The animals were uncared for. All food, all necessities became excessively dear.

Because of the fall in production, prices in towns rose at once by almost fifty per cent. In some cases they doubled and even quadrupled. Iron, salt and clothing cost twice–now and then four times–what they had in the previous year. Fish, which had been the cheapest edible flesh, rose so in price that it went beyond the reach of the majority.

For almost a generation afterwards there were not enough priests for the parish churches. Monastic establishments were crippled until nearly the end of the century. But the pestilence had not ended. Twelve years after the first outbreak there was a second, almost as severe (they called it *pestis puerorum* because it chiefly attacked children). In 1367 there was a third, in 1375 a fourth, and in 1390–91 a fifth. In a little over forty years, as least as many died as there had been people alive when the epidemic started, so that in spite of a slow growth in population that had been going on ever since the Norman Conquest, by the year 1400 there were only about half as many alive in England as there had been sixty years before.

We know about the tolling bells, the carts for the dead, the bodies tumbled helter-skelter into pits. We can imagine the looting, the occasional savagery, the *Schadenfreude* of survivors. In any one place the sickness burned away for six or nine months, so for six or nine months no man ever knew when he rose in the morning if he would live to climb back into bed that night.

And since the members of any society are interdependent, the confusion must have been out of proportion to the number of the dead. The tinker did not arrive at the door. The alewife had no ale, and the town tavern lost three-quarters of its trade. On the farms, cows bellowed to be milked and oxen to be given hay. The alderman sitting in council felt a twinge in his chest and dared not speak, and the thief vomited blood in the alley. In the cities rubbish piled up in the gutters for lack of men to sweep, and goods on the wharves for lack of ships to take them away.

Since very few had reserves of ready money, many must have starved. But the effects were cumulative. If no one slaughtered the pig, there was no tallow for candles. If no one cut or carted wood, there were no fires to cook by or for heating. And since whoever was able to run away from his pestilence-stricken village did so, the roads were crowded with destitute men, some alone, some with their families, some pulling waggons piled with whatever they owned, some eventually lying down in the ditches to die. And since morality, justice and the observance of custom normally depend very much on a stable society, there was inevitably a greater overturning of values than had occurred in perhaps the whole of English history.

Fashions swing and quickly return. Standards, once lost, take generations to be revived, and the plague set changes in motion which were in a generation to damage not only the fabric of society, but the economic well-being of the nation and even the stability of the crown. It hastened the end of villeinage and the decay of the landed gentry. It accelerated the rise of cities, the growth of a new mercantile class and the beginnings of a new, entrepreneurial nation. In the ferment that followed the terrible eighteen months, there was suddenly a great deal of money to be made. And people came to the surface who knew how to make it.

Not only this. There had been dissatisfaction at the political power of the church. It had grown generation by generation ever since the Norman invasion. Now suddenly people became aware that in the greatest crisis of their lives the church had either turned a blind eye or been powerless to help. If God had not created John Wycliffe, by 1355 the commons would have had to create him or somebody remarkably like him.

According to a register of the abbey at Gloucester, barely a third of the population was still alive.[8] This is probably going too far, but whatever the true figure, the casualties can only be compared with what we imagine would be those of an atomic war. As frightening as anything else, perhaps, was the fact that no one had even the vaguest idea what had caused the infection, or what could have been done to cure it. To be sure, the ecclesiastics thought they knew.

Ther been...cloudes as I seide, that ben clene withoute watir. And such letten [stop] the liht of the sunne. For they [the clouds] been endurynge and ever semeth to regne and regneth noht. And suche, for defaute that the sunne mai not come doun, genreth corrupte eir; and so pestilence sueth.[9]

Or the plague had been brought about because, like the children of Israel, England had forgotten the Mosaic commandments. There was no respect for parents.

And yf this lessoun hadde be tauht and ykept in Engelonde, I trowe the londe hadde ystonde in more prosperitie than it hath ystonde many [a] day; and it may be for vengeaunce of the synne of unworschepynge and despysynge of fadres and modres, God sleeth children by pestylence, as ye seeth al day.[10]

Even Langland considered the plague a punishment for moral failings.

Reson reuerentliche . by-for al the reame
Prechede and prouede . that thuse pestilences
War for pure synne . to punyshe the puple.[11]

Long after the epidemic had subsided, preachers continued to point out that 'that man that mekell swereth shall be fulfilled wyt grett sykenes'. And indeed, the years of the Black Death remained a watershed in people's minds, like those of the First World War in modern Europe. 'Since the pestilence time,' Langland had said, 'priests can no longer make a living in their parishes, so they wander to London.'

Master Robert Rypon of Durham wrote that before the pestilence men were simply dressed. But afterwards England became infected with the pride of the French. The times were surfeited with finery and colour, and that caused the many thefts and extortions that had changed the very character of England. In a word, the old virtues looked to be dead. Simplicity, honour, goodness were things of the past.

England in 1350 was a nation so disorganized that hardly a man knew from one day to the next how he would go about his business. Even human relationships were not what they had been. Langland writes that many couples have married since the plague, but that the only fruit of the marriage is foul words. Their children are blows and quarrels.[12]

Tens of thousands were unemployed, and for the moment unemployable. The prices of commodities in the towns had risen faster than at any time in history, and to make matters worse, 1353 was a year of such drought that practically no rain fell from March until the end of July. Corn was so dear that the poor never bought it at all, and since there was no grass for the cattle, meat became outrageously expensive too.

It was, as I have suggested, the landowners who suffered most, for their income from rents and the peasants' labour fell markedly. Although their crops rose in value, they were forced to reduce the acreage they planted. In any case, the food they grew had in the past done little more than make them self-sufficient; only a small proportion had ever been sold.

By contrast, the manufactured articles they had always imported from the towns were often doubled and quadrupled in price. Ever since the time of Edward I, wages had remained more or less stable, and the price of comestibles had steadily risen. Now suddenly the shoe was on the other foot. Thus reapers and harvesters had used to be paid an average of three-halfpence a day. Now they demanded two and three times as much. Carpenters and masons charged double, and, as we shall see in a moment, wages kept rising, year by year.

William Rees examined the accounts of the little manor of Caldicot between Newport and Chepstow, and he found that its receipts increased after the plague by some twenty-five per cent. But its annual expenditure rose by some sixty per cent, so that an annual net profit of £17 13s. 10d. fell in spite of serious inflation to £12 11s. 0d. It was no wonder that many a landlord found it necessary actually to sell some of the villein services on which his livelihood depended. The income from heriots may for a short time have risen, but even so, villeins were worth less dead than alive.

In the beginning, so great was the dearth, the villein fared no better. 'I have not a penny,' says Piers Plowman, 'to buy a pullet or a goose or any pork. All I possess is two green cheeses, a little curds and cream, some oat cake and a bit of bread made of peas and beans for my children.'[13] The average price of beans, incidentally (and they were the peasant's staple diet), rose from 1s. 4d. to 8s. a quarter.

So in London proclamation was made that thenceforward a hen or a rabbit must not be sold for more than 4d, four larks for more than a penny, a shoulder of mutton for more than 2½d., or a leg of pork for more than 3d.[14] But even these prices were four times what they had been.

In the cities whole shopping streets were deserted, but that vacuum would in time be filled. On the land the emergency was more dangerous, for labour was in terribly short supply. Bailiffs went out with redoubled force to assert whatever powers they had over the villeins that remained.

Above *'Sic transit gloria mundi'*; a contemporary view of the Black Death. Here it is the high-born who are reflected as worm-infested skeletons. (Trustees of The British Museum)

Left Lanterns thought to be of the fourteenth century. (London Museum)

Above Chaucer's physician. He kept close hold of what he had earned during the Black Death, 'for gold in physic was a cordial'. (The Mansell Collection)

Below Part of a green-glazed jug with a grotesque human face. (London Museum)

But villeins could not even get their own crops into the ground. So, since on many manors the work days had already been remitted in exchange for rent, the employers tried with an eagerness they had never felt before to hire labour.

There were thousands of men, suddenly either rootless or ambitious, wandering the roads. Others might be enticed off neighbouring manors by a promise of higher wages. But every bailiff was in competition with his neighbour, and for the first time in English history the peasant came into his own. In the end, he took the revenge that any man hitherto deprived would take when the tables had at last been turned.

Wages doubled, then doubled again. Not even Langland was in sympathy with so revolutionary a situation, for he points out that:

Laboreres that haue no lande . to lyue on but her handes,
Deyned nouht to dyne a-day . nyht-olde wortes.
May no peny-ale hem paye . ne no pece of bakoun,
But if it be fresch flesch other fische . fryed other bake,
And that chaude or plus chaud . for chillyng of her mawe.

Unless the peasant is paid high wages, Langland goes on, he quarrels and bewails that he was born a labourer. He complains against God and grumbles at common sense. He curses the king and his council for making such laws to oppress him.

And by oppressive law is meant the Statute of Labourers, whereby in 1351 it was ordered that wages be pegged at the rates that had been common before the pestilence. Not only could a workman be fined or imprisoned if he demanded more than the law allowed. He could in some circumstances have an F for falsity branded on his forehead. As for prices, they had to be kept 'reasonable'.

But the Statute might as well have tried to stem a tide in the Channel, and the only excuse the government had was that no one could really have been aware which way the tide was flowing. At least they recognized that the inflationary force came from two directions, for not only was the labourer fined if he demanded higher wages: the employer was

---

* Labourers that have no land to live on but their hands deigned not to dine for the day on night-old greens. Nor did penny ale satisfy, or a piece of bacon. But only fresh meat or fish, fried or baked, and that *chaud* or *plus chaud* to take the chill off their bellies. *Piers Plowman*, B. VI. 309–13.

We ought not to miss the poet's irony in writing *plus chaud* as the gentry would have done, to imply that the peasant is getting above himself.

C

fined too if he offered more than a penny a day for haymaking or more than 3*d.* for reaping.

The attempt was hopeless before it was tried, however, for the peasant could no longer have lived on the old wages and the landowner was in no position to bargain. If he offered no more than the permitted maximum his work force would migrate *en masse* to some neighbouring bailiff who acted with fewer scruples. If he invoked the Statute, the men he needed in the fields would be fined or imprisoned, and prisoners cut no corn.

Even so, various peasant leaders were brought up before the justices because they had actually begun trying to form unions. One Walter Halderby of Suffolk, for example, had demanded–and received–8*d.* a day for reaping, and he had *advised various groups of labourers not to take less.*[15]

Nevertheless the law was enforced whenever courts had the practical power to enforce it. To be sure, very few ploughmen ever worked again for a penny a day. But without the Statute, inflation might have been worse than it was. At least it inhibited the wilder demands, and in any case it was not the peasant but competition between employers that made a 'wage freeze' impossible.

For the landowner, almost the only saving factor was the old doctrine that serfdom existed in the blood. On several occasions the courts found that a master was entitled to reclaim his villein even though the man had already entered into a contract with another employer. Rights of property took precedence, in other words, over subsequent contractual agreements.

Of course, in the main, peasant and lord both had an interest in breaking the law. Nevertheless, the antagonism between them became polarized. Each side now had a ground, a principle to stand on. Seeing the first signs of prosperity in free labourers, the villein became mutinous. As for the free man, he took to roaming from village to village in search both of higher wages and of wider opportunities. When he could not find them, he turned thief.

If employers chide them for poor workmanship, [we read in the Rolls of Parliament] or offer to pay no more than the Statute requires, they simply run away and leave not only their work, but their very homes. They wander from shire to shire and town to town so that masters are unable to find them. Many of them use staves to enforce their will, and so they turn into criminals. They form bands and steal from the poor in villages. From day to day the thieving and pillaging of these servants increases.

Langland had written with huge pity about the poor in little cottages. He had even said of himself at one time, 'I am dwelling with Deth', and that he ate 'as Hunger me hote [called] til my belly swellyd'. But now even he became indignant.

Ac ich warne yow werkmen . wynne whyle ye mowe,
For Hunger byderwardes . byeth hym faste;
He shal awake thorw water . wasters to chaste.
Ar fewe yeres be fulfilled . famyne shal aryse,
And so seith Saturnus *. and sent yow to warne.*
*Thorwe flodes and foule wederes . frutes shullen faile.**

In a word, even the stars would fight against them. Indeed, the astrologers had ascribed the arrival of plague itself to the conjunction of Saturn with other planets, and Saturn brought not only misfortune, but cold winters, floods, much thieving and early death. Now the thieving, the death, the cold were here. Only the floods were lacking, and they, in fact, never arrived. The peasants' rebellion itself flared up, not when matters were at their worst, but, as with most rebellions, when conditions had begun to improve.

In the meantime, as Trevelyan pointed out, 'Flights of villeins formed as marked a feature in the later fourteenth century as the flights of negroes from the slave States of America in the early nineteenth.'[16] There was a determined and almost universal–though uncoordinated–effort on the part of the servile class to break free. And the effort, which was at first only an accumulation of individual actions, gradually became easier. For as I have already said, there was an acute shortage of labour in the towns too, and a man who fled to London or Norwich or Bristol, or to any one of the rapidly expanding cities could–at least for a time–find work almost wherever he liked.

So because the cities wanted labour while every bailiff in the country was desperate for the same thing, the escaped villein, instead of being treated as an outlaw, was welcome wherever he went. He was not even aware of the change he had brought about, but the death of serfdom, though it was to take many decades, had now become all but inevitable.

So many tenants had either died or absconded that it became impracticable to work the land in narrow strips as before. So the fields

---

* And I warn you, workmen, win while you may, for hunger is hitherward hastening fast. He shall awake with water to chasten the wastrels. Ere five years be passed, such famine shall arise, and so saith Saturn, sent to you for warning, that through floods and foul weather the fruit shall fail. *Piers Plowman*, C. IX. 344–9.

were redivided. Holdings became larger, and hedgerows began to be planted to do away with the old, difficult boundaries. Or, when not enough men could be found even to cultivate what arable land had been cultivated before, the hard-pressed landowner turned arable into pasture and raised sheep.

And although no one could possibly have foreseen it, sheep were to prove the foundation of England's later agricultural prosperity. Not only that. These changes ensured that, unlike France and Germany, England came to be farmed, not by a large number of peasant proprietors, but by a small body of large landowners. The estates did not really begin to be broken up until after the First World War.

There were other changes. Before 1349 the nobility and the gentry had written and talked amongst themselves almost entirely in French. Very few poems–and they were almost all written to be recited–had ever been written in what today we call Middle English. School lessons had been conducted in French too. The tutors of gentlemen's children had generally been imported from France.

But the plague had driven great numbers of the foreigners home to districts where the disease had already spent itself, and the nation drew in upon its own body and began to live on its own intellectual resources. Italy had not really been discovered yet. The English renaissance had not yet arrived when in 1356 it was ordered that thenceforward all cases before the sheriffs' courts must be conducted in the language of the common people. In 1363 Parliament was opened in English too. The earliest known will in the vernacular was made in 1387.

By then a schoolmaster named Cornwall had already 'som del ychaunged matters', and begun teaching in English. It was unheard of, but by 1385 the practice had become almost universal. Indeed, Trevisa says that in his day [*c.* 1387] boys knew no more French than their left heel. Even earlier–soon after the middle of the century–just as church dogma began to be questioned, so the poets, the unacknowledged legislators, began turning back to the old language, to the one that had used to be spoken only by serfs and common men.

The result, of course, was a flowering in literature finer than any England was to see again for over two hundred years.

CHAPTER FOUR

ThAN LONGEN FOLK TO GOON ON PILGRIMAGES

As early as 1285 Edward I had promulgated what became known as the Statutes of Winchester to control people who were not wandering labourers at all but simply thieves, and by the time of the great mid-century migrations such thugs and footpads had greatly increased in number. Indeed, as early as 1348–before the outbreak of the plague–the Commons had again taken note that 'throughout all the shires of England, robbers, thieves and other malefactors, both on foot and on horseback, ride the highways in divers places'.

So a journey became more dangerous than in the old days, when the greatest risk had been that of accident. Chaucer's pilgrims rode in a body for mutual protection. They had an armed knight for company, and a miller strong enough to break a door by running at it with his head. Most businessmen travelled with a retinue of protectors, but even then the state of the roads made a journey of 80 or 100 miles arduous in the extreme.

In theory, landlords employed peasants to keep the neighbouring highways passable. But this was work unprofitable to both master and man, so it was often neglected. To be sure, the great roads had been built by the Romans, and these had been in use for over 1,000 years. Except for the ruts, they were still in tolerably good condition.

Bridges were under the protection of various saints. Very often a tiny chapel would have been erected on the riverbank, and there alms would be collected as a tariff from passers-by. Bow Bridge in London, for example, though it was not built until later, was until 1839 under the protection of St Catherine, London Bridge itself under that of St Thomas, and the tariffs or tolls were supposed not only to support the 'hermit' or the priest who collected them, but also to provide funds for the repair of the bridge itself. But more often than not, repairs were never made, and the money was swallowed up by the man who collected it. Sometimes the bridge itself was held to be the proprietor of certain lands, and the beneficiary of their revenues. But inanimate bridges do not go to law to enforce their rights. So ruts in the stone carriageway deepened year after year. Piers were damaged by floods. Balustrades were swept away, and the money to repair them had invariably disappeared, no one could ever say where.

In 1334 one Robert le Fenere, parson of St Clement's in Huntingdon, complained that a certain Sir Adam (by his title, a priest) had taken the alms and offerings for himself, but would not spend a penny on repairing the bridge. Even London Bridge, famous all over England, with its tower from which hung the heads of traitors and criminals, with its chapel, its cellarage in the piers, 'a continuall street,' wrote Lyly, 'well replenyshed with large and stately houses on both sides, and situate upon twentie Arches, whereof each is made of excellent free stone squared, everye one of them being three-score foote in height, and full twentie in distance one from another',[1] even this bridge, first built in 1176, whose houses were by their rents to have kept it repaired forever, was within a hundred years so dilapidated that messengers were sent scurrying all over the country, hunting funds with which to have it repaired.

In January 1281, Edward I begged for haste (London Bridge was falling down), but money and materials arrived too late. Early in February 1282, five arches suddenly collapsed and were gradually carried away by the stream. And this was so great a shock to the national pride, it was talked about and argued with such horror, that our children remember it in their nursery rhymes even today. There is a tradition that when the new piers were finally erected they had children buried in them because 'silver and gold will be stolen away', and therefore 'we must set a man to watch'.

In those days there were still wolves in England. Thus little Red Riding Hood. In 1376 a clerk was drowned in the Severn when the bridge collapsed (he was carrying a hundred marks of the king's money and a mark was two-thirds of a pound) but his body was never found, for the wolves had eaten it. In Nottingham, according to a local complaint, the Heybethebridge was in ruins. Horsemen had been drowned, and even carts had fallen through into the Trent. At Shoreham the long bridge fell into the river, even though certain of the Archbishop of Canterbury's tenants had been ordered to repair it. On at least three occasions the bridge over the Tweed at Berwick collapsed, and the bridge over the Teign at Newton Abbot had to be rebuilt at least four times.

As I have said, the principal highways were usually in tolerable condition. But lesser roads had often degenerated almost beyond repair. We never notice the culverts over which we travel today; but in the fourteenth century culverts did not exist, and spring freshets, instead of being channelled underneath the road, flooded the highway itself, so that a traveller who did not know his way could wander off the firm surface and suddenly find his horse mired up to the belly.

In 1339 the opening of Parliament had to be postponed because so few barons, knights of the shires and other citizens had been able to get to London.

Yet [Jusserand remarks] they had good horses, good coats, thick cloaks covering the neck, reaching up just under the hat...no matter, the snow or the rain, the floods or the frost had been strongest. While battling each one against the weather which hampered his journey, prelates, barons or knights, must have been obliged to stop their animals in some isolated inn, and as they listened to the sound of the sleet on the wooden panels which closed the window, feet at the fire, in the smoky room while waiting for the retreat of the waters, they thought on the royal displeasure at their absence.[2]

To be sure, the clergy considered it an act of charity to repair what highways they could. The great monastic houses sometimes owned enormous herds that had to be moved to market, so they too sent workmen out, at least on to the roads they needed. The Abbey of Meaux, near Beverley, kept 2,500 sheep, 98 horses and 515 oxen. Above all, the merchants who shipped produce to and from the towns had to be certain that their carts could travel without being overturned into the ditches. Great, square, two-wheeled vehicles they were, and carriage of goods cost 2*d.* a ton-mile.

The king and his entourage were almost perpetually on the road, travelling from one country house to another. Edward III had his Clivedens as well as Edward VIII. So along these pitted highways the rich, four-wheeled carriages rolled, like nineteenth century covered wagons, each pulled by three or four horses and guided by a postillion. They had no springs, these vehicles, only solid beams resting on the axles, the whole framework surmounted by a kind of tunnel for the passengers lurching slowly along at two or three miles an hour.

Judges, bishops, king's messengers rode past now and then with jangling entourages, and fine ladies on horseback, always riding astride, never (until late in the century) in side saddles. And many a peasant child would hear the jingling of bridle bells and go running out to see what great personage was riding God knew where, from limbo perhaps, towards some unimaginable paradise at the end of the journey.

Most city streets were paved with cobblestones, and in the centre of the road there was generally a 'kennel' or ditch, down which ran waste from the adjoining houses. These stank, of course, particularly in hot weather, and sometimes they were clogged to overflowing, but at least there was firm footing if one stayed near the wall and ducked under the ale stakes that projected seven feet out from tavern doorways over the roadway.

In a patent of Edward III, dated 20 November 1353, it was ordered that the high road running between Temple Bar (at the city wall) and Westminster out on Thorney Island be paved, 'for it is so full of holes and bogs...and the stones [are] so damaged and broken that travel has become dangerous for men and carriages'. So each proprietor was made responsible for the road in front of his house out as far as the ditch. In 1356 a toll was levied–a penny per cart, a farthing per horse–on all vehicles and all laden beasts that went in or out of the city. But in spite of that, Fleet Street and the Strand were not paved for another hundred and eighty years, not until 1533.

The inns were little better, except that at least the money paid contributed in some way to the traveller's comfort. The simplest were of course the rude ale houses, each with its bush or stake over the door. We have heard of the one that Elynour Rummynge kept. Langland describes another one slightly better, a place we would think of today as a drab public house in some squalid part of town. He introduces Glutton on his way to church when Beton, the alewife, calls to him from the door.

'I haue gode ale, gossib,' quod she . 'Glotown, wiltow assaye?'
'Hastow auhte in thi purs . any hote spices?'
'I haue peper and piones,' quod she . and a pounde of garlike,
A ferthyngworth of fenel-seed . for fastyngdayes.'
Thanne goth Glotoun in . and grete othes after;
Cesse the souteresse . sat on the benche,
Watte the warner . and his wyf bothe,
Tymme the tynkere . and tweyne of his prentis,
Hikke the hakeney mon . and Hughe the nedeler,
Clarice of Cokkeslane . and the clerke of the cherche,
Dawe the dykere . and a dozeine other;
Sire Piers of Pridie . and Peronelle of Flaundres,
A ribibour, a ratonere . a rakyer of Chepe,

A ropere, a redyngkyng . and Rose the dissheres,
Godfrey of Garlekhithe . and Gryfin the Walshe,
And vpholderes an hepe . erly bi the morwe
*Geuen glotoun with glad chere . good ale to hansel.**

But our observer did more than set the scene. The drinking lasted all that day. Clement, the cobbler, threw down his cloak and offered it for sale. Hick, the hackneyman, added his hood, and a great chaffering followed over what the author calls these 'pennyworths'. But it was all settled in the end, and the proviso made that whoever was unsatisfied had to buy Glutton a gallon of ale. And even though ale was expensive, a penny a gallon for the ordinary and fourpence a gallon (a modern 40p a pint) for the thicker variety called pudding ale, their capacities must have been enormous. The bargaining and drinking went on all afternoon.

---

* I have good ale, gossip, quoth she. Wilt thou try it, Glutton? Hast thou ought in thy purse [he asked]? Any hot spices? I have pepper and peony seed [she said], and a pound of garlic, a farthing's worth of fennel seed for fasting days. [All this, we learn later, took place on a Friday.] Then goes Glutton in, with great oaths after. Cicely, the shoemaker, sat on the bench. Wat, the warren keeper, and his wife also. Tim, the tinker, and two of his apprentices, Hikke who hired horses, and Hugh, the needle seller. There were Clarice of Cock Lane and the clerk of the church, Dave, the ditch digger and a dozen others. Sir Piers of the prayer stool and Peronelle of Flanders, a fiddler, a ratcatcher, a streetsweeper of Cheapside, a ropemaker, a lacquey and Rose, the dish seller, Godfrey of Garlic Hithe and Griffin, the Welshman, and auctioneers, a heap of them, early in the morning. With glad greeting they gave Glutton good ale in earnest of their cheer. *Piers Plowman*, B. V. 310–26.

Vivid as the scene is, and the crowd not unlike that in a similar establishment today, there are one or two touches a modern reader might easily miss. Thus Sir Piers is a priest, yet he sits next to Peronelle (or Petronilla), and Peronelle was the proverbial name for a bold and flashy woman. If she came from Flanders, she is by implication a whore, and if Langland had not intended this to be understood, he would have given her either a different name or a different place of origin.

In Riley's *Memorials*, p. 535, we read a proclamation of 1393 which states that 'affrays, broils and dissensions have arisen in times past...by reason of the frequent resort of, and consorting with common harlots at taverns [and] brewhouses...and more especially through Flemish women who profess and follow such shameful and dolorous life, and...we do command...on behalf of our lord the king and the Mayor and Aldermen of the City of London that any such woman shall not go about or lodge in the said city, or in the suburbs thereof, by night or by day; but they are to keep themselves to the places thereunto assigned, that is to say, the Stews on the other side of Thames, and Cokkeslane, on pain of losing and forfeiting the upper garment that she shall be wearing, together with her hood every time that any one of them shall be found doing to the contrary of this proclamation'.

So the fact that Clarice of Cock Lane and the clerk of the church are also sitting side by side in this disreputable company ought not to be lost on us. Indeed, in his last version of the poem, in what is called the 'C' text, Langland adds three others to the crew, a hayward, a hermit and the hangman of Tyburn.

There was laughyng and louryng . and 'let go the cuppe',
And seten so til euensonge . and songen vmwhile,
Tyl Glotoun had y-globbed . a galoun an a Iille.
His guttis gunne to gothely . as two gredy sowes;
He pissed a potel . in a pater-noster while,
And blew his rounde ruwet . at his rigge-bon ende,
That alle that herde that horne . held her nose after,
And wissheden it had be wexed . with a wispe of firses.
He myhte neither steppe ne stonde . er he his staffe hadde;
And thanne gan he go . liche a glewmannes bicche,
Somme tyme aside . and somme tyme arrere,
As who-so leyth lynes . forto lacche foules.
And whan he drowgh to the dore . than dymmed his eighen,
He stumbled on the thresshewolde . an threwe to the erthe.
Clement the cobelere . cauhte hym bi the myddel,
For to lifte hym alofte . and leyde him on his knowes;
Ac Glotoun was a gret cherle . and a grym in the liftynge,
And coughed vp a caudel . in Clementis lappe;
Is non so hungri hounde . in Hertford schire
Durst lape of the leuynges . so vnlouely thei smauhte.
With al the wo of this worlde . his wyf and his wenche
Baren hym home to his bedde . and brouhte hym therinne.
And after al this excesse . he had an accidie,
That he slepe Saterday and Sonday . til sonne yede to reste.
Thanne waked he of his wynkyng . and wiped his eyghen;
The fyrste worde that he warpe . was, 'where is the bolle?'*

London streets were raucous with the cries of tavern keepers, hustlers loud as barkers at country fairs, calling in passers-by. Langland writes

---

* There was laughing and louring and 'let go the cup'. And so they sat till evensong, and now and then they sang, till Glutton had gulped down a gallon and a gill. His guts began to grumble like two greedy sows. He pissed a couple of quarts; it took as long as an Our Father, and blew the round trumpet at his backbone's end. So that all who heard the trumpeting held their noses after, and wished he had been stopped up with a bit of furze bush. He could neither step nor stand until he had his staff. Then he began to go like a glee-man's bitch, sometimes to one side and sometimes a step backward, like a man laying nets in hope of catching fowl. But when he drew near the door, then his eyes grew dim. He stumbled on the threshold [thresholds were raised to keep the water out] and fell to the ground. Clement, the cobbler, caught him by the middle in order to lift him and set him on his knees. But Glutton was a great lout and grim in the lifting, and he spewed up a mess into Clement's lap. So fiercely it stank, the hungriest hound in Hertfordshire would never have lapped up his leavings. With all the woe of this world, his wife and his serving wench bore him home to bed and got him up into it. And after all this surfeit he had a fit of slug-gishness. So he slept Saturday and Sunday till the sun had gone to rest. Then he woke up of his slumber and wiped both his eyes. The first words he uttered were, 'Where is the bowl?' *Piers Plowman*, B. V. 344–69.

about cooks and their servant boys who stand at the doors of inns and shout, 'Hot pies! Hot. Good pork and geese. Come, let us dine!' Taverners called out the same to them. 'White wine of Alsace, red wine of Gascony. Rhine wine and Rochelle wine to help digest the roast!' 'A taste for nowt', they shouted, and meanwhile the ditchers and dykers came ambling by, bad workmen, Langland calls them, who spend the day singing, 'God save you, Dame Emma', or very likely pissing their potels into the kennel in the middle of the road.

Of course Chaucer's tavern where the pilgrims arrive at the start of the *Canterbury Tales* was of a far higher order, for the travellers were made very comfortable indeed. In fact, the Tabard in Southwark and its host, Harry Baily, were known to many hundreds of passers-by on the way down to Canterbury and Dover. Two hundred years afterwards Thomas Speght that wrote 'whereas through time it hath bin much decayed, it is now by Master J. Preston, with the Abbot's house thereto adgoyned, newly repaired, and with convenient rooms much encreased, for the receipt of many guests'.[3] And indeed, since it lay only about a quarter of a mile from Shakespeare's Globe, it is more than likely that Shakespeare dined there too. At any rate, Chaucer reports that:

And to the soper sette he us anon,
And served us with vitaille at the beste.[4]

But then those pilgrims were of an entirely different order from Clement the cobbler, and Clarice of Cock Lane. Chaucer's nun fed her little dogs with roast meat, white bread and milk, and she herself would hardly have been satisfied with less.

The very poor who had some legitimate business on the road–or the very rich–would now and then be put up at a monastery, the poor because monks were required to give them charity, the rich because any well-to-do monastic establishment could offer considerably more comfort than travellers would be likely to find at an inn.

The inn would have rushes on the floor, a long, common table and sleeping quarters that often had to be shared with whoever else happened to put up there for the night. One expense account has survived–of two Oxford students who travelled with their four servants from Oxford to Durham in 1331, and from it we can get some notion how dear such establishments normally were, particularly if we compare the prices the students had to pay with wages current before the great inflation. On one particular winter's day, for example, they were charged fourpence for bread, twopence for beer, a penny farthing for wine, fivepence halfpenny for meat and a farthing for gravy, the total a little over twopence a head, or a modern £1·70.

Their beds, on the other hand, cost only twopence for the party. But fuel and candles, plus fodder for the horses, cost another twelvepence farthing. So supper and a night's lodging cost each of the travellers about four times a ploughman's daily wage. Condiments would have been extra. Thus at one inn they were charged a halfpenny for pickles and the huge sum of fourpence (a modern £3·55) for sugar. But then, sugar had to be imported, for beet sugar did not exist.

Complaints about excessive charges must have been as frequent in the Middle Ages as they are now. In the 23rd year of Edward III, 'hostelers and herbergers' were adjured to sell food at reasonable prices. Four years afterwards a statute demanded a reduction in 'the high and unwarranted price of victuals all over the country demanded by innkeepers and other retailers to the great harm of travellers.'[5]

In his enchanting *English Wayfaring Life*, from which I have already quoted, Jusserand writes about a manual of French conversation in which a servant is sent ahead to engage rooms. He tells the landlord that he hopes 'there are no fleas or bugs or other vermin'.

'No, Sir, please God,' the host replies. 'I make bold to say that you shall be well and comfortably lodged here, except for the fact that we have a great plague of rats and mice.' Rats could not be avoided, but a decent landlord got rid of the fleas by changing the rushes frequently.

In the same handbook two travellers compare notes about the lodging at another inn. 'Undress and wash your legs', one of them warns. 'Then dry them with a cloth and rub them well so that you can be rid of the fleas that have lept upon your legs. There are masses of them in the dust under the rushes.' He has scratched his own shoulders, he says, until the blood flowed.

Langland quotes it almost as a proverb: to have as much pity on poor men as a pedlar has on cats. There were no shops, of course, in the country, so the pedlar's business lay chiefly with villagers. In his saddle bags he carried not only such articles as the peasant could not manufacture himself–pins, knives, musical instruments. There were pewter pots and dishes too, cotton cloth from Egypt that had travelled in Flemish galleys, vessels of Cornish tin, camphor, sugar out of Sicily and Egypt (it came by way of Venice). From nearer home he brought such simple luxuries as gloves, purses, girdles, laces and Flemish embroidery in scarlet, yellow or green to tempt the girls. And he was a particularly welcome visitor because along with his goods he brought news and bits of gossip from places perpetually beyond the countryman's horizon. 'Old pots to mend', he called in the village street. But his own pots and hood often looked as if they needed mending more than those of his customers.

Or there were the footsore friars–but we shall hear about them in a moment. Most colourful of all were the pardoners, and since every bit of evidence we have bears out the accuracy of Chaucer's description, these must generally have been shrewd, hard, fast-talking salesmen who lived by playing on the almost universal fear of hellfire and retribution. They had brought to a fine art the knack of trading safety and the promise of miracles in return for hard cash. Even this trade, however, had its roots deep in medieval church history.

'Indulgence' was the word. In the beginning there had been penances, so many *Aves*, so many psalms recited, so many strokes of the lash to wipe away sin. But very early these penances had begun to be commuted by priestly authority and made easier. A month on bread and water could be exchanged for the singing of 1,200 psalms while kneeling, or 1,600 standing. Gradually, those who could afford it were allowed to escape a given penance altogether by making a cash payment instead.

Thus, as early as the seventh century, Theodore, Archbishop of Canterbury, had actually published a tariff of commutations, and in 1095 Urban II had granted a plenary indulgence, a forgiveness of all sins, to those who would volunteer to go east and fight the infidel.

But gradually a new theory came into being, the theory of 'treasury', first officially promulgated by Clement VI in a bull of the year 1350. According to this teaching, since the virtues of Christ were infinite and those of the Virgin and saints superabundant, they constituted an illimitable storehouse of goodness which might be drawn upon like a bank account by true believers who were in need of it to outweigh the sins they had already committed. In return for this invaluable credit, which could ease a man's conscience and weave his very being into the fabric of the church, which could absolve him from penances and guarantee the remission of hundreds, perhaps thousands of years in purgatory, he was asked only to give up a small part of the worldly goods which he had perhaps sinfully acquired.

With this the pardoner came into being, and he turned out to be the most vivid, indeed the most bizarre, of all figures in the medieval landscape. Those licensed by the church, the men who kept accounts and handed over the takings to their superiors, were soon far outnumbered by an army of professional rogues who, acting solely for their own profit, neither kept records of what they were paid nor set limits to what they promised. All vows, all perjuries, all hindrances to advancement, such an illegitimacy or excommunication, could be nullified, all penances could be remitted in return for cash on the barrel.

As early as 1340 the Bishop of Durham had had reason to complain of those who 'make a jest of our power, and distribute indulgences to the people. They dispense with the execution of vows, absolve those who are perjured, murderers as well as usurers and other sinners...and in return for money, grant remission for crimes that have not been atoned for.'[6]

Pope Urban V in a bull of 1369 writes of men who 'go into church on some holy day at the hour when people are accustomed to give offerings, and...make their own collections, speaking until it is no longer possible to celebrate mass'. And obviously the money was kept by those who collected it. But they did more. Very early they realized that a miracle in the hand was worth any number in the bush. So in Boccaccio we read of one who actually owned–he could show it to them–a feather from the angel Gabriel's wing, a feather dropped by accident in the very chamber where Mary had heard the Annunciation. And when in the middle of this pardoner's harangue somebody stole the feather and substituted a fistful of dead coals, the trickster was not troubled for more than an instant. No, he cried. He could do more. Instead of the feather, he would show them some of the coals that had actually been used to grill St Lawrence.

Henry III was once sold a bit of stone in this manner. It had been marked with the imprint of Christ's foot, and it was finally deposited, along with a phial containing some of the Saviour's blood, in Westminster Abbey.[7] Edward III paid a hundred shillings (£1,000 in modern money) for a vest which he was solemnly assured had once belonged to St Peter.

It was not only simple pardoners who practised frauds. One cardinal visiting England during the reign of Richard II wiped out excommunications, and even absolved penitents from whatever vows they might have made to travel to Jerusalem–on condition that the estimated cost of the journey be handed to him instead.

Chaucer's pardoner earned something like 100 marks, or about £66 a year, which even after the mid-century inflation we may take to be worth about £3,500 today. As I have pointed out, there is so much other evidence to confirm what Chaucer wrote that we are probably quite justified in drawing on Chaucer himself for the man's *modus operandi.*

He rode among the company of pilgrims with his smooth yellow hair spread over his shoulders, and on his lap a wallet crammed full of pardons, come all hot from Rome. He owned a scrap of the Virgin's veil, he told them, a bit of St Peter's sail and a jar of pigs' bones which he convinced the gullible were the bones of saints. He even had a miraculous mitten, he said, which, if a man would only put his hand into it, would multiply whatever harvest he had sown.

> *Lordinges, quod he, in chirches when I preche,*
> *I peyne me to han an hauteyn speche,*
> *And ringe it out as round as gooth a belle,*
> *For I can al by rote that I telle.*
> *My theme is alwey oon, and ever was—*
> *Radix malorum est cupiditas.*[8]

He tells the congregation where he comes from, shows the pope's bull with its waxen seals dangling, speaks a few words of Latin to impress them—and then pulls out his relics. And he can earn more in a day with these bones and bits of cloth, he says, than the parson earns in two months.

How those illiterates must have crowded round him and gaped! When he thundered out his warning about secret sins, sins too shameful ever to have been confessed, the guilty must have felt the cold in their very bowels. Sins were rotten teeth burning in the mouth. Had anyone there—and his eyes would rove from face to face, stare at them one by one—eyes bulbous as a hare's—had any woman there made a cuckold of her husband?

He would pause to give their consciences time to work. Which of them had slipped into his neighbour's house and acted the secret thief? Who was the drunkard? They had all learned their ten commandments. Which had they broken? If such a one there were, let him come up, make offering in God's name—and by the authority of the bull he held in his hand he would absolve him.

When he had them all on tiptoe with expectation, when they had begun to cast covert glances at their neighbours, then he would rise towards his climax. He would stretch out his neck to east and west. He would point—at this one and that. He would gesticulate to lend force to his words.

> *Myn hondes and my tonge goon so yerne, [briskly]*
> *That it is Ioye to see my bisinesse.*
> *Of avaryce and of swich cursednesse*
> *Is al my preching, for to make hem free*
> *To yeve [give] her pens, and namely unto me.*
> *For my entente is nat but for to winne,*
> *And nothing for coreccioun of sinne.*
> *I rekke never, whan that they ben beried,*
> *Though that her soules goon a-blakeberied!*[9]

But he goes further. He becomes particular. He has already listed some of the famous sinners in history, but now he stings them by naming sins specific to certain individuals in his audience. He could, if he wished, betray the guilty, but he will not shame them. As he says this, a flush creeps up the face of the girl in the red smock. The reve moistens his lips with a nervous tongue. That heavy-browed woman lowers her eyes, and even the curate starts twisting his fingers in his lap.

What if a sinner is contrite, but cannot pay? Then the pardoner will take silver spoons and rings. Cupidity is the root of all evil. Has he not said it before? Will they—and now he is in full voice—will they, for the sake of useless worldly goods, risk their immortal souls?

Then abruptly he changes tack. He makes his voice quiet and, beckoning them nearer, starts telling them a few old stories. Simple people, he tells his fellow pilgrims, love the well-worn tales. They can retain them in their minds and retell them over and over again.

And all this time, there in front of the sinners' very eyes, lies the fragment of Peter's sail that the pardoner is actually touching with his hand. There stands the little phial that contains the blood of Christ. God only knows how many dangers, how many accidents it has avoided on the long journey here from Jerusalem! And it costs only a penny or two to touch one of these, to touch the nearest thing in the world to God—and buy absolution. If afterwards one should happen to sin again, he or another pardoner will return. So in spite of a world full of temptations and an eternity pregnant with danger, there is hope.

That pardoner worked hard for his living. By his own lights he struggled as endlessly as the peasant to make ends meet. But the real fortunes were earned by the custodians of the holy shrines. No tramping the muddy roads for them. People travelled half-way across the world to worship in front of the relics they had preserved, of St Thomas at Canterbury, of Edward the Confessor at Westminster, of the Holy Cuthbert at Winchester, of Holywell, of Glastonbury and its miracu-

Above The knight, a true and perfect gentleman (Ellesmere MS). (The Mansell Collection)

Below Small costrel (a sort of canteen which was suspended from the belt by its flap or 'ear'; the pilgrim's bottle') made of decorated leather. (London Museum)

Above Pilgrim badge of St Thomas. (London Museum)

Below Ewes being milked. The hurdles behind which they have been penned are remarkably like those in use until well into the nineteenth century. Luttrell Psalter. (Radio Times Hulton Picture Library)

Tumblers and acrobats from Strutt's *Sports and Pastimes*. (Radio Times Hulton Picture Library)

Above Children's games from Strutt. It does look remarkably as though nothing much has changed. (Radio Times Hulton Picture Library)

lous thorn, with its church founded by Joseph of Arimathea, of Walsing-ham where they kept a phial containing the Virgin's milk.

Now, saints had often been popularly created, not because of their holiness, but because they had been political rebels and thus, to simple peasants, men to be adored. Latin hymns had been composed to Simon de Montfort, and this had much annoyed Henry III. In 1323 Edward II had written to the Bishop of London that 'people crowd round a panel erected in your church of St Paul's, and there are to be seen statues or painted images, notably that of Thomas, late Earl of Lancaster, a rebel and our enemy. Without any authorization from the Roman Church, our subjects venerate and worship this image, and maintain that it there works miracles.'[10]

Some shrines could boast miracles without number, and these were the most popular places. At others there would have been numerous wonderful cures. At still another, the blood of Christ had been seen to liquefy. At a fourth, the stone statue of the Virgin had raised its hand in blessing. And the popularity of various holy resorts went by fashion. As the decades passed, holy places rose or fell in the popular estimation, and as at modern Lourdes, a huge industry was built up in the sale of souvenirs.

Of course many of the pilgrims were men and women quite sincerely moved by faith. I have seen such people crawling on their bellies up to the shrine of the Virgin in Czestochowa in Poland, hundreds at once moving towards the altar, beating their heads against the stone floor of the nave, women in scarlet, blue and yellow, with big, brown hands that had been twisted by manual labour now lifted in supplication, the brown, rapt faces streaked with dust and tears.

So it must have been at Canterbury, where during the fourteenth century the offerings at the shrine of St Thomas came to three and four hundred pounds a year. Some had walked scores, perhaps hundreds of miles. Others, more well-to-do, had come on horseback. To hire a horse from London to Rochester cost twelvepence. It cost as much again from Rochester to Canterbury. And at the shrine of St Thomas they bought little pewter flasks as proof that they had been there.

At St James's Compostella they bought emblems in the shape of shells, at other shrines, medals bearing images of the saint's head, and wore them pinned to their clothing. On the road they would perhaps have met some old man who lay in a ditch, rigid with devotion, arms stretched out in the form of a cross. Some hermits ate thistles to mortify the flesh. At one shrine they found a nun whose paralysis had been cured, and who sang all day in a quavering, pitiable voice to witness the truth of the miracle that had been vouchsafed her. And of course there were the innumerable beggars they encountered by the roadside or in the doors of churches, crying out 'to haven reuthe and pitee', while they showed their sores or twisted limbs.

Somewhere in a *Dialogue* of Erasmus there is a character who asks, 'I pray you, what araye is this that you be in? Me thynke that you be clothyd with cockle shelles, and be laden on every side with bruches [brooches] of lead and tynne.' And there were many such. When news came, good or bad, a man would kiss one of the medals he was wearing, much as his modern equivalent touches wood or crosses his fingers. Indeed, there were even professional pilgrims, people who wandered from shrine to shrine in a perpetual round, begging on the way. Jusserand says, 'The pilgrim had by calling a great experience of men and things; he had seen much, but with what he retained he mingled a world of imagination, born of his own brain.'[11]

Langland puts it more sharply.

Pilgrimes and palmers . plihten hem to-gederes
For to seche seint Ieme . and seintes at Roome;
Wenten forth in heore wey . with mony wyse tales
*And hedden leue to liyen . al heore lyf aftir.**

Higden in his *Polychronicon* says much the same thing about 'pilgrims and palmers that faste con lihe [lie].' And many of the wild tales current all through the Middle Ages, about mermaids and strange beasts, 'the Anthropophagi, and men whose heads do grow beneath their shoulders', very possibly originated among pilgrims whose legs had not travelled as far as their imaginations.

Some were ambitious indeed. Not for them the patient crisscrossing of England, staff in hand, iron-tipped to pin down the devil, hooked at the other end to gather sinners as a shepherd gathers sheep. No, they obtained the king's passport at any one of a dozen ports, crossed the Channel from Dover or Sandwich (the fare was sixpence, or two shillings if one had a horse) and journeyed on to Cologne or Paris, or perhaps to Rocamadour in Guyenne. The sword of Roland was said to be kept there. Or they might travel to Compostella in Spain via Southampton,

---

* Pilgrims and palmers pledged themselves together, and went to seek St James and the saints at Rome. They went forth on their way with many wise tales, and had leave to lie all their lives thereafter. *Piers Plowman*, Prol. A. 46–9.

perhaps in the *Marie de Southampton*, licensed to carry a hundred passengers, or the *Sainte Marie de Blakney* that took sixty, or by any number of others.

As soon as they reached the open sea 'their hearts began to fail', says a doggerel rhyme of the early fifteenth century, for the big, awkward ships pitched and rolled fearfully in rough weather. But once on dry land again, the pilgrim's world expanded to an extent he had never imagined possible. The Knight of La Tour Landry, who compiled a book of instruction for his daughter, tells her she ought to 'plucke no browes, nother temples nor forhead', and also that 'ye wasshe not the here of youre hede in none other thinge but in lye and water'. In fearful warning he adds that in the Church of Our Lady at Rocamadour he had seen the 'tresses of ladies and gentille women that hadde be wasshe in wyne and in other thinges forto make the here of coloure other wise thanne God made it'.

The farther east a man went the greater the indulgence he might count on. Look at the holy Veronica in Rome–if the pilgrim has come across the sea to do so–and the reward is 12,000 years' freedom from purgatory.

As a matter of fact, in Rome one could find almost anything that had ever been mentioned in the Gospels. There were Aaron's rod and the table of the Last Supper. At Santa Maria Maggiore there stood the portrait of the Virgin by St Luke. Miraculously, it is also to be found in Czestochowa. I myself have seen enough pieces of the true cross to build a moderately large house, and of course in the Middle Ages there must have been more, for a good many will have been destroyed in the six hundred years intervening–by infidels, unbelievers and dry rot.

In Venice the pilgrim had a chance to stare at an ear of St Paul, one of the wine jugs from Cana and a tooth out of the mouth of Goliath. And in Venice he could take ship for the Holy Land. If he stopped in Cyprus, he might, as an Englishman, even be received by the king. One traveller in 1393 wrote to Richard II from Nicosia that 'all the subjects of the King of England are his friends'.[12] Another reports that 'the Venetians send every year five galleys to the Holy Land'. And a certain William Wey, mid-fifteenth-century Fellow of Eton College, actually put together what can only be called a guide book, listing the best hostels, giving the exchange rates of money and at the end adding a collection of useful foreign phrases. He recommends that the traveller take 'a cage for half a dozen of hennys or chekyn to have with yow in the galley', as well as half a bushel of corn with which to feed them. Laxatives, saffron, pepper and other restoratives are also recommended. He tells his readers to beware of eating fresh fruit, for it can 'gender a blody fluxe, and yf an Englyshman haue that sykenes hyt ys a maruel and scape hyt but he dye thereof'. He warns against thieves, advises how to choose a donkey and gives suggestions about tipping in Jaffa.[13]

If all this grandeur lay far beyond the imagination of the poor villein we last saw gaping at his itinerant pardoner, so was at least half the ecclesiastical magnificence he might have seen round him at home in England, even though by the fourteenth century most of the great cathedrals had already been built. But we shall come to them in good time.

As a fitting coda, however, to what little I have had time to say about pilgrims–and Jusserand tells us far more–we ought to hear a word from that old Benedictine, Higden, who died in 1364, for he was writing about his contemporaries, and he might as well have been writing about Victorian England. His countrymen, he says, 'are curious to know, and forever ready to tell what wonders they have seen...and that is why they have spread themselves so far over the earth, for they consider every land they inhabit to be theirs'.

All this time the great waggons full of merchandise rumbled along the roads from town to town. The friars, the pilgrims, the rich merchants, the landlords wandering the wrinkled, many-coloured landscape from one to another of their estates, the beggars, the occasional great lady, the halt, the blind, the whores, the scavengers, the peasants on their way to market, the messengers, the priests with jingling bells–all these travellers drifted through a countryside unhedged and wild, the hamlets small and miles apart, the taverns poor, expensive and sometimes hours away from each other.

In January the unblemished snow stretched away into the distance as far as one could see, and riders narrowed their eyes against the wind. In July the dust rose into the horses' nostrils thick as midsummer midges. And in every copse, some of that workless, itinerant throng might be lurking, the bands of destitute men who in the years after the plague made life dangerous for anyone rich enough to carry a purse at his belt.

From Berwick down to Devon men were leaving the land in ever-growing numbers. They were like migrant animals. No individual had any idea that he was part of a pattern. He had been set moving by the plague and by all the various urges that accompanied and followed it. And as I hope I have made abundantly plain, he had started a revolution that was not only in the end to overturn feudal society but to rearrange the agricultural and indeed mercantile structure of the nation.

With so many dissident wanderers fleeing the known and the hitherto accepted, we have to extrapolate out of our not dissimilar experience. Today in the late twentieth century we too see all around us the breaking up of systems–and not only in England–that have lasted a hundred or a hundred and fifty years. In this spinning time of ours, when nobody knows what the next decade will bring, we too are watching a centrifugal pilgrimage of many people out of the safe centre of our social organism into a rootless and more satisfying world of their own.

The difference is that in Chaucer's England the rout was begun by labourers who saw no other physical possibility, for they had been driven by exhaustion to terror, privation and despair. Like some of our own contemporaries, they too must have talked and argued, year in and year out in a hundred huts and hedgerows and taverns. Often they must have foundered in a host of half understood abstractions.

'When Adam delved and Eve span,' never started with old John Ball. It was in all likelihood a line of Richard Rolle's, who had lived about eighty years earlier. But it survived; it hung in the air, and it made respectable people afraid. These wanderers too, stole, drank, killed, copulated in shabby rooms. How many pregnant, parentless girls there must have been!

When the peasant disappeared off the land, when hired labour became expensive and hard to find, the landowner was of course faced with difficulties quite new to him. Prices may have soared in the towns, but the price of farm produce did not actually rise for the producer all during the period 1350–60. As I have already explained, in the long run the landlord had no choice. He had to change his whole method of farming, to turn arable land to pasture and stock it with sheep–sheep which were, incidentally, smaller than today's and provided a lighter fleece.

Gradually, but with growing momentum, a trade in wool developed, and a first step was taken towards the day when England would be incapable of feeding herself as France and Germany have always done. Woolfels began to be exported from Newcastle and London to Flanders and the Rhine. The first of the great stone barns was built to house fleeces. St Blaize was patron of wool combers, and his festival, 3 February, began to be celebrated with carnivals and processions in Bradford and in various other great centres of the wool trade. 'The wool of Britain,' it was said, 'is spun so fine that it is in a manner comparable to the spider's web.'

For some years Flemish weavers had been scenting the future and moving over to England. Now the king invited dyers, fullers and other wool workers in far greater numbers to emigrate out of Flanders. In the beginning the export of woollen cloth was prohibited, but within a very few years that was changed, and wool became known as 'the flower and strength and revenue and blood of England'. In 1353 the staple was first established, and thenceforward woolfels had first to be collected at one of ten cities from Newcastle to Exeter and Bristol, there to be graded and weighed. Englishmen were in business in the modern way.

The first of the great commercial fairs was established. The organizers closed all the shops in a given town. Nothing was allowed to be sold except at the fair, and whole streets in the fairground were given over, each to its particular trade, to the workers in iron, copper, tin, brass, silver, gold, to cloth, wool, leather, jewellery, to provender of various sorts. There the mummers, the jugglers, the tumblers, the beggars and mountebanks would come rambling, dusty-legged from the highways, hunting for whatever odd pennies they could find. Shakespeare's pedlar in *The Winter's Tale* haunted 'wakes, fairs and bear baiting', and a famous thief he was, selling ribbons, laces, gloves, broaches, bracelets and heaven knows what besides.

It was then that the first great fortunes began to be made, not out of the production of goods–and here was a great change–but by buying and selling. Landowners had never been rich in money, only in land. But all in a single generation the first mercantile families that possessed both real power and hard cash were established, the de la Poles of Hull, for example, who eventually became Earls of Suffolk, or the Canynges of Bristol. William Canynge had been a merchant, a trader overseas and five times mayor of the town. Or there was Nicholas Brembre, the London man (of whom we shall hear a good deal), or William Walworth, who eventually owned not only a thriving trade, but half the brothels in Southwark (the Bishop of Winchester owned the other half), and who almost single-handedly put down Wat Tyler's rebellion, or the Philpots or the de Stodeyes or a host of others.

They not only made enormous fortunes. They supported a government naturally conservative, and in some cases they were able so nearly to control both mayoralties and Parliament that they all but became the government themselves. They became able to lend what would today be millions to Edward III and to his grandson, and in many important respects to put themselves beyond the law.

In a word, feudalism was dying because circumstances made it die, and in the course of a single generation capitalism began to take its place. Not only was the feudal landlord suffering a terrible diminution in both power and property. Not only was his erstwhile tenant and villein migrating to the cities and increasing the number of consumers (as opposed to agricultural workers), and thus providing profit to new masters. But that villein had begun to acquire enough money to fend for himself, so the great merchant guilds began devising ways of helping him spend it.

It was in this way that the Black Death brought about a revolution, a revolution, most importantly, that fed upon itself, for a man who a generation before had hoped only to feed his family began to be aware of luxury on every side. And so he began demanding a share of it.

In the generation between 1350 and 1375, not only did Englishmen begin to see what a fortune there was to be made in wool, in trade and in the creation of monopolies, but the trade itself began breeding the type of adventurer who was in time to expand it in a score of different directions. Here was the beginning of the great English merchant navy, for whose advantage so many subsequent wars were to be fought. Here the great fortunes began that eventually subsidized exploration and the expansion of an island into an empire.

Napoleon was not altogether wrong when he called England a nation of shopkeepers. It was in this third quarter of the fourteenth century that the shopkeepers began to come alive and understand how to take advantage of their opportunities. It was then that (for lack of a better word) an individualism was born that was to make England what she eventually became.

In time these things might very well have happened anyway, as they did in the Hansa towns, for example, and in Marseilles. But in fact, they happened on a nationwide scale nowhere else in Europe. And it is odd to reflect that only a strange concatenation of circumstances in the middle of the fourteenth century put the Lord Chancellor on his woolsack today.

CHAPTER FIVE

IF GOLD RUSTE, WHAT SHAL IREN DO?

There were priests, Langland tells us, who after the pestilence went off to sing for souls in London, 'for silver is sweet'. Chaucer's parson, on the other hand, stayed at home and took care of his flock.

> *This noble ensample to his sheep he yaf,*
> *That first he wroghte, and afterward he taughte;*
> *Out of the gospel he tho wordes caughte,*
> *And this figure he added eek ther-to,*
> *That if gold ruste, what shal iren do?*[1]

He was, so far as the literature is concerned, a most uncommon man Yet we dare not, if only in the name of accuracy, ignore the hundreds, perhaps thousands like him who wrought and taught in utter obscurity, who moved about their little worlds, inwardly aware of a splendour and complexity unlike any we can understand, but which in a hazy way we equate with the great beauty there was in the Middle Ages.

Today we accept intensity as normal only when it is applied for political ends. We see it in a Cromwell, a John Ball, a Lenin, a Garibaldi (to take four men of utterly different temper). But many a simple medieval cleric wept with the same depth of feeling that he had been born too late for the blissful days when Christ had actually walked on earth, when one might have stood in a crowd and heard his voice, or felt his mantle touch one as he passed.

'*Ve michi, ve michi,*' their hearts said, like Chaucer's on his deathbed, for having through weakness and inadequacy fallen short of what they knew to be the human potential. In many a simple lyric, they and men like them sang softly and joyfully about the tears that stirred in them with pity for the world.

We know that priests like this existed, but they left no record. Their purpose was not to leave records, but to do in the world what could only have been done in heaven. So, each in his own obscure place, they wrought and taught, preached convoluted sermons, and tried, Sunday after Sunday, by argument and example to make their congregations feel a touch of glory. They failed because men cannot be argued into seeing visions.

Such intensity of spirit is uncommon in any age, even in a time that builds Chartres or the stained glass of Canterbury or the great visionary prophets of Bamberg. It is the ordinary that mostly survives, one of their sandals, perhaps, propped in a glass case with an inscription telling us nothing whatever about the man who wore it.

The man who *did* leave records, most often left them because he came to the attention of his superiors as careless, abominably taught and utterly undistinguished. In 1281 Archbishop Peckham wrote that 'The ignorance of the priests casteth the people into the ditch of error'. His predecessor, Archbishop Langton, had referred to priests as dumb dogs. Indeed, large numbers of them had been drawn from the peasant class and simply by reason of their advancement had secured a precarious foothold on the fringes of a more affluent society. But most had neither the income nor the dignity to sustain it.

As Richardson points out,

A great many vicars...received but five or six Marks and even less a year, and although rectorial incomes ruled higher, yet there were some who must have been very badly off indeed. We go far wrong if we consider the stipendiary chaplains and assistant priests as forming the lowest paid grade of the body of priests and beneficed clergy. Below them came the unbeneficed minor clergy, a little above them the perpetual vicars and poorest rectors of the really valuable churches.[2]

Such a vicar might have a stipend about four times that of a simple ploughman, or approximately ninety shillings a year.

Latin he knew, or at least enough Latin to read services, which were never conducted in English. But one Dean of Sarum found during a visitation that five different clergymen serving some fifteen parishes were quite unable to construe the central portion of the mass. A curate who had been five years a priest proved to be no more than barely literate. The rich, the learned, the big of heart rarely chose to stay long in rural parishes. And therein lay one basic difficulty of the medieval church, that most of its priests lacked a quality concomitant with its aspirations.

If we can believe the authorities, the troubles had not always been of this order. According to Bede, and Bede was not only immensely learned (he taught Latin, Greek and Hebrew) but perceptive as well, the seventh- and eighth-century clergy had generally been held in great veneration by their parishioners.

The religious habit was held at that period in much honour, he wrote, so that wheresoever any clergyman or monk happened to arrive, he was joyfully received by all the people as God's servant. And if they happened to meet him in the road, they ran to him, bowing, and were eager to be signed with his hand or blessed with his mouth. On Sundays people travelled eagerly to the church or to the monasteries, not to feed their bodies, but to hear the word of God, and if any priest happened to come into a village, the people flocked to him to hear the word of life. Priests and clergymen went into the villages for no other purpose than to preach, to baptize, to visit the sick and in short, to take care of souls.[3]

Early preaching was generally done out of doors, perhaps in a market-place, perhaps at a primitive holy well or on some convenient stretch of green. A stone cross would often be raised at such a place (coincident-ally, it was often at the site of a pre-Christian shrine), and some of them are still standing–at Eyam in Derbyshire, for example, and in Ruthwell on the Solway Firth.

After a time a chancel would be added to protect the portable altar. When the priest had gone so far and thus created a permanent place of worship, his parishioners would be expected to build a nave to cover themselves during inclement weather. And in fact the word 'nave', is derived from the same Latin as 'navy', for the church likened itself to a ship tossed by frequent misfortune. Finally, between the separately built chancel and nave an arch would be erected to separate worshippers from what was considered the holy place, and nevertheless enable them to hear and see the service being conducted.

Some of the great Saxon landowners built churches on their estates, and indeed, Domesday Book, compiled some thirty years after the Conquest, lists about 1,700 of these, almost as many as there were in the early nineteenth century. In such rustic churches the jurisdiction of the priest would be precisely as wide as the lord's property on which he had been hired to serve. And there, eventually, lay one of the troubles, for the priest, depending just as he did in the eighteenth and nineteenth centuries on the goodwill of his patron, inevitably found himself adopting the patron's point of view.

In Saxon times the clergyman seems generally to have been a man of some learning. Very often he was a younger son of the lord himself and had been educated to take what was considered his proper place in the church, much as in the nineteenth century a boy was often brought up a Spartan to prepare himself for a commission in the army.

But after 1066 these Saxon priests, clerical officers in a homogeneous society, were gradually replaced by Normans, and the Normans had no particular ties with those they served. They had come, not as missionaries, but as place-seekers. Then, too, the country began to be sprinkled with monasteries administered from abroad and owing allegiance, not to the peasants on their land, but to the Church in Rome. A new wind blew into the English world, less parochial, less evenly tempered to the sheep, but conceived in a vast classical erudition, in a so-called science of theology, in a religious scholasticism that had touched the Saxons hardly at all. Everything changed. Everything became less simple.

Norman abbots now and then disapproved the opinions and contravened the acts of their Saxon predecessors. Saxon monks were gradually replaced by men born in France, or even in Italy. Thus the church hierarchy changed as the political hierarchy had changed. But most important—at least as far as the common people were concerned—the rectories were taken over by new, foreign priests who felt little except contempt for their Saxon flocks.

William's Domesday Book had been compiled chiefly in order to determine the rights and, above all, the revenues of the crown. But even before the conquered property had been listed and evaluated the duke's followers swarmed into the farthest reaches of the kingdom to seize whatever was of value. That was what the Conquest was all about, and the difference between the old order and the new became almost immediately apparent. From Canterbury to the smallest rural parish, new men brought about changes. It probably did not seem important to them—for it was a brutal age—that these changes accentuated and indeed perpetuated for many generations the differences between the two nations. By the middle of the fourteenth century almost every poet—and poets were, if not the legislators, at least the commentators on the time—pointed out in anger what a vast gulf had opened between laymen and ecclesiastics.

Boys went up to the universities far earlier then than now. The average age at matriculation was no more than fourteen or fifteen, and by the early thirteenth century there were over 3,000 undergraduates at Oxford alone. Poor scholars who had been born to serfdom and had no other livelihood went back to their fathers' cottages during the holidays and worked in the fields as they had always done. The long vacation lasts from haymaking to harvest even now. Others travelled the country from town to town, from monastery to manor house, begging alms, and it was almost everywhere recognized as an act of piety to help them.

But we have to become able to see these people in terms of their modern equivalents, the laughing, ribald, songmaking, drinking, fornicating young–the clerk in Chaucer's *Miller's Tale* is a particularly vivid example–who wandered the roads in piebald tunics with feathers in their hats, arguing whatever you liked, from Aristotle and theology to mathematics and the science of alchemy with interlocutors for whom they felt nothing but a half-humorous contempt, who sang to their guitars in taverns and tumbled the girls, who got into endless scrapes, swore by the latest fashions and were, as they have always been, the new idea.

And if this life led to what looked like the eventual security of a priesthood, they must have waked sadder and wiser men when they finally got into harbour. No more tavern tales and tricks played on the miller. No more singing 'Come hither, love, to me', and decking one's coat with flowers. If one took the girls, there'd be leyrwite to pay in the morning.

Ordination generally followed receipt of the minor orders as acolyte, subdeacon and deacon. But before he could be ordained, our clerkling had first to acquire a 'title', that is, a place in which to exercise his ministry, and a stipend with which to support himself. This required an eye for the politic word, a knack for being able to ingratiate himself. He might be given one of the parishes. He might become a member of some religious house. He might not want to preach at all, but to enter the civil service, though for a peasant boy this was all but impossible.

Even so, the number of ordinations was very large. In one diocese–that of York–there were 271 priests ordained in the year 1344-5, and everywhere, not only here, there had to be frequent dispensations granted, permissions to ignore the canonical obstacles, which were servile condition, illegitimate birth, what was called personal blemish and, most often to the point, insufficient learning.

And when after all the struggles he finally moved into his vicarage, what did he find but ignorance all round him, ignorance positively maddening to one who had lived with his peers in the great world? His parishioners were idle oafs. They gambled, they drank, they cheated him even of the tithes that gave him his miserable living, and towards each other they acted with a brutality which, if they were Christians, should have been utterly foreign to their natures.

What wonder that the priest either fled to seek a well-paid chantry, or else sank into an apathy much like that of the peasants under his care? Many a young vicar must have heard with a pang the little bells jingling to indicate some fashionable gentleman riding by, for they reminded him of the promise of his own youth, never to be fulfilled.

What became of him? The Hereford visitation of 1397 is crowded with evidence. In only 44 of 281 parishes does the report state that all is well. In many of the others the priest is charged with immorality. He is a fornicator, an adulterer. He has stolen women away from their husbands. At Weston it is reported that he is absent for weeks on end, and no services are held. At Cowarne the chancel is in ruins, the windows are broken and the roof leaks. At Werley the rector pastures horses and ducks in the churchyard. In Colwall the chaplain has forged a will and made himself beneficiary of a parishioner's estate. The vicar of Eardisley is a common usurer; he is also thought to be sleeping with the maidservants. The rector of Wentnor frequents the local tavern day and night. In North Lydbury the vicar has committed adultery with one Johanna Staltogh. At Clun the chaplain has refused the sacrament to a dying man, is living with a married woman and has two children by her. The chaplain of Kilpeck is actually a heretic. He conjures up familiar spirits. In Shelsley the priest, a certain Richard Sterre, copulates in the church itself. Chaucer's poor parson begins to sound an extraordinary man.

Once a man had been ordained, he had reached a certain station in life, even though he might actually be serving in some hamlet where his father and brothers worked as villeins in the fields. It was still a struggle, however. The sense of class distinctions was very strong, and Langland sets down the not uncommon feeling that a man ought to live in the station to which he has been born.

> Hit by-cometh for clerkes . Crist for to seruen,
> And knaues vncrouned . to cart and to worche.
> For shold no clerk be crouned . bote yf he ycome were
> Of franklens and free men . and of folke yweddede.
> Bondmen and bastardes . and beggers children,
> Thuse by-longeth to labour . and lordes kyn to seruen
> Bothe god and good men . as here degree asketh;
> Some to synge masses . other sitten and wryte,
> Rede and receyue . that reson ouhte spende;
> Ac sith bondemenne barnes . han be mad bisshopes,
> And barnes bastardes . han ben archidekenes,
> And sopers and here sones . for seluer han be knyghtes,

And lordene sones here laborers . and leid here rentes to wedde,
Lyf-holynesse and loue . han ben longe hennes,
*And wole, til hit be wered out . or otherwise ychaunged.**

The priest might have risen above his origins, but his house in the village was often no better than those of his peasant neighbours. Unless he managed somehow to break free, he had achieved all that a man with his particular connections could achieve, because for him, as for most people, the fourteenth century was a prison, and very few indeed were ever released into a society wherein a man might rise by his own merits.

The cottage would have one long room, with a hearth at one end and probably a pair of firedogs. There would be a dais where his chair and table stood. He would own a bench, a few stools for visitors and a board propped up against one wall that could be set up on trestles if they stayed to dine. In a small, separate building he would have a buttery, storeroom and kitchen. And there would be a servant. If he were a little better off than the average he might have bought a tapestry to hang across one wall and, unlike his peasant neighbours, he would be provided with rushes to strew on the floor.

Here he would eat and sleep, read, compose sermons and be visited with the endless ugly complaints of his parishioners. If, on the other hand, by luck or by usury or by wheedling the rich, he found some way of living a little more grandly, of providing some colour to gild the drabness, then he was censured for living too well.

Often enough he wore no sober grey or black, but went about with his hair grown long, wearing a bonnet to hide the tonsure. In a word, he tried to look like a man of the world. He would appear in a short coat and scarlet gown, perhaps with a silver belt at his waist and a baselard or dagger at his side. In a catalogue of the benefactors of St Albans Abbey there are coloured portraits of a number of such men.[4] Richard Threton wears a gown and hood of bright blue, lined with white, and his shoes are scarlet. John Rodland, Rector of Todyngton,

---

* It is fitting that clerics serve Christ and untonsured fellows do carting and labouring. For no cleric should be given the tonsure unless he be born of franklins and of free men and of folk who are married. Bondmen and bastards and beggars' children, for them is labour suitable, to work with the lord's cattle, to serve both God and good men as their rank requires. Some should sing masses, or else sit and write, advise and be advised whatever reason offers. But since bondmen's children have become bishops, and the children's bastards archdeacons, and soapmakers and their sons in return for silver have been made into knights–with lords' sons for their labourers, men who have lost their rents in wagers… holiness of life has long ago vanished, and will remain lost until these things be out of style, or otherwise are changed. *Piers Plowman,* C. VI. 61–73, 80–1.

appears in green gown and scarlet hood, the Rector of Little Waltham in pink and purple, and still another gentleman is shown in pink lined with blue, and with silver at his shoulders.

> *Sire Iohan and sire Geffray . hath a gerdel of syluer,*
> *A basellarde, or a ballokknyf . with botones euergylte.*[5]

In his instructions for parish priests, written in 1303, John Myrc had strictly forbidden them to go about dressed as laymen, and in 1342 the Archbishop of Canterbury had written that

The behaviour of clerks ought to be an example and a pattern to lay folk. But the abuses of these clerics, greater than they have ever been, in neglecting the tonsure, in manner of clothing, in trappings for their horses and in many other ways have created an abominable scandal among the people. Men who hold positions of ecclesiastical dignity... allow themselves to be seen with hair spreading over their shoulders as if they were women. They walk about, dressed not like clerics but like soldiers...their hair curled and perfumed, their hoods decorated with lappets of enormous length, wearing beards, with rings on their fingers. The belts at their waists are studded with precious stones. Their purses are enamelled, and they are armed with knives as long as swords. Their hoods are of green or red. Hunting horns hang about their necks, and their capes and cloaks are so decorated with fur in wild disregard of the canons that one can see little or no difference between them and laymen.

It is easy for us, with the benefit of hindsight, to see that the old simplicity, the original Christian purity of life, had simply gone out of fashion. But we would be only partly right. The individual priest, beset with the day-to-day cares of his village life, could have had little idea of the larger picture. Every class, the clergy, the peasantry, the nobility, the commercial, royalty itself, was trying to break free of limitations that must have seemed stultifying and repressive. The great merchants, as we shall see in a moment, were amassing fortunes and living both more dangerously and more luxuriously than any class in post-Roman western Europe had ever done. Edward III struck the gold noble, the most magnificent coin that had ever been minted in England. Richard II dressed more flamboyantly than anyone had done in a thousand years. The wars in France were being fought at greater cost than any since the time of the Romans. The peasant was about to unleash a rebellion against intolerable conditions, and even the plague, the Black Death, had struck on a scale commensurate with the times, and killed more people in a single year than had ever been killed in one year in all of recorded history.

The missionaries at the close of the dark ages and the Saxon priests who followed had lived in a far less perplexing world. The new medieval society was on the point of explosion. In spite of superficial certainties in men's minds, England was highly unstable, and although it achieved its fourteenth-century flowering in the arts–in poetry, in music, in architecture, even in dress–a flowering so far unparalleled in its history, it was already part way down the road to decay, and in the crises to come was going to have to learn–in what eventually became good English fashion–not to reason, but to muddle through.

By the middle of the fourteenth century, so much had the village priest been divorced from those he had come to serve that peasants would often cross themselves in holy dread when they met him in the road. When he was rich, as Coulton points out, he naturally attracted more envy than those of noble birth, for he had demonstrated a contradiction in purposes. When he was poor, unless he possessed the conspicuous virtues of Chaucer's parson, peasants looked at him only with contempt.

I shall have something to say in a moment about what he preached, for at a time when the law was an enemy and political eloquence did not exist, it was only from the pulpit that the revolutionary ferment then working could be adequately expressed. The great and real priests were, unlike their country brothers, the editors of the age. They said not only what was in men's minds, but, almost as important for our purposes, they left us in their surviving sermons a gloss on the society they served, more vivid and perhaps more accurate than any other we have found. They were big men and spoke in a big language.

But I want first to interpolate another development which, though it flowered a generation or so after Chaucer's time, had its beginnings while he was alive, and helped bring about the changes that were then so strongly in the wind.

The church relied not only on preaching and good works to drive home its lessons. It used every tale the peasant might ever have heard; it used the old pagan festivals, the dancing, the laughter, the primitive re-enactment of historic events to show its audiences the bloody pieces out of which it had been formed. The fall of Adam, Nebuchadnezzar mad and eating grass like an ox, the cozening of Samson by his wife, the tribulations of Job, the sufferings of the martyrs, the purity of those who had learned to 'pierce the palace of heaven with a paternoster', the deaths

The Rector of Little Waltham,
John Rodland, Rector of
Todyngton, and one
Richard Threton, three priests
vividly characterized by the
illuminator of Cotton MS Nero
Dvii. (The British Library Board)

The fourteenth-century priest's house in Prestbury, Cheshire. (Radio Times Hulton Picture Library)

of kings–all these began to be dramatized so as to make plain even to the dimmest attention what the church wanted to make part of people's emotional baggage.

It is a truism that to see a thing acted makes a sharper impression than to hear it told. When some ninth- or tenth-century priest first conceived the idea of dramatizing–let us say–the discovery of the empty tomb on Easter morning, he no doubt sent his congregation home with a sharper understanding of the story. We have to imagine the mass interrupted by a little scene beside the altar, a scene in which actors representing the three Marys come to the sepulchre, and are there met by an angel who stands with wings outspread and cries, '*Non est hic. Surrexit.*' Then, to the bewilderment and growing delight of the congregation, the priest lifts a curtain to reveal the empty tomb. There are the bandages, there the stone in which Christ lay, there the frightened women.

Gradually, year by year, as the possibilities of such a representation become clear, the scene at the tomb is expanded, and we have the beginnings of a Passion Play. We see Herod, frightening as the devil himself, we see the journey into Egypt. Or else, with a star rising behind the crucifix, we are shown the inn and the host explaining that in all Bethlehem there is not a room to be had. Then comes another scene, with the manger, the miraculous birth, the arrival of the shepherds and of the three wise men from the east.

The idea is taken up by some enterprising bishop. His cathedral can provide not only a more glorious setting for the drama, but clergymen and a choir, both to take part in the drama and to sing. Then, if friars preached, not in church, but in the churchyard or at the market cross, why should not the play be acted either in the porch or on a stage set up in the town? And now the whole panorama of Biblical history–paradise crowded with angels, the harrowing of hell, kings, courtiers, martyrs–can all be represented.

The important point was that the stories were as familiar to the audiences as bread and cheese. And gradually, as the plays began to be presented, not in Latin, but in the vernacular, and as laymen (generally members of the various guilds) began to stage their own versions–there are records of such productions in more than a hundred towns–not only did the productions become more ambitious; the stories themselves, because the actors wanted to entertain, began to be altered in the interests of the drama itself.

The Virgin Mary might be seen pulling a sinner up out of hellfire with her own two hands. Or a scene would be turned into farce that no

D

historian–and certainly not the Bible–had ever intended. Or the most flagrant anachronism would be introduced in speech or dress, simply to give the scene pungency. In *Noah's Flood*, when Noah asks his wife to go into the ark, 'By Christ,' she answers, 'not or I see more need.'

The plays became so huge that performances (with the actors in masks) very often had to be started at dawn so that from the fall of Lucifer to the Last Judgement the entire day could be given over to their unfolding. Between sunrise and sunset a man might watch the whole epic, from the beginning to the ending of the world.

'Alas,' cries Satan, 'that ever my mother me bare!' And one by one the damned cry out at the thought of the sins they have committed which are going to earn them nothing but torment until the ending of the world. They were drunkards, they were pitiless to the poor, they murdered, they were luxurious, covetous, vain, lecherous, proud, idle and given to worldly pomp. They robbed holy church, they cheated men out of their land, and now they are going to burn in the devil's belly.

> *Alas! now fallen is my flower,*
> *Alas! for sinne is no Succower;*
> *No silver may me save.*

> *Alas! that euer I was Emperour!*
> *alas! that euer I had Towne or Tower;*
> *Alas! I Buy hard my honour:*
> *Hell paynes for it I haue.*[6]

Laughter, pageantry, pain, the frequent sudden awareness of truths almost too poignant for expression, the terrible temptation of Eve, the death of Abel, the slow talk of Abraham and Isaac:

> *Father, I am full sore afraide*
> *to see you beare this drawen sword...*

> *Wold God, my mother were here with me!*
> *she wolde knele vpon her knee.*[7]

Balaam and his ass, Moses upon Sinai, the slaughter of the innocents, the slow, splendid and frightening death of Christ, and at the end, the purgation, the pity and fear. It must on many occasions have been more than horrifying to see scenes and stories acted, every word of which one knew to be true, and, above all, pertinent to one's own situation, for it was the history of the struggle to know God.

But the Mysteries were also the beginning of the secularization of the church. 'The plays,' says Greg, 'from being ecclesiastical became human, from being Latin became vernacular, from being cosmopolitan, became national.'[8] Not that either Miracles or Mysteries were staged without facing serious opposition. 'In the old tyme,' Bromyard writes late in the century, 'men and women were ful glad to make them clene in sowle from all maner of unclenenes of syn. But now-a-dayes that solemnyte ys turnyd to syn and unclenenes, not only in pryde but all the vii dedely synnys, and in ouhtbragyng, drynkyng, wakynge, playing veyn plays with al rybawdry and all harlotry.'[9]

The priest who dressed in scarlet and blue, the pardoner who sold heaven for a handful of silver, the pilgrim hunting salvation everywhere except at home, all these were similar expressions of a sense that the old, lonely theology evolved during a period of hundreds of years was no longer pertinent to what many in the fourteenth century thought of as their modern world.

The church had looked to have a monopoly of the same incontrovertible truth and the same unassailable virtue that modern science and modern capitalism seems to some of us to possess. It is only in this light that we can appreciate how momentous, and indeed terrible, a change the coming reformation must have looked. It is no wonder that John Wycliffe, who began it during Chaucer's lifetime, had his bones disinterred, burned and scattered to the winds, or that Jan Huss, who continued it, was betrayed and burned at the stake, or that Luther, who all but completed it, was known without question to have been the offspring of the devil and a nun.

CHAPTER SIX

Fish have to swim

We have looked at our simple village priest through the eyes of his superiors, but most of them did preach, and we could certainly judge them more fairly if we were able to read what they said. But with some few exceptions, what they said was never written down, and it is reasonable to suppose that many of them simply picked their sermons out of the numerous manuals that had been written to teach them what to preach in the first place.

Thus John Peckham, a Franciscan Archbishop of Canterbury, had late in the thirteenth century composed his *Constitutiones*, a Latin treatise for the instruction of the clergy. Fifty years afterwards it was translated into English by Archbishop Thoresby for the benefit of priests whose Latin was too execrable for them to understand it. And there were other tracts and primers, many of them. 'Don Gaytrige's Sermon', one of the most famous, was gradually expanded with *exempla* and argument so that it could be used as a preaching text for almost any occasion.

> *Loke thou moste on thys work;*
> *For here thou myhte fynde and rede*
> *That the behoveth to conne nede,*
> *How thou shalt thy paresche preche.*[1]

The book instructed its readers to give lessons to their congregations four times a year on paternoster, ave, creed, the commandments, the virtues and the deadly sins. No simple priest was thought able to speak with his own tongue.

But it is the more original preaching that really concerns us, for it not only holds up a mirror to the time; it lets us hear the voices of such vigorous and intelligent men as Bromyard, FitzRalph, Brinton, Waldeby, Alkertoun and many others, who not only quoted chapter and verse in castigating their fellow clerics, but expressed themselves in vivid and sometimes emotional language about the social and political evils of their time. Indeed, the whole known world was their province, from astronomy to botany, history and a sometimes mythically interpreted zoology.

As Professor Owst* pointed out, many of the phrases and proverbs we use today appear in their sermons–to grease someone's palm–many hands make light work–enough is as good as a feast–to run with the hare and hunt with the hounds–the apple never falls far from the bough–a maid should be seen, but not heard–pride goeth before a fall (though a similar phrase appears in *Matthew*, xvi. 18)–or love me, love my dog, though this last is actually attributed to St Bernard.

'With three thynges the material sunne is maad derk fro men,' runs one such. 'That is, with nyht, and with cloudes, and with the eclipce...ye schulleth understonde that the derknesse of the eclipse if of no defaute in the sunne, as it semeth in mennes siht. But, as clerkys seyn, whan the moone is directli betwixe the erthe in which we dwellen and the sunne, than is causid the eclipse. Riht soon, whan men of holi cherche, that is, prelates and prestes, which principalli shulden take liht of kunnynge of the sunne or cristis lawe, as the moone of the sunne, beth directli bitwixe it and the comen peple, with al hire power stoppynge and hidynge from hem the verrei knowing ther-of, than is causid a greet goostli eclipse of the sunne of cristes liht and his lawe in cristen mennes soules.'

In the same way drawing on current scientific speculation, the great Bromyard, probably a Herefordshire man, who became lecturer in theology at Cambridge, in his *Summa Predicantium* compares hypocrites to falling stars. Elsewhere the adder, 'the old serpent', who lays one ear to the ground and stops up the other with his tail, is likened to the sinner who will not listen to the priest's exhortations. The enquirer into forbidden matters, on the other hand, is like the eagle that 'flieth hier than othur birdes. He may also se farthur, [yet] he fedeth hym oft on stynkynge careyn [carrion].'[2]

Over and over again, animal fables are used to point moral lessons. The partridge calls in the hawk to save him from the kite, and suffers

---

* I must in all justice add here that it is Professor Owst who has written the very nearly definitive work on medieval sermon literature, a great deal of which has never been printed. I have leaned heavily on Dr Owst's researches in what I have to say on the subject. The manuscript sermons I mention are those he has uncovered and transcribed. MS. Add. 41321, fol. 9b. Owst, *Literature and Pulpit*, p. 190.

accordingly. The pelican is Christ, for his blood has the power to bring the dead back to life. Even classical literature and myth are plundered to furnish *exempla*. Mercury closes the hundred eyes of Argus so that he may safely steal the cattle that Argus is guarding. The eyes are compared to priests, who ought never allow themselves to be beguiled, but instead should keep watch in every direction to save the souls in their charge.

Elsewhere the story is told of a dying man too nearly moribund to make a sign whether or not he wishes to be given the sacrament. The priest tries to rouse him, but in vain. So a friend offers to make the man respond. He lays his hand on the treasure chest at the foot of the bed, and at once the sick man gapes and raises an arm to protect it.

Exempla provide some of the liveliest efforts to use the natural world for the purpose of pointing moral lessons. Dr Owst, in a letter to *The Times* of 24 November 1928, announced his discovery in one of the Harleian manuscripts of a sermon containing a remarkable similarity to the story of Bunyan's pilgrim so many centuries afterwards. A man charged with sin, says the preacher, is like one carrying an enormous sack while he tries to walk a plank over an abyss. He hardly dares take a step forwards. If 'he bere longe the sak of synne and he susteyne hit tyl he be ded...he falleth down into the swole [pit] of helle'. But if during his lifetime he had only known how deep the chasm was and had cast down his sack while he was still able to do so, he would not have fallen into the pit.

As I said earlier, in their zeal to speak the truth, some are not even afraid to attack the church itself. Archbishop FitzRalph, a most remarkable scholar, eighty-eight of whose Latin sermons have survived, speaks of prelates, greater and lesser alike, who are...fornicators, adulterers of many mistresses. Others are drunk every day of the week. Still others are plunderers of the church, and pass on goods they have stolen to their own sons and daughters, whom they call nephews and nieces.[3]

Bishop Brinton of Rochester, one of the most reasonable and fiery men of his age, preaches about clerics who crucify Christ daily. 'So ambitious are these ecclesiastics,' he says, 'that if they already have a fat living they must have a prebend. If they have one prebend, they want several. If they have several, then they want to be made bishops, and at last, being given a bishopric, they want to be made bishops at court.'[4]

How dare a priest celebrate the communion, men ask, while his bed is still warm with a prostitute's body? How dare people preach charity who sell the goods of the poor that have been given them in tithes? Those hypocrites, the elegant priests, are compared in one sermon, not with men, but with apes.

But it was not only sinful clerics they attacked. Sixty or seventy years earlier in the *Speculum Laicorum*,[5] there had been a story about a steward with a wicked tongue, a man so harsh to his lord's tenants that he quite impoverished them with his extortions. When he was dead he appeared to one of those same tenants, 'dressed all in black, sticking out of tongue and with his own hand cutting it into pieces with a razor. Then he would throw the bits back into his mouth, shoot out the tongue, quite whole again, and cut it up once more. When later he lifted up his cloak, the dreamer saw that his body looked like blazing iron.'

The great Bromyard again, speaking of the rich, says that 'their fulness was our hunger, their merriment our misery, their jousts and tournaments our torments. It was with our oats and at our expense that they had these things. Their plenty was our scarcity, their feasts, their delights, their pomps, vanities, excesses and superfluities were our fastings, our penalties, our wants, calamities and spoliation.'[6]

Certes it semeth [says another], that it may not be withoute grete outrage and synne that oon person schal have for his owne body so many robes and clothinges in a yere, of diverse colours and riches, thorgh whiche many pore men and nede persones myght be sufficiantly susteyned and clothed as charite asketh. And yit, hif suche robes and clothes, after that thei have wered hem as longe as hem lust, were afterward yeven to the pore nedy, and for love of God, yit schulde it somwhat helpe to the soule. But thei beth yeven comounliche to harlottes, mynstrelles, flaterers, glosers and other suche; and that is grete synne.[7]

The rich man ate the poor, said Wimbledon, preaching at St Paul's Cross in London, and how much more strongly can one express it? 'Children, be stille,' said the ploughman to his infants lying at the end of the furrow. And the preacher cries out for a paternalism by which the poor man will at least be given cast-off clothing. It was probably the best one could have hoped for.

But morality often had no need to thunder. Sometimes it stepped quietly, but held no less firmly to the point. 'It is told of oon that was an evyll doere,' said a preacher, attacking men's vanity, 'and so prowde that his neighbores myght not lyve in pease for him: there came to him a riche man and a good man of that same contre, and asked hym why he was so prowde. The tother answerid and seide—"for he was a gentillman".

"It is sothe," saide the tothere; "thou arte a Gentillman on thy fadres syde. But thy modre was a strumpet.""[8]

Luxury, avarice and pride, over and over they are attacked in stories that provide specific illustrations. Bromyard, for example, writes of those who feed their dogs more plentifully than they do the poor, and whose dogs turn up their noses at white bread while the poor would greedily devour the bran. Indeed, after some great banquets, bread is actually brought in for the hounds, and what is left over is handed to the poor outside the gates. 'The wickede pride amonge lordes and knyttes, says a preacher, 'that causeth this oppressinge of the pore peple, maketh now so gret a noyse and soun that it is a gret clamour in al this rewme, in everi schire thereof, of the extorcioneris that dwellin therinne...' It is 'herd in to the heres [ears] of god in hevene, as it was of the cheldern of Israel'.[9]

Not that the nobility alone are censured. Bromyard and many others have a good deal to say about the peasant too. He is equally guilty of pride and avarice, ill-clothed though he may be. 'For ofte tymes pore men gruccheth ayenst god and holdeth hemself more worthy, and to have more mede byfore god than thylke [those] that be more at ese.'[10] No matter what one possesses, says another priest, be it little or much, one wishes to have more. Do not the poor sometimes pass on false coin to their neighbours? Do they not grumble at God, at the bad weather, or because of dear years or crops that have failed?

Indeed, the *Speculum Laicorum* is even more specific. A wretched ploughman, it says, who used to be happy with a good white kirtle and a russet gown, has now quite changed. He has become more demanding. Now he must have a costly doublet and a gown and a gay hood and wear a tippet as though he were a squire. If he is not given a dagger in a silver sheath along with his wages, he refuses to work. And we have to remember that this compilation was written before the time of the Statute of Labourers.

Marriage is generally evil too, they say, not necessarily because it permits sexual gratification, but because it is so often entered into out of greed. 'Mony [many] wedd hem wyvys for her worldly goodes', we read. 'Som had lever to take an olde wedow, though sche be ful lothe-lyche and never schall have cheldren. And fro the tyme that he hathe the mocke [the muck] that he wedded her for, and felethe her breth foul stynkynge and her eyen blered, scabbed and febyll, then they spend apon strompettes that evyll-getyn goodes. And sche shall sytt at home wyth sorowe, hungry and thrusty.'[11]

How maidens ought reasonably to act is beautifully spelled out in a sermon too long to be quoted here verbatim. The preacher tells a story about a princess whose father thought her old enough to marry. So he invited hundreds of suitable men from all the countries of the earth, and asked his daughter to walk amongst them and choose whichever she liked.

So the girl did as she was bid, looked at and talked with them all, and then made her decision. 'If I marry one of you because he is rich,' she said, 'the riches will make us greedy for more, or else fearful of losing what we have. So we shall be very unhappy. If I marry a man because he is handsome, when his beauty fades I shall have lost the thing for which I married him. If I marry a man because he is a brave knight, why, he is the one most likely to be killed in battle. So I shall marry none of you.' And falling to her knees, she folded her hands in prayer and looked up to heaven. Whereupon the roof was opened and a great light shone through, for she had been accepted as the bride of Christ, in whom alone there is no danger.

Even kissing and cuddling are evils, says one preacher in a famous passage, for they are like the three inducements that a tavern keeper uses to drum up trade. First he hangs a pretty garland out to draw men in. Then he gives them a free taste of his wine, and that is the equivalent of those 'unclene kyssynges, clippynges and other unhonest handelynges'. And at last, after the taverner 'hath yeve men a tast, he bryngeth hem to a place where thei may drynke aftur here plesaunce...and even so dothe the flesshe, for aftur clippynge and kissynge and unclene towchynge, he bringeth thise unclene pepull to some plase that pleases hem, wher thei mai make her cownauntes of sensuall love'.[12]

Who in all history was a stronger man than Samson, they ask, wiser than Solomon, holier than David? Yet behold how women undid them all! 'Nyce maydenes,' the preacher tells them, 'that walketh aboute in medes and in fayre places, ledynge daunces and syngyge, as it were schewynge [showing] hem selfe to lese her maydenhode, and makynge sorwe that they have ybe so longe maydense', these are the temptresses. 'For it byfalleth [behoves] maydenes to be in stilnesse and in cloos [confinement] as our lady seynte Marie was whenne the angel came to hure and fond hure in a pryvy chambre and nouht stondynge ne walkynge by stretys.'[13]

Who wants women, anyway? They are so contrary, so quarrelsome, so disobedient that one husband who had grown tired of his wife's habit of contradicting simply left her two boxes of sweets when he had to go on a journey. One was wholesome, and one poisonous. On no account, he told her, was she to touch the poisoned ones. But of course she refused to obey, and by that means he got rid of her.

But women go further. They deck themselves with hair that is not their own, and colour their faces to borrow a complexion that God never intended. Only two sorts of people ever wear masks, Bromyard points out, those who act in plays and those who are out to commit robbery. Women who thus cover what God made and wander about the town to entice men achieve exactly what they intend. They fill the hearts of the beholders with lust, and thus damn souls that God both created and redeemed.

If we are to believe the preachers (and there is plenty of other evidence), copulation, drunkenness and swearing were so common as to be almost commonplace. The drunkards 'ofte as thei goth homward toward hire beddes, their drencheth hemself in dichis [ditches] bi the weie. And thouh thei comen hoom unti hire chambre, their leteth the candel falle and brenne hire bed, hemself and hir wyfe, hire children and alle hire godes', we read in one sermon.[14]

Master Rypon of Durham, a contemporary of Chaucer, complains that although men fast during Lent, as indeed they should, they take to drink instead. 'Fish have to swim', they cry, laughing. So they swallow a bit of herring or salt beef to excite a thirst, and then they drink and fall to obscenity and quarrelling. At last they fight and sometimes kill each other. And the next day, those who did manage to stagger home cannot go to church, for they have hangovers. Indeed, Langland confirms all that the preachers say.

> I haue made vowes fourty . and for-yete hem on the morne;
> I parfourned neure penaunce . as the prest me hihte,
> Ne ryhte sori for my synnes . yet was I neuere.
> And yif I bidde any bedes . but if it be in wrath,
> That I telle with my tonge . is two myle fro myne herte.
> I am occupied eche day . haliday and other,
> With ydel tales atte ale . and otherwhile in cherches.*

The evidence all points one way, to suggest that it was an age when men, both rich and poor, drank heavily, fought at the drop of a hat and forni-

---

* I have made forty vows, and forgot them in the morning, never did my penances as the priest required, nor was ever right sorry for my sins. And if I told my beads, except when I was angry, what I said with my tongue was two miles from my heart. I fill up every day, holidays and others, with idle tales in the ale house, only now and then in churches. *Piers Plowman*, B. V. 404-10.

cated with considerable energy. And the drunkards whom the preachers
describe reeling home at night along dark streets, singing and shouting,
attacking the occasional passer-by, surely these are Milton's 'sons of
Belial, flown with insolence and wine'. A Puritan thought, a Puritan
expression of it, and it makes one realize how much of Puritanism was
already audible in the sermons of fourteenth-century Catholic priests.

The disparity between the peasant's life and that of his betters was
evident even in church. The peasant stood or knelt on the stone floor
of the nave, where there were neither pews nor benches. His masters sat
in the chancel. In many cases, the lord not only had his own chapel,
but insisted that inferiors be excluded. One chaplain of Erleigh was
reprimanded for admitting the simple folk of nearby Sonning into such a
private chapel when he said mass, for he was actually entitled to admit
no one except the lord, his lady and their freeborn servants.

But it was not only lord and villein who had to observe social distinctions. Chaucer's host, Harry Baily, remarks that his own wife goes mad
with rage at any imagined snub, if some neighbour, for example, refuses
to bow in her direction when their eyes meet during the service.

> *When she comth home, she rampeth in my face,*
> *And cryeth, 'false coward, wreak [revenge] thy wyf.*
> *By corpus bones! I wol have thy knyf,*
> *And thou shalt have my distaf and go spinne!*[15]

People shouted and shoved at each other in church for positions they
considered suitable to their social standing. There is a vivid picture of
this in Langland where Wrath makes confession.

> *Ich haue be cook in here kychene . and the couent serued*
> *Meny monthes with hem . and with monkes bothe.*
> *Ich was the prioresse potager . and other poure ladies,*
> *And made here ioutes of iangles . 'dame Iohane was a bastarde,*
> *And dame Clarice a knyghtes doubter . a cokewold was hure syre,*
> *Dame Purnele a prestes file . prioresse worth hue neuere;*
> *For hue hadde a childe in the chapon-cote . hue worth chalenged at eleccion.'*
> *Thus thei sitte, tho sustres . som tyme, and disputen,*
> *Til 'thow lixt' and 'thow lixt' . be lady ouer hem alle;*
> *And thenne a-wake ich, Wratthe . and wold be auenged.*
> *Thanne ich crie and cracche . with my kene nailes,*
> *Bothe byte and bete . and brynge forth suche thewes,*
> *That alle ladies me lothen . that louen eny worscheap.*

Among wyues and wodewes . ich am ywoned sitte
Yparroked in puwes; . the person hit knoweth
How litel ic louye . Letice at the style;
For hue hadde haly bred er ich . myn herte by-gan to chaunge.
Afterward after mete . hue and ich chidde,
And ich, Wratth, was war . and wroth on hem both,
Til aither cleped othere 'hore' . and of with the clothes,
*Til bothe here heuedes were bar . and blody here chekes.**

The brawling was not confined to the church, of course. After service, out they would go to the churchyard, where buskers and stallholders had set up a veritable fairground. There the afternoon would be whiled away in gossip and gambling, pudding ale and fights. Of one parson it was reported that he never encouraged people to think of the church as a holy place, for he stored his corn in the building, and even brewed his beer there.

If these examples are suspected of having been picked out for their luridness, one need only look at any eighteenth-century history. Fighting and drunkenness there have always been, but only in some Hogarthian gin alley will the sheer despair and the sense of remediable wrongs have bred such a universal flouting of convention. No wonder the peasant fought, or the priest fled to the city, or stored his corn where he could, or drank, or dressed like a soldier, or toppled the occasional serving wench head over heels in the straw.

No wonder the peasant tried to avoid paying at tithing time, for although a quarter of his donation was intended to go to the poor, very few quarters ever got there. Bishop Lyndwood of Hereford may have written that 'they who pay not the personal tithes are damned', but Gower wrote that a monk was nothing but a bailiff in a cowl. Chaucer's

---

* I have been cook in their kitchen, and served the convent many months. Aye, and the monks too. I was the prioress's soup maker, and that of other poor ladies, and stirred their soups with wrangling. Dame Joan was a bastard, and Dame Clarice a knight's daughter, with a cuckold for a father. Dame Pernel was a priest's whore, and never should be prioress. She'd had a child in the hen house, and will be accused at election time. Thus they sit, these sisters, now and then, and argue, till 'thou liest', and 'thou liest' is lady over them all. Then I, Wrath, awake, and look to get revenges. I shout and I scratch and claw at them with my sharp nails. I bite and I beat and show such filthy manners that all the ladies loathe me if they feel any reverence. I sit amongst wives and widows, parked in the pews, and the parsons knows the truth, how little love I have for Letice at the style. She had the holy bread before me and my heart began to change toward her. And later, after dinner, she and I began squabbling, and I, Wrath, was wary and angry with them both. Till they called each other whore, and off with their clothes, so that both their heads were bare, and their cheeks bloody. *Piers Plowman,* C. VII. 130–50.

poor parson, loath to excommunicate for non-payment of tithes, is almost unique in the literature of the period.

'In justice is great profit', ran the proverb, and the average priest's justice was much like that of the landlord. But there was another side to the coin. If the priest was often as poor as the peasant he served, the exceptional man was sometimes moved by the same sense of a need for radical change. John Ball was a priest before he became a revolutionary, and died by being disembowelled in Coventry. Another revolutionary, John Wrawe, had been vicar of Ringfield, near Beccles. He ended his days on a Suffolk gallows because he, too, had been filled with a sense of injustice, and with a zeal for socialist reform five hundred years before his time. In many a village the priest was the ringleader in spiritual, and eventually in political rebellion. Dreary and interminable fulminations against the seven deadly sins, or a righteous parroting of paternoster, Ave and creed were by no means all that they had to offer. And my suggestion that this is so is borne out by the fact that when the rebellion came, it was never directed against village priests, against any priests at all with the exception of Archbishop Sudbury and those few who were hated because they were also landlords.

In a word, no one point of view was representative of the whole church. As we shall see in a moment, a fundamental schism was already developing among its most learned members. By the same token, no one reaction to that church was typical of peasant thinking, except that hungry people are rarely paragons of devotion.

All his life the villein had been taught that he was not only dirty and unworthy; he was black with sin. The priest who might have explained why did nothing of the sort, but spoke an unintelligible jargon. It was all a muddle of abstractions, whereas pagan custom and superstition are nothing if not concrete.

The peasant understood Christ. Christ had suffered and died. He felt sympathy for saints; they had had kings and rich men for enemies. The Virgin was a mother; she had loved her son, and that, too, was understandable. And all these figures could work miracles, so one ought not to offend them.

His own Twelfth Day fires, his Plough Monday, his blessing of the corn, his Midsummer and Midwinter ceremonies, these also were good. They spoke to an inexplicable inward part of him. They made the seasons spin. But if the church bells were as strong as the priest said they were, why could they not be rung to drive away a thunderstorm at haymaking? If exorcism of evil was done by the hand of God, why did the priest not use it to destroy the caterpillars that were eating his cabbages? In fact, in this respect the priest did sometimes bow to his demand. Between 1120 and 1501 there are some eighty-six instances recorded when animals were formally excommunicated.

But there were other fundamental misunderstandings, which no priest could satisfactorily clear away. Why, at the last sacrament, was a wafer more useful than the pinch of earth that had always been put into a dying man's mouth to call him back to the earth from which he had come? If a priest could marry a couple in the sight of God, why not an old man, wise as weather? From time immemorial, village elders had taken young lads and girls solemnly aside and asked each of them three times if they really wanted to be wed. Surely such a marriage was as real as any the church could solemnize.

As for those cursed tithes, surely the priest was lying when he said they were shared with the poor clergy and destitute laymen. One could see with one's own eyes that they were shared as the wolf shares whatever he has killed. He eats what he can to grow fat, and the rest he carries home and hides in the earth.

Yet what was one to do? Life, as any fool could see, was uncertain and full of trouble, and the hellfire on the other side of death was as real and almost as immediate as the night.

CHAPTER SEVEN

A SPARE, FRAIL, EMACIATED FIGURE

The peasant's only friend among clerics, or at least the only one with whom he felt at ease, was the friar, even though, as the proverb had it, 'This is a friar and therefore a liar.' It was the friar who preached mainly at the market cross, the friar who lived in the slums among those who most needed him, the friar who was almost the only medieval figure to court popularity among common people. If he did it for money, no matter. If he was sometimes a rogue, at least he was a rogue on the side of the angels. So when a wandering friar came to the cottage door and talked comforting words about the peace of heaven, it was almost beyond human power not to give him a farthing for the joy he brought. He did not chatter the ununderstandable Latin of the rector, but was full of one's own saws, one's own little jokes, all in the vernacular.

Chaucer's friar looks to have been almost the prototype. 'A wanton and a merry man', the poet calls him, a most important fellow, not dressed like some poor scholar in a threadbare cloak, but decked out like the pope himself, in double worsted, and yet he lisped, 'to make his English swete upon his tonge'. When he played on the little harp after he had sung them a song, then,

> *His eyen twinkled in his heed aright,*
> *As doon the sterres in the frosty night.*[1]

The begging journeys he made from village to village were the business of his life, and clearly his methods had been developed by long experience. He knew the taverns well in every town, we read. He knew the hosts and barmaids better than he knew the sick.

> *For un-to swich a worthy man as he*
> *Accorded nat, as by his facultee,*

To have with seke lazars aqueyntaunce.
It is nat honest, it may nat avaunce
For to delen with no swich poraille,
But al with riche and sellers of vitaille.
And over-al, ther as profit sholde aryse,
Curteys he was, and lowly of servyse.
Ther nas no man no-wher so vertuous.
He was the beste beggere in his house.[2]

Over eighty years ago it was said of the friars that 'The medicine, the science of the time were in their hands, and from 1220 they mixed themselves up, both by preaching and in society, with the crafts of the merchantman; and interlarding all their speech with French words, made these words common among the crafts and the middle class, till they [the words] stole in even to the Creed and the Lord's Prayer.'[3]

Chaucer's friar had married off many a young woman at his own expense, perhaps because he had already made them pregnant. So, being a man of the world, he could hear confession with a far more sympathetic ear than could a mere curate.

He was an esy man to yeve penaunce
Ther as he wiste to han a good pitaunce;
For unto a povre ordre for to yive,
Is signe that a man is wel y-shrive.
For if he yaf, he dorste make avaunt,
He wiste that a man was repentaunt.
For many a man so hard is of his herte,
He may not wepe al-thogh him sore smerte.
Therefore in stede of weping and preyeres,
Men moot yeve silver to the povre freres.[4]

And surely that was the point of the business. To give money to the poor friars was a good sign that a man was sorry for his sins. And the friar could offer not only worldliness and personal charm; he had a hatful of pretty presents to give the cottage wives who met him at the door.

At the other extreme was the monk, and unless a peasant happened to work on a monastic estate he would normally never have met such a man. But who of us does not remember Chaucer's picture of one, 'an out-rydere that loved venerye [hunting]', and

...whan he rood, men mighte his brydel here
Ginglen in a whistling wind as clere,
And eek as loude as dooth the chapel-belle.[5]

above A monk preaches outside a church. (The Fitzwilliam Museum, Cambridge)

below An embroidered velvet cope, the long semi-circular cloak worn by ecclesiastics in processions; fourteenth century. (Crown copyright, Victoria and Albert Museum)

Above A feast. (Bodleian Library, Oxford)

Below left Bone combs, each about three inches long. Probably made in the fifteenth century, but similar ones were used in the fourteenth. (London Museum)

Below right Embroidered purse of a type used in the thirteenth and fourteenth centuries. (London Museum)

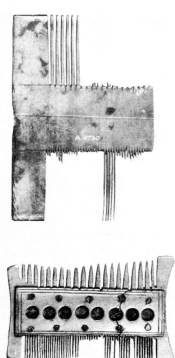

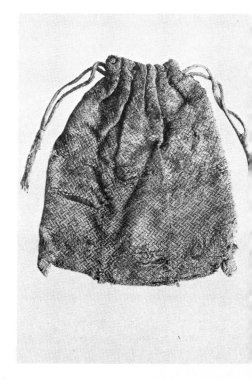

Above The friar of the *Canterbury Tales*, 'a wanton and a merry man'. (The Mansell Collection)

Below The monk. One might 'hear his bridle jingling in the whistling wind as loud and clear as a temple bell'. (The Mansell Collection)

Above A monk in Worcester Cathedral, spade in hand. (The Mansell Collection)

Right Early fourteenth-century silk embroidery on linen, bearing the shields of arms of English families. (Crown copyright, Victoria and Albert Museum)

His sleeves were edged in fur, the finest to be had, and to fasten his hood under his chin he wore a gold pin in the shape of a love-knot. He kept greyhounds that flew as swiftly as birds, and 'many a deynteee hors hadde he in stable'.

This ilke monk leet olde thinges pace,
And held after the newe world the space.
He yaf nat of that text a pulled hen,
That seith, that hunters been nat holy men.[6]

But of course it is too simple to look at monastic life only through Chaucer's eyes, for his portrait is the portrait of an individual, and the ramifications of monastic life were very many indeed. One need only read Jocelin's *Chronicle* to see that life in the cloister was remarkably like life in the common room of some great public school, where men of diverse abilities, but sharing a common purpose, live in a microcosm of their own making. If one remembers that there were well over 2,000 religious houses in the island, houses of varying degrees of wealth (or poverty), that these belonged to several different orders and were controlled by abbots and prioresses of an almost infinite variety of characters, it will be clear how nearly impossible it is to present any picture that pretends to more than a fraction of the truth.

'I know myself most naked in all parts', writes Lydgate, the old monk of Bury, and one likes to imagine it was his honesty and simplicity which, in spite of his long-windedness, made him by far the most popular poet in the generation after Chaucer's death. Lydgate had been ordained priest by the Bishop of Ely in 1397.

At school he had preferred work to play, he says of himself, had stolen apples and amused himself stupidly by counting cherry stones. Later he had travelled in London, Paris and perhaps in Italy, been poor, seen much of men and manners. But for the greater part of his life he had lived in Bury, composing his interminable bookish ballads, his *Guy of Warwick*, his *Fall of Princes*, his verse histories of saints. 'The nightingale sings at the top of the tree before it dies,' he says, and the very dullness, prolixity and sweetness of a man like Lydgate, who loved so many things, is enough to make us look at the monastic life of which he was a part with unexpected sympathy.

There were idlers, poets, copyists, hunters, musicologists, cooks, gardeners, scholars, historians and lechers among them. One monk (the story is to be found in several manuscripts) was so enchanted by the sweet singing of birds that he cried out to God to be allowed to sit quite still and listen for two hundred years. It was monks who wrote down their lives of the saints and filled them with invention, with wonders, with touches of innocence unlike anything to be found except in the works of the major poets. There was St William, who absent-mindedly hung his cloak on a sunbeam, or St Francis who floated in the air during meditation, or St Rumald who died at the age of three days.

The monastic life was, in theory at least, ordered beyond the dreams of anyone except a philosopher. The bell for the night office rang between two and three in the morning. We have to imagine the dim and splendid columns, the paintings half seen against the walls, the figures of saints or of noblemen in stained glass windows, reflected, perhaps almost caricatured in candle light as the good men rise out of their beds and robe themselves to go to prayers, the gilded tombs that come into view as they file into chapel. This, in one of the great houses.

Or the place might be no more than a small, damp cloister with earthen floors and windows that looked out over the rooks' nests in the trees. Whichever it was, the quality, the very nature of its life was determined by the abbot who, in the words of St Benedict, took Christ's place in the house. Able though he might be, devout and deeply committed to his calling, he was forced willy-nilly to become in large measure a political animal too. Without an acute sense for manœuvre he could neither control the complex organism he was in charge of, nor achieve the financial stability it needed to survive.

What was equally important, he had been taught from his earliest childhood that all men were guilty of sin, and this developed a cynicism in the examination of motives, a dourness, perhaps, unlikely to receive fresh ideas gladly. He normally accepted none. He expected evil, he expected impure motives, he expected chicanery and false dealing in the world around him, and he was not often disappointed. Above all, if he was intelligent he soon learned that to impose goodness by prescription is both useless and, in a curious way, immoral.

When the night office was concluded the bell rang for lauds, 'the praise of the morning', and then at six or seven o'clock for prime and for early mass. Then came morning mass, the Chapter, when brief excerpts were read from the martyrologies, complaints of negligence or indiscipline were heard and punishments handed out. After that followed what was called the parliament, high mass, dinner and the going to daily work. Late in the afternoon came vespers, then the small collation, compline and, with nightfall, the end of the day.

Unlike friar, priest, pilgrim or pardoner, the monk had no obligatory contact with the outer world. Except when he travelled on to the estate to collect tithes (if the monastery possessed an estate) he rarely met anyone except the members of his house. He often had a fine library. Canterbury had 698 volumes. At St Albans the great Thomas of Walsingham was master of the scriptorium. Durham possessed not only some 60 volumes of civil and canon law, but a vast collection of classical authors as well. He had the cloisters to walk, the gardens to tend. He had manuscripts to copy. Indeed, he developed to a very great art the technique of illumination, and in several houses men were busy collecting materials for laborious and remarkably accurate chronicles.

Music there was, but amidst all the complex antiphony, few of the gay little tunes that might have caught the fancy of lay contemporaries. Instead, they gossiped; they enjoyed the pleasures of the table. They hunted the hare and the deer. As Chaucer says of his monk, 'He was a lord ful fat and in good point.'

In France, in Italy, in Germany his contemporaries were living much the same sort of lives. He could not have imagined differences of any real moment between the nations. Ideas about human rights would have seemed to him not so much unthinkable as unreal. For time stood still, and, as Langland had said, if there was anywhere a heaven on earth, it was here, when for hours on end the pens scratched in the scriptorium. It was here, during the holy silences in the middle of the mass, in the warmth one could imagine glowing on men's faces at prayer, in walks along the colonnades, at vespers, even in the dusty light that shone in through the high clerestory windows. Never perhaps in all of western history has time stood still so satisfyingly and to so little effect.

But the great ecclesiastic who was to start drawing this whole world into the future was already at work. And he was the most remarkable and arguably the most brilliant man of his age.

John Wycliffe had been born about 1328 up in Yorkshire, and after a lonely and (it seems) introspective childhood, he grew up into what was to become a typical Yorkshireman, blunt, independent and possessed of a certain angularity, both in speech and in body.

There were few serfs in Teesdale. Independence was in the blood. The Lollard, William Thorpe, knew him in old age (we shall come to the Lollards by and by), and said of him that he was 'a spare, frail, emaciated figure, in conversation most innocent'. Of himself Wycliffe wrote that he had a quick temper which he tried not always successfully to control. Even his enemies (and he had many) described him as 'the flower of Oxford', and for the last thirty years of his life–he died in 1384– he fought with tongue and pen–in the end he even made a disastrous stab at politics–to carry the vast, corrupt body of the church, pope and all, back towards first principles.

'Medievalism was sick unto death,' someone has said, 'but she was dying hard.' Wycliffe took up arms against what he saw as the perverse dogma and superstition of the church and against the possession of temporal power (what was in fact political power), by the clergy. It was degrading, he insisted, that spiritual leaders should seek to amass material wealth. It was evil that £13,000 a year should be transported out of the country to the pope at Avignon, and that much of it should be spent to equip French armies fighting against England. So he argued for the disestablishment of the church, for the prohibition of pluralism, but, above all, for the separation of spiritual and secular powers.

About 1340 he came up to Oxford, a university even then so conscious of its distinction that it claimed to have been founded by Alfred the Great, and thus (with a sad ignorance of chronology) to be a thousand years old. Cambridge, with a fine effort to seem superior, claimed King Arthur as its founder, and was thus quite obviously older.

In those days students were allowed (and indeed expected) to carry weapons on the journey from home, although these had to be surrendered on arrival. And Wycliffe, travelling for the first time in his life, would have seen sights which to an adolescent boy probably looked every bit as bizarre as those of Acre to a crusader. There were friars trundling their portable altars from town to town, beggars (one carrying his tongue, said to have been cut off by thieves), mountebanks, frauds, jugglers, horse dealers, men with performing dogs, conjurers pulling countless odd-ments out of empty hats, gamblers with 'queaks'–chequerboards whose white squares were sunk imperceptibly lower than the black.*

---

* The game was played by rolling dice or small stones on to a board. If the white squares were depressed, most of the stones would settle in the depressions. When the board was turned over, when in other words the tables were turned, the black would be depressed, so the dishonest gambler, knowing which side was which, would manage to win on both. The tongueless beggar was John Warde who, with his confederate, Richard Lynham, was eventually arrested in London. He carried an iron hook and pincers with him when he begged, as well as a piece of leather edged with silver, on which was written, 'This is the tongue of John Warde'. The two men simply roared whenever they opened their mouths, and gave bystanders to understand that they were innocent traders whose tongues had been pulled out with the pincers and hook they held in their hands.

He would pass taverns with ale stakes projecting out over the road, and arrive at last in Oxford itself, not yet the city of dreaming spires, but still the largest place he had ever seen. Carfax was 12 ft lower than it is today, and there was a sewer or kennel running down the centre of the street. In Broad Street there were piggeries, and pigs wallowed in the mud.

On 18 March 1301 the king had written to the bailiffs and mayor that 'the air is so corrupted by the broken kennel and pavements that an abominable loathing is diffused among the...masters and scholars'. Eight years earlier, in 1293, brewers and bakers had used the foul water of the Trillmill stream to make ale and bread, even though many 'houses of easement' had been built over it.

At Oxford Wycliffe discovered in himself a passion for physics and mathematics. There he met William Rede, who built the library at Merton and was to become Bishop of Chichester, Simon Bredon, also of Merton, and John Ashingdon, three of the finest mathematicians of the day. If he learned little Greek, he did in fact read Hebrew. He studied optics, and if he never mentions Roger Bacon, who had described how the still uninvented telescope and microscope could be made, he was perfectly aware of Bacon's principles, for he wrote that faith, like lenses properly arranged, allows us to see things far off as if they were near, and to read minute letters as if we were young men.

He interested himself in astronomy, and particularly in comets. At a time when most men thought the earth to be flat, he not only knew that it was a sphere, but that when it was noon in England it was midnight in the antipodes. He made a study of Roman civil law and of English statute law, had a complete understanding of the voluminously preserved Aristotle, and was conversant with the work of Plato, Avicenna and Averrhoës of Cordoba.

He acquired a deeper knowledge of St Augustine than did perhaps any of his contemporaries, and he must have known almost by heart Peter Lombard's great medieval textbook, *Sentences*, 'wherein the profound mysteries of all scriptures are contained'. In a word, he made himself master of the most complex of medieval sciences, which was theology.

Late in the 1350s he became Master of Balliol, and in his lectures, vivid (he believed in a prose *nude et apte*), and perhaps for that very reason precise in doctrine, delivered in front of enormous audiences, he began gradually to evolve the ideas which made him in time the most controversial figure in England. For they struck at the very roots of the contemporary church, and this was not, we must remember, the Church of England, or even the Church of Rome, but the Church Universal.

He attacked its corruption, the political power of the papacy, its support of and profit from feudalism, which was slavery. He maintained with increasing vigour as he grew older the doctrine that for the church to hold property was both sinful and a negation of its purpose. By that token, the government, the *politici*, would be right if they deprived the church of its revenues. For the Christian, lay or cleric, depended immediately and individually on God, and not on any temporary reinterpretation of God's will as promulgated in papal doctrine.

In all this he expressed the current temper, not only of the poor and dispossessed, but of many simple ecclesiastics who were as disgusted as he by the place-seeking and peculation on every side.

Transubstantiation he had originally accepted. But gradually he changed his mind, perhaps primarily because he had become aware to what mundane purposes it was put, that it was used to secure the veneration of the ignorant. In the end he was able to declare it a positively horrible idea that a priest could manufacture the body of Christ. It was a false miracle, he wrote, performed for unworthy purposes. As Trevelyan remarks, 'The Eucharist always presented to him a mystery. He believed the body was in some manner present, though how he did not clearly know; he was only certain that bread was present also.'[7] Down in Cornwall, Ralph de Tremur had said to the priests far more bluntly that 'Ye adore like idiots the work of your own hands. For what doth a priest but gape over a piece of bread and breathe upon it?' St Peter, he had said on another occasion, was nothing but an empty-pated rustic.

More to the practical point, Wycliffe wrote that clerics whose work is to interpret God to their parishioners 'couchen in softe beddis whanne othere men risen to ther labour and blabren out matyns and masse as hunteris, withouten devocion and contemplacion; and hien faste to mete richely and costly arrayed of the beste, and then to slepe. And soone a-noon to tablis [anon to gambling] and chees [chess] and taverne... and by these prestis and their wantonnesse moche peple is brought to lecherie, glutonye, ydelnesse and thefte.'

It was the old complaint. But there were superb exceptions, and Wycliffe cherished them. For purity and simplicity there was Thomas Bradwardine, called *Doctor profundus*, author of a work on geometry, another on practical arithmetic and a third on squaring the circle. As a young man he had written cogently in his *De Causa Dei* about one of the vexed problems of the day, that of free will. And Bennett shrewdly remarks that his 'subtle arguments were not easily apprehended, but had a similar attraction for thoughtful men to those raised in our own day by relativity or dialectical materialism'.[8] Bradwardine, a Merton man, happened to be at Avignon in 1349 when he learned that he was to be consecrated Archbishop of Canterbury. Being in the profoundest sense not only a teacher, but a humble man, he walked the 540 miles to Calais at the rate of 20 miles a day, and (as Workman points out) under an August sun. He was fifty-nine. In September he reached London, but a week later he was dead of the plague in Lambeth. Even Chaucer, who seldom praises clerics, compares him to St Augustine.

'Good Master', had been his prayer,

'my only Master, thou who ever since my youth hast taught me all that I have learned of the truth, and all that, acting as thy pen I have written of it, send down upon me now also thy light, so that thou, who hast led me into the profoundest depths, mayest also lead me up to the summits where rests thy inaccessible truth. Thou who hast carried me into this huge, broad sea, bring me also into thy harbour. Thou who hast led me into this wide and trackless desert—my guide, my path, my final purpose—lead me also until the end. Show thy little child how to unravel the knot of thy words.'

On Friday, 14 May 1361, Wycliffe became rector of Fillingham, just north of Lincoln, and two years afterwards he inherited the manor of Wycliffe near which he had been born. In 1368 he was rector of Ludgershall, and there for the first time in his life he became truly aware of the terrible hardship in which the peasant lived, when bedridden 'couching in muck or dust', when healthy borrowing money with which to get drunk, when married copulating with anonymous women in the hedgerows. He writes that he has seen men lend and even sell their wives.

In 1362, after the second plague, England had the worst harvest in a dozen years, and prices rose higher than they had in living memory. It was to be the first of fourteen successive years of scarcity. In 1363 there were three suppliant kings, guests at the English court. The Black Prince, heir to the throne, was the hero of the nation, and unquestionably the first among Christian knights in Europe. The great victory at Sluys in June 1340 and another at Winchelsea ten years afterwards had given England mastery of the narrow seas. English longbowmen seemed invincible, for Crécy and Poitiers had been fought in the lifetime of any adolescent boy.

But—it was a way she had—England kept sending out armies to fight the previous war. Now, however, instead of offering pitched battle as they had used to do, the French retired upon heavily fortified towns and brought their livestock with them in behind the walls. So the new English armies found they could neither live off the land nor draw the heavily armed French cavalry into the old traps. Week after week the elusive enemy followed instead, cutting off stragglers and foragers. At Poitiers so many prisoners had been taken that according to Froissart they outnumbered their captors two to one. King John was almost killed in the press of English knights trying to seize him in order to claim his ransom. After the Battle of Sluys the fish were said to have been so sated with the dead that if God had given them the power of speech they would have spoken French. But now England began to fall upon evil days. The ransom and the booty stopped coming in. Money to pay the soldiery became harder to find. The splendour went out of the war, and within a handful of years it became apparent to any reasonable intelligence that the nation itself was in decay.

Not only was there economic chaos at home, and with the decline of the vast manors a real measure of poverty. Not only were the roads unsafe (King Peter of Cyprus was actually attacked and robbed on the road between London and the channel coast). Not only were new mercantile factions rising rapidly in London, groups of speculators who had banded together to amass huge fortunes, but these men had begun to exercise political power in proportion to their wealth. Fortunes turned on the continent too. In June 1369, Edward III once again proclaimed himself king of France, but by now he had no real armies left, and no money to pay them if he had.

Edward of Woodstock, the 'Black Prince' to later historians, had fallen ill during his disastrous Spanish campaign when he had marched over Roland's pass at Roncesvalles and his army had wasted away with Spanish fevers. In 1370, Aquitaine, which for eight years he had ruled with a measure of success, rose in revolt, and on 19 September, no longer able to sit his horse, he conquered and in unknightly fashion massacred the citizens of Limoges. It was the last of his victories, and in the following spring he returned to London, never to set foot abroad again. He was a dying man.

The king, his father, had become old too. He acquired his last mistress, the greedy and ambitious Alice Perrers, and the great, brown, berry-bearded king who thirty years before had been the nation's hero, sank in his early sixties into senility.

Of all his conquests in the north of France only Calais remained, in

Aquitaine only Bayonne and Bordeaux. But still that war with France went on, a war in which, as one historian wrote, 'the whole nation persisted with an infatuation blind to all disaster'.[9] In April 1370, there were fears of an invasion on the Sussex coast. In August a French fleet appeared off the North Foreland, and London expected to be attacked. Near Rochelle the Spaniards won a naval victory that lost England the mastery of the seas. In February 1372, there were very real fears of an invasion from Scotland, and in July the Welsh castles had to be repaired 'to repel the malice of the French'. So at the end of over a decade of disaster England stood alone, without allies, saddled with an old, extravagant king and with its only potential leader dying. In 1366 Edward had paid £350 for one embroidered vest. Now it must have seemed to reasonable men that the nation was on the verge of anarchy.

In August 1371 the men of Shoreham made a piratical attack on a ship from Dordrecht, boarded the vessel, murdered the crew, its passengers and even the few women aboard and carried the cargo ashore. A few months earlier the citizens of Winchester had begun pulling down disused churches to cart the building materials away. The town of Truro was reported 'almost uninhabited and wholly laid waste'. But the old king, stubbornly continuing the war—perhaps trying to revive the old spirit of optimism—had begun borrowing money on every side.

In an effort to halt what can only be called a flight of capital, a law was passed that prohibited the sending of gold and silver out of the country. At the same time, because politics and religion were inextricably intertwined, an order was made to arrest any messenger who brought in a papal bull. In 1373 the deportation of all alien friars was ordered, and in a desperate effort to dam up disaster, John of Gaunt, younger brother of the Black Prince, set out from Calais on 4 August with an army of 15,000 men determined to drive the French back, perhaps for the last time.

With the French retiring before him, he burned and pillaged his way through Picardy, Champagne and Burgundy. Brutal, ruthless, endlessly ambitious, he was nevertheless a man born to fail at whatever he set his hand to. In Auvergne his baggage train was swept away by the autumn floods. His men began to desert, and those who stayed began dying of hunger and cold. By Christmas–the ultimate degradation–there were English soldiers begging in the streets of Bordeaux.

By the mid 1370s John was back in London, however, and with the heir to the throne confined to his bed and the king all but moribund, he became leader of what was known as the court party. He began like an old cat purposefully to organize the parliamentary rats.

In his prologue to *Piers Plowman* Langland writes of a mock council among the rats, for the cat was playing with them dangerously and knocking them about. One of them remembers that he has seen men wearing bright collars round their necks. If they could buy a bell and tie it round the cat's neck, they might at least have warning whenever he drew near. To this they all agree. So the bell is bought and attached to a collar, but not one of them can be found who will dare to hang it round the cat's neck. And even if one did, says a mouse, there would only come another cat to scratch at them and bite them, even though they crept under the benches. So the cat scratched away and no one dared defy him.

With his friends, certain noblemen and a handful of the great merchants, John began making corners in wool and foodstuffs, amassing a power at home which had continually eluded him abroad, and allowing the national defences to rot.

It was with this man, a man loathed by most of the common people of England, that Wycliffe, who had begun to despair of achieving spiritual reform by any other means, made a political alliance. Probably he would have acted more wisely if, like us, he had had the advantage of hindsight.

In all charity we can only think that Wycliffe was precisely what his contemporaries said he was, an utterly apolitical man willing to take whatever steps seemed feasible for the realization of his spiritual aims. For it cannot too often be repeated that the affairs of church and state were all but one. The doctrines according to which men acted were so interwoven with theological thinking that in the last analysis the questions of the day were largely theological.

Thus Parliament decided, quite mistakenly as it happened, that five times as much gold was being sent annually to the pope at Avignon (who was supporting the French armies) as ever went to the king in London. So to the reformer, the man anxious to have the church disestablished, the church was conducting a civil war and contradicting its own principles in doing so. Worse, it was involving itself in material affairs and acting against the spirit in which it had been founded.

More than once Wycliffe had said in the pulpit that 'Clerics should not be allowed to discharge secular duties.' Or in another context, 'If any monk fails to keep to the poverty he first professed, I dare to say that he is not a follower of St Benedict, but a dangerous apostate, a disciple of Antichrist.'

In his vast treatises on divine and civil dominion he had tried to determine the jurisdictional limits of church and state, and in the course of discussion had touched on the nature of kingship. It ought not to be conferred by heredity, he thought, but by grace. By that token worldly priests, not having been chosen by grace, were members of an alien sect. For the important thing to look for in a man was not his rank or the splendour of his vestments, but the way he lived. And if this doctrine caused conflict in either church or state, well, there were true peace and false peace, and the only true peace was founded in God. True peace was not based on tolerance of evil. It could never rest simply on a failure to resist one's enemies.

He considered whether or not serfdom was admissible when it meant the impoverishment of some and the enrichment of others, and decided that slavery on a hereditary basis was wrong, for distinctions of rank ought to depend purely on distinctions in virtue. Thus the possession of rank or property by the unvirtuous was a sin. By inference, the good peasant might steal from the wicked lord. And although Wycliffe did add that in worldly terms the good had to leave the wicked in possession, his doctrine was spread abroad without his concomitant warning that to put it into practice would be wrong, for it involved the doing of evil.

But on one matter he was clear. The secular power—and this was thought to be one of his great heresies—should take steps to deprive the ecclesiastic of power he has abused. If this were done the people would be relieved of much oppressive taxation. If doing it led to excommunication, such excommunication would be without effect in the sight of God, for it had been pronounced as a punishment for acts that were not spiritual in their nature.

Thus he protested against the numerous excommunications to enforce payment of tithes. Tithes ought to be collected by the secular arm, regulated by secular law. If they were paid to the clergy, the clergy should simply have acted as almoners for the poor, but there were priests who used the money for their own ends. And if, by reason of this reform endowments had to be forfeited, if the clergy were deprived of its possessions, it would be forced to rely, not on temporal, but on spiritual power. This would be right and good, for popes and cardinals might err, but neither popes nor cardinals were necessary for the government of the church. In fact, a worldly pope was a heresiarch and ought to be deprived.

Wycliffe tried to define the limits of a just war. He protested against luxury in dress and about the giving of grand dinners. 'If every parish had a saintly rector,' he wrote in his *Civil Dominion*, 'there would not be so much arable land lying fallow, or so great a dearth of cattle. The realm would possess an abundance of every sort of wealth.' But now we had nothing except hirelings who fretted because of the civil as opposed to the spiritual rule of the clergy. The peasants were lazy, indifferent to what ought most to concern them, the tillage of the soil. And why? Because they had no spiritual leaders. The land was not theirs, and they stole what they could because there was no resident spiritual squire to act as overseer. They were like horses without bridles. As for the clerics, they rivalled the secular lords in their luxurious habits, and the secular lords in their turn sought to outshine the clerics. But if tenants were to own the temporal wealth they worked at, there would not only be an increase in production. There would be an increase in marriages too. There would be more children, and according to Aristotle these were the factors that made a republic grow.

Ideas like these were so frighteningly revolutionary that it is no wonder Wycliffe was not unlike a modern Marxist in the eyes of the establishment. He threatened the power of the landlord, the political privileges of the church, the hereditary basis of the monarchy, the conduct of the war, the apportionment of property and property's doctrinally established right to levy taxes on people to whom those taxes brought no benefit.

He attacked the politically oriented papacy, for 'God entrusted the sheep', he wrote, 'to be pastured, not to be shorn'. But Arnold Garnier, the pope's collector, 'keepeth a great hotel in London with clerks and officers thereto as though it were a prince's custom house, and thence he transporteth to the pope over £13,000 a year'.

Fourteenth-century church income has in fact been estimated to have amounted to £270,000 annually, a third of the gross national product, this quite apart from tithes, collections and the sale of indulgences. And the only individuals in England from whom tithes were not collected were usurers, jongleurs and prostitutes. So much had Rome gained control of internal affairs in the island that alien cardinals had been appointed Dean of York, Dean of Salisbury and Dean of Lincoln. Another was Archdeacon of Canterbury. The Archdeacons of Durham, Suffolk and York were foreigners too. And Wycliffe maintained that these aliens maintained their power by betraying both king and commons and by robbing the poor.

John of Gaunt was for many good reasons a supporter of the monastic orders. But he was not only utterly lacking in principle; he was a bungler. Having now made new alliances with some of the rich

London merchants (for there, as I have said, lay one of the great centres of political power), he determined to remove the bishops from their posts as officers of the crown, and to put his own creatures in their places. By adopting Wycliffe's doctrine of disendowment he could both double the size of his own estates and gather support from the baronage by offering to let them share in the spoils.

Time-honoured Lancaster indeed! Shakespeare's portrait was inaccurate to a degree, for whereas he seems to have drawn on Holinshed for much of his material (and Holinshed's description of John is reasonably accurate), when he wrote the Duke's magnificent speeches in the second act of *Richard II*, he looks to have taken his ideas from an anonymous sixteenth-century play called *Woodstock*, and here the Duke had been turned into a noble and high-minded counsellor.

In any case, the result of Wycliffe's alliance could have been foretold. Gaunt consolidated the episcopate against him and Wycliffe lost much of his popular support. Worst of all, reform became identified with political manœuvre, and neither protagonist gained any of the ends he sought.

The Good Parliament of 1376 had some of the grossest peculators arrested and impeached. Under the leadership of Peter de la Mare of Hereford the knights of the shires made common front. There were only seventy-four of them, but they wielded far more power than the city members, and they had determined to assert their strength and break the political sovereignty of the great mercantile houses in London.

The cash wealth of these men had given them enormous influence because the crown was in perpetual need of money. But Parliament had at its disposal a formidable militia composed of apprentices and other workmen. It had the man in the street behind it, and it relied on this support to protect it from John of Gaunt and his friends.

The members were not actually adherents of any political party. They were a party in themselves. They sensed their power, that it was a matter of now or never, and they decided in cold reason to put an end to the corruption that had stuffed public taxes into private purses, to put down the growing anarchy in the countryside, to see that the war abroad was conducted more efficiently, and to reform and tax the church.

In all this (except for the last) they were antagonists to John of Gaunt, and they were determined to bell the cat with all possible speed. For with Edward III nearly powerless, with the Black Prince on his deathbed and his son, Richard, nothing but a boy, they feared that by one means or another John would contrive to have himself crowned. This they were determined to prevent.

Under the leadership of their Speaker they took the first step and refused the grant of taxes that had been demanded by the crown. The king was in need of money, they maintained, only because his advisers and his privy council had pocketed the money themselves. The second step was to frame the charges on the basis of which they intended to ask for the impeachment of the guilty.

Chief among these was Richard Lyons, the great merchant who had collected extravagant sums of money by abuse of his position in the privy council. He was a vintner, farmer of petty custom, and had both levied and collected duties which Parliament had never authorized. In an attempt to save himself, he had a barrel filled with gold coin, marked it 'sturgeon' to allay the suspicions of the carters and sent it to the Black Prince in Kennington. It was contemptuously returned.

The charges against the other accused were so many and so various that to describe them fully would be to expand my account out of all proportion. The most important was Lord William Latimer, Keeper of the King's Privy Purse, Warden of the Cinque Ports and Constable of Dover Castle. He had taken bribes to betray certain English strongholds on the French coast. But he managed to suborn the witnesses, so they never appeared against him and he was finally adjudged guilty, not of treason, but of peculation.

Then there was John Pecche. He had been Lord Mayor and a Member of Parliament, and was one of the Company of Victuallers. It was in food that the huge fortunes were being made, and a monopoly of any sort was illegal. But Pecche was a leader of what one can only call a Mafia that had been ruling the city for years. On 26 November 1373 he had obtained a monopoly in the retailing of sweet wine. But not satisfied with this, he had thenceforward extorted an illegal tax of 3s. 4d. on every tun, and it had made him very rich indeed.

Adam de Bury was a skinner, had been mayor from 1364 until 1366 (when he had been summarily removed), and again in 1373. In 1367 he had managed to obtain a pardon for sedition, for fraud in the exchange of the king's money and for the suspiciously sudden death of a colleague.

Sir Richard Stury (one of John of Gaunt's creatures), Alderman Roger Elys and Lord Neville were the others. Neville was Lord Latimer's son-in-law and heir. He had been busy for some time buying up the king's debts at enormous discounts. Then, by virtue of his position on the Privy council board, he had paid himself the face value of these debts out of the exchequer.

In the midst of the bitter—and indeed dangerous—trials (the whole city was in ferment), the Black Prince began rapidly sinking. During his last days the door to his chamber was left open so that all who wished might come to take their leave of him. Sir Richard Stury was one of these visitors.

'Come, Richard,' the prince called to him. 'Come and look at what you have long desired to see.'

The soldier, the living legend, the Philip Sidney of his age was ending his days a bitterly disappointed man. Crécy and Poitiers, where he had fought with such daring and imagination, might as well have been nothing but a dream. 'It was twenty years,' says Trevelyan, 'twenty years since, brought to bay behind the vineyards of Poitiers with a handful of English gentlemen and archers, he had destroyed the chivalry of France and led her king a captive to London.' Now his country was in decay. The gay, lecherous, hard-drinking, splendid and colourful court was sick and poor, and the prince's small son surrounded by greedy men and in danger which he could do nothing to forestall.

'God pay you according to your deserts,' he said when Stury protested. 'Now leave me, and let me see your face no more.'

On 6 July 1376 the Good Parliament was dissolved, having (the members thought) accomplished what they had set out to do. The malefactors were fined or banished or imprisoned. But two days later the Black Prince died, and the attack on John of Gaunt and his adherents had spent its force.

The duke was too devious a man to use violent means for undoing the damage that had been done him. He simply picked the next parliament and used underlings to do it for him. We have to understand that members were not elected. They were simply chosen—either by important men in the counties or else by sheriffs in the towns. So of the seventy-four knights of the shire who had sat in 1376, only eight returned the following year. Yorkshire, Derbyshire, Lincoln, Sussex, Kent, Dorset, Wiltshire and Gloucestershire all sent members nominated by the duke.

Latimer was recalled from exile and his ludicrous fine of 2,000 marks remitted. Lyons and Pecche were released from prison and a poll tax of fourpence on every subject over the age of fourteen was imposed to help pay the costs of the war. Naturally, it bore heaviest on the poor.

At about seven in the evening on 21 June 1377 old King Edward died of a stroke after a reign of fifty years. He had been there so long that hardly a soul living could remember his father. He it was of whom Froissart had written that 'his face shone like the face of a god, so that to see him or dream of him was to conjure up joyous images'. Now his mistress stole the rings off his fingers and went home to her acquiescent husband. The golden age was finally over.

Meanwhile Wycliffe, the Hebraist, the mathematician, the scholar and reformer, was himself suffering attacks from every quarter. He had not only entered politics; he had entered it with allies for whom he could have felt little sympathy. So now he began preaching in London too.

The church had perverted the doctrines on which it had been built. The Host had become God. Ceremony had taken the place of reality. Elaborate choirs detracted from the meaning of what they sang (Augustine had first said this), for the music delighted more than the lifting of the soul. Great buildings took one's mind away from worship.

They needed great preachers, he said, and little ceremonies. Friars preached, but only to swell their collections. A sermon ought to be a mighty instrument for reform, for making people aware of a personal relationship with God. Masses, pardons, penances were simply substitutes for a genuine sense of individual responsibility.

As for images, if they gave the mind a point to fix on, well and good. But in fact they often made poor parishioners more conscious of the saints they represented than of the nature of saintliness. For it was not canonization that sent men to heaven. It was the acts by which they had lived. One ought not to pray even to Mary, warm and beautiful though she had been, but to God. If one says that Christ's church must have a head on earth, it is not a pope who ought to be head. It is Christ.

The pope tried to have Wycliffe arrested and brought to Rome for trial. Hitherto, the church had had men arraigned in English courts, but now Rome was determined to assert its supremacy, and in an attempt to gain allies in high circles Gregory declared that Wycliffe's heresies were not only ecclesiastically but politically revolutionary. He had at any cost to be silenced. The rebel refused to listen. He would not go.

Indeed, Wycliffe, indefatigable even in old age, was already broadening his attack. Years before he had begun sending out his 'poor preachers' to spread his doctrines to every village in the country. Now in the last quarter of the century these threadbare, hollow-cheeked enthusiasts began setting up their pulpits in markets and little towns, at crossroads, in the hamlets, and they grew in numbers until they became a serious embarrass-

pedlar offers his wares. From the *Codex Mannesse* in Heidelberg University Library. (The Mansell Collection)

Hawking, the sport of kings. Notice the gauntletted left hands and the beagle-like dogs used as retrievers. (The Mansell Collection)

ment to the established church. There were even women among them, though women had always been frowned on as preachers, not so much because of their incapacity as for the fact that Eve had been a woman and her tongue had brought the world nothing but trouble.

They preached to audiences of the poor, these Lollards,[10] to those who had themselves been disestablished, and using Wycliffe's own words, they hammered out his denunciation of all that he had found evil in the church he served. Wycliffe prepared tracts for them, and the outlines of sermons. Poor they may have been, but they did not beg. They practised obedience as if they had belonged to one of the more formal orders. Above all, they mingled with the poor as their master bade them.

Their teaching was of the simplest, the Lord's prayer, the ten commandments, the seven deadly sins. Wearing russet robes, without purse or sandals, but carrying a long staff and a few pages each of Wycliffe's translation of the Bible into English (even this was revolutionary), they kept perpetually on the move so that unlike established churchmen they would not be 'tied to one place like a dog'. The Archbishop of Canterbury called them sheep in wolves' clothing. Others complained that they preached without being licensed. Even the poor friars attacked them as 'heretical idiots'.

They taught by fable, by stories out of the saints' lives, by parable and, above all, by scripture. 'Pray not to the saints, but to God,' they said. 'Whanne we maken our praioris herteli oneli to god for [a] thyng that is due…thouh we make no special praieres to the seyntes, yet natheless alle the seyntes that ben in hevene ben redi to praie for us to god.' Let a man only 'kepe the commaundementes of god and lyve vertuousli'; that is the way to heaven.[11]

But the poor preachers did not stop at that. They could cite chapter and verse out of the world around them. When they preached about the 'Caesarean clergy', the pluralists, the absentee rectors, they could cite the Bishop of Salisbury who in 1352 had been absent from his see for forty years. They could call to mind Philip Beauchamp, the protégé of Queen Philippa, who had been created Canon of Southwell at the age of six, and who by the time he was fourteen had been granted fourteen separate preferments. They could remind their congregations that one of their antagonists, William, Bishop of Winchester, had had to summon over forty vicars for not residing in their parishes.

It is hard for us to put ourselves in these people's places, and to realize how heatedly such things were argued. In the twentieth century perhaps only a militant trade unionist or an Arab nationalist or a Jew in Israel can understand the intensity with which the fourteenth century disputed matters of religion, and the sheer anger and sense of outrage with which either the Wycliffite or the established ecclesiastic looked on his opponent. There were 8,500 parish churches in England. According to the poll tax records for 1381 there were 25,883 regular and secular clergy, and in addition, 1,952 who had taken inferior orders as deacons and acolytes. Ignoring Durham, for which there are no figures, England and Wales supported a total of 30,350 clerics, one for every 65 of the population. Today, with a population twenty times as large, clergymen of all denominations number only about 40,000. As I have already said, a third of the gross national income went to the church, and Wycliffe considered this not only economically but ecclesiastically indefensible.

For, as a result, one had hunting parsons clad in furs 'with fat horses and gray saddles'. As for the immorality of these parasites, even the church had to recognize that it existed. In 1364 a synod in Ely had ordered that no one offer hospitality to priests' concubines 'except on a journey'. A London synod of 1330 had forbidden priests to use church funds to buy houses for their mistresses. Between 1378 and 1403 three London priests had had to be pardoned after courts had convicted them of murder. In 1382 a priest willed his breviary to such of his brother clerics as happened to be imprisoned in Newgate.

And, of course, since the cities were far smaller, since in a sense everyone knew everyone else, such cases were common gossip. But Wycliffe could go further and recount the history of one of his greatest antagonists, William of Wykeham.

In his youth he had been a notary. At the age of twenty-seven he became keeper of the manor of Rochford in Hampshire. Two years later he was clerk to the sheriff. At thirty-three he rose, no doubt by reason of his amiability, to be clerk of the king's works at Henley and Easthampstead. There he was charged with transporting stone and timber for building and with paying the men's wages. In the same year he was offered similar work at Windsor, and he was clerk of the king's works there until 1362 when he was nearly forty. So at the onset of middle age–far from being an ecclesiastic–he had never in his life been more than a supervisor of buildings, a notary and, in 1356, keeper of the king's dogs.

But he had obviously long had his eye on a church benefice as a reward for his labours. In 1357 the Bishop of Ely had been implicated in a murder, so the temporalities of the see were put into the king's hands, and almost at once–without his even having taken orders–Wykeham was made rector of Pulham in Norfolk.

That was not enough, but he had to wait for the second plague of 1361–2 before he could go higher. That year four bishops died, and the king, being now able to advance him, poured a whole fistful of the suddenly vacated benefices on him, even though he had still not been ordained.

'Manners makyth man' indeed. On 12 July 1361 he was made a prebend of Hereford, on the 16th of the same month, of Abergwilly and Llandewybrewi, and on the 24th of Bromyard collegiate church. By 16 August he was prebend of Salisbury, by the 24th prebend of Beverley Minster, and on 1 October of Oxgate in St Paul's. On 24 October he became clerk of the exchequer, and on 22 November prebend of St David's Cathedral. On 5 December he was at last made an acolyte, and on the 20th of the same month prebend of Wherwell Abbey in Hampshire.

In 1362, on 12 July he was finally ordained priest. By the 15th of the following month he had become prebend of Shaftesbury Abbey, and by 20 August of Lincoln Cathedral. The next year saw him canon of the collegiate church of Hastings on 3 February and of the Royal Chapel of St Stephen's, Westminster, on 21 April. On the 26th of the same month he became Archdeacon of Northampton, but he resigned the post to become Archdeacon of Lincoln instead on 23 May.

By 31 October 1363 he was canon of York, by 5 May 1364 keeper of the Privy Seal, and thus, for all practical purposes, Prime Minister. On 13 October 1366 at the age of forty-two he became Bishop of Winchester, and a little less than a year later, Chancellor.

As early as 1365 Froissart had written of him that 'a priest called Sir William de Wican reigned in England...by him everything was done, and without him nothing'.[12] It was true. By this time he held simultaneously the richest ecclesiastical and the best-paid civil office in the kingdom. With these and the rents he shared with Sir William Walworth of the brothels in Southwark, he had an annual income of £2,000, or about a quarter of a million pounds in modern money.

In 1376 he was impeached on five separate counts of peculation and taking of bribes, and on one of these counts he was convicted. So his revenues were seized and he was banished from London. But within seven months he was allowed to return and his property was handed back to him. According to a monk of St Albans, he had bribed Alice Perrers to have the verdict against him set aside.

One has only to look at these men, the knights, the bishops still lying in effigy on their tombs, to see what a tough, bull-necked race they were. With their broad shoulders, their forward-jutting chins, they might for all the world be athletes past their prime. Good living has added jowls to the ruthless and much-satisfied faces and a certain weightiness to the musculature of their more athletic years.

Bishop Courtney lies in Canterbury, Wykeham at Winchester, Bishop Ralph of Shrewsbury in Wells, and it is not easy to distinguish churchmen from the rough, semi-literate soldiers with whom they made common cause. They have energy even in repose. They stand four-square with swords at their sides. Or else they lie with palms laid devoutly together on their breasts. These were the men with whom the brilliant, frail and innocent Wycliffe was at war until the end of his life.

CHAPTER EIGHT

LONDON, THOU ART
THE FLOUR OF CITIES ALL

For over five hundred years the great landowners had been operating in a closed society. Each estate had formed a little community, gathered first for mutual defence, then growing to become a self-supporting economic unit. Lord and peasant built and thatched their dwellings, lighted and warmed them, made their own clothing and spread their boundaries to accommodate gradually increasing numbers.

Tallow came out of the pig, fuel out of the forest, cloth from home-grown flax, leather from hides, wool from one's own flocks, water out of the wells. And if salt or iron, sometimes tools or clay or dyestuffs, had to be imported, these could in times of poor harvest be treated as superfluities. At its happiest such a community had had small need of the outer world.

In Saxon England or in Carolingian France there were cities, to be sure, but they were not cities in our modern sense, that lived by devoting themselves to commercial activities. Instead they were military strong-holds, centres of legal and governmental administration, and as such they lacked two attributes of the city as we know it, or indeed as Chaucer would have known it. They had no middle class and **no** communal organizations. In the earliest times they had simply been enclosures wherein people gathered for certain religious ceremonies or when there was a threat of war.

But gradually as city chieftains took up residence with their entourages of servants and guards, merchants established themselves nearby to provide goods that these unproductive people needed, and small artisans, carters and shipbuilders to transport the materials that travelled in and out. With the advent of Christianity came bishops and lesser ecclesiastics, builders, gardeners, various craftsmen and menials, and eventually a weekly market was established to which peasants brought produce from the surrounding countryside.

In course of time these places became centres of trade, one city with another. By the end of the tenth century there were merchants from Cologne, from Dinant, from Flanders and Rouen regularly coming in to the port of London. Englishmen sailed up into the Baltic with cargoes bought in shares by merchant adventurers who divided the profits in proportion to their investments. But voyages were long and sometimes perilous. If a vessel was to be adequately loaded to cover expenses money had to be borrowed, and although money generally cost about twenty per cent, there were enormous profits to be made if things went well. But all this time the city had remained a comparatively small unit, dependent for its own needs on farmers in the immediately surrounding countryside.

At first, as in Greece and Rome, the major urban area in a country–be it Paris, London or Cologne–had been the administrative centre for an entire tribe. But as populations increased and occupations became diversified, the court found it more often necessary to travel out to other centres where minor chieftains or smaller administrative groups had established themselves. By the time of the Middle Ages English kings were crossing and recrossing the country in almost continuous travel, putting up either at the great abbeys or on the estates of powerful retainers. So the centres to which they travelled grew too, and in time acquired mercantile establishments of their own, or became episcopal seats.

The growth of towns did not at first disturb the autonomy of each of the many hundreds, perhaps thousands of manorial units. Being self-sufficient, they lived from season to season in what must have seemed a divinely established equilibrium.

Gradually, however, the cities grew too large to be supported by their suburbs; they became lodestars for migrant workers. Trade over great distances increased because the highest profit lay in carrying merchandise from places where it was abundant to places where it was scarce. Cotton had to come from Egypt, sugar from Sicily, tin from Cornwall, wine from Burgundy or the Rhine, woven wool from Flanders. By the year 1150 the merchants, like the kings, were continually on the road. They began to be known as *piepowdrous*, dusty-footed, and to the landed gentleman living in a hierarchical world, stable, traditional, bound to the turning seasons, they seemed not only upstarts, but active dangers to a society that had not changed since any man living could remember. The merchant had too little respect for social status; he loved hard cash, and this love began creating ferment and uneasiness in a world whose greatest virtues had been its stability and its independence.

Pirenne phrases it very simply indeed.

The nobility, he writes, never had anything but disdain for these upstarts come from no one knew where, and whose insolent good fortune they could not bear. They were infuriated to see them better supplied with money than themselves; they were humiliated by being obliged to have recourse in time of trouble to the purse of these newly rich... The prejudice that it was degrading to engage in business remained deeprooted in the heart of the feudal caste up to the time of the French Revolution.[1]

As a matter of fact, it lasted longer. Even as late as 1914 it was thought demeaning to be or to have been engaged in trade, and when Chesterton wrote about the wicked grocer he was expressing a contempt for tradesmen that had lasted eight hundred years.

The church disapproved of the new class, too. 'The merchant can please God only with difficulty,' St Jerome had written. Profit-seeking was avarice, speculation a sin, for the early church depended for its livelihood on a feudal organization composed of innumerable self-sufficient units which had no interest in profit or expansion. In a word, landowners were gentlemen; usurers, merchants and adventurers were not, and the distinction survives, even though the medieval merchant's answer became something of a proverb. 'The usurer goes not to heaven,' it ran, 'but without usury he goes to perdition.'

The contempt that their betters felt for them may in part account for the fact that medieval entrepreneurs often underwent a deathbed repentance and left vast sums for charitable purposes. They had themselves buried in magnificent tombs, though many had no doubt started as serfs. But no matter what colour the earth they had originally had on their hands, their peripatetic lives had turned them into aliens wherever they went. Jews, Flemings, Lombards, Englishmen, no matter what they were they had no heritage. Unlike almost anyone else, they had no roots, for they lived not on or by the land, but on the strongbox, by the rattle of coins and on a system of mercantile alliances they had built up with other expatriates like themselves. The merchant of Venice borrowed money of the Jew, and although the terms looked cruel, the profit to be expected no doubt seemed worth the risk.

Now, as the cities grew, as merchants brought in food from the hinterland and imported hitherto inaccessible goods from abroad, the demesne lords often found it profitable to grow more crops than they needed for their manors alone. Hay, grain, leather, indeed whole droves of cattle, vegetables, flax, timber and whatever else they produced began moving into the market towns, and finally as trade began to be worth more money, into the cities themselves.

The little, scraggy sheep from the west came in to Shepherd's Bush in London, the cattle, also far smaller than those of today, to Notting Hill or Smithfield which, incidentally, was not named after anyone called Smith, but had originally been 'smooth field', *campus planus*. Kentish coals were carried into Croydon, wine from overseas to the Vintry where it could be unloaded from the ships, fish into Billingsgate. The very names of Cornhill, Bread Street, Cow Lane, Carter Lane, Fish Street, the Poultry, Seacole Lane, Leather Lane and many others make their origins self-evident. London grew by what it fed on, and as the market expanded and began to require butchers with their bloody-mouthed dogs, drovers, innkeepers, farriers and a host of artisans and servants, it not only demanded a much increased production in the countryside, but caused many a rural landlord–in return for ready money–to remit feudal services just at a time when those services were beginning to be most needed. It caused the villein to cast about for ways to escape his bondage, because for the first time the city offered him the possibility of both freedom and advancement.

But although the growth of the mercantile middle class first offered the peasant enfranchisement, it also created divisions between capital and labour that time has only exacerbated. For as the city–Bristol, York or London–attracted men from the country, as the number of trades and occupations grew, as the merchants became richer and more influential, as the gulf widened between their origins and their current prosperity, so the gulf grew between them and the men whom they used and who depended on them for a livelihood. In the end, it was not a man's work, but his rate of consumption that really mattered to the mercantile powers. So in a very little while the former villein found himself on the same treadmill as before. This time his only possible escape lay in trying to emulate his master.

Gradually, the process became self-perpetuating. Rural industries fell on difficult times, for whatever they did, from weaving or spinning to iron work, could be done more cheaply and thus more profitably in the towns. Thus, goods manufactured in the cities would be transported back for sale to the rural populations. Goods from overseas began to seem current necessities, and by the middle of the fourteenth century the village was devoted solely to agriculture, the city to manufacture and commerce.

In such a trade the rustic is always at a disadvantage. Food was comparatively cheap. Manufacture became a near-monopoly and its products were dear.

As cities grew the agricultural land on their outskirts began to be swallowed up by new building. London edged out beyond its walls, to Holborn and Highgate, to Westminster and Knightsbridge, and it followed inevitably that whereas in the eleventh and twelfth centuries economic and political influence had been based on the ownership of land, after the Black Death it came to be based largely on the possession of money.

The nobility, however, were not willing to remain in cities among the new upstarts. But now, as those cities, particularly London, began to be given over to crowds of workmen and merchants struggling for economic survival, they started moving out to the country where landowners had sometimes fallen on evil days and become not unwilling to sell. So one by one the great houses in London were either taken over by the newly rich, or else turned into tenements where immigrant workmen lived crowded, sometimes four, five and six to a room.

To many it must have looked as though in a remarkably short space of time the lovely, patriarchal world had all but died, and any man old by the time of Richard's accession in 1377 could (and probably did) complain that nothing was as it had been. Since his boyhood the world had been going downhill. The vulgarity and ostentation he saw around him made it quite clear that the past was dying and the future unlikely to have anything in it of delight.

Gradually London–and we shall be talking principally about London –became a rowdy political and economic battleground. As for the villeins, even if the city had made them technically free, they were actually as badly off as before. As serfs they had suffered exactions and privations, some of which I have listed. As workmen they found themselves living in a hitherto unknown urban squalor. Very often they simply became vagabonds and preyed on each other in much the same way as Dickens' characters did in the heydey of the industrial revolution.

Nor was that all. One of the most miserable features of London mercantile life in the fourteenth century was its corruption. Party struggles and sporadic attempts at reform achieved nothing at all. By 1375 the city was firmly in the hands of an oligarchy closely connected with moneyed coadjutors abroad. Its members monopolized the offices of mayor and aldermen; they monopolized the supply and sale of foodstuffs. They bribed the king himself with a succession of loans, and with only infrequent interruptions became the virtual rulers of England.

In the main these capitalist adventurers belonged to one of the five great guilds, the vintners, the fishmongers, the grocers, the mercers and the goldsmiths. But we must not think of them as doing only the work of the guilds they represented. Thus we read in Stow that in 1377 'John Philpot, a citizen of London, sent shippes to the sea and scoured it of Pirates, taking many of them prisoners'. And he did in fact capture one 'pirate', a Scot named Mercer, who had fifteen Spanish ships in tow.

But Philpot was a grocer, and in 1378 he was elected mayor. Or, again Stow, we learn that Nicholas Brembre, four times mayor, was beheaded, or that in 1356 Mayor Picard, a vintner, feasted four kings, all on one day.[2] Now Stow was not always accurate, but what, we ask, have grocers and vintners risen to if they kill pirates, entertain kings or lose their heads on the block like gentlemen?

Brembre and Philpot had become, by then, not so much tradesmen as what we should call city bosses or gangsters in control of private armies. They were brothers-in-law, for they had married daughters of the enormously rich John de Stodeye, and in the last twenty years of his life Brembre amassed a quite remarkable amount of money. As well as six manors in Kent, three manors in Middlesex and certain houses in St Albans, he owned property in twelve separate London parishes.

He was not only a grocer, but a pepperer (spices were imported in large quantities) and a dealer in iron, wines, woad (a blue dye for cloth) and wool. His international financial dealings were almost bizarre in their complexity. Nine-tenths of them, like the proverbial iceberg, lay hidden even in his own day, and will thus never be known. But certain of his dealings are still on record. Thus in 1382 a certain merchant of Venice owed him £1,250. In 1383 two merchants in Lucca owed him £729 3s. 4d. At various times he lent the king, Edward III, sums close to £1,000, and to Edward's grandson, Richard II, he personally advanced £2,970 between 1377 and 1387, or something like £600,000 in modern money. And Brembre was not a banker. The money was his own private property, it was over and above money tied up in houses and goods, it was money he could spare–and it was in cash.

I make note of this fortune, or such parts of it as the records disclose, simply to make plain with what sort of men we are dealing. The ploughman's penny a day or the smallholder's four or five pounds a year for his wheat set Brembre's fortune into some kind of perspective.

He was called a grocer, but of course he was far more. Common retailers were called regrators. He was actually a wholesaler on an enormous scale. And, as grocer, he was on the side of the victualling guilds with whom the non-victualling fraternities maintained a continous rivalry. In 1373 a certain John Northwold, mercer, was actually killed 'at a wrestling' on Blackheath. On Sunday, 7 March 1378,

before the hour of Noon a conflict arose at Westchepe between certain persons of the trade of Goldsmiths and others of the trade of Pepperers, from a certain rancour that had existed between them; by reason of which conflict, no small affray arose throughout the entire city; and that too while the Bishop of Carlisle was preaching in St. Paul's Churchyard; in which place, because of such conflict, and the wounded fleeing thither with very great outcry, no little tumult and alarm arose.[3]

To exacerbate the tension, to bring the rivalry out into the open as it were, a change was made in the electoral law in 1376, so that common councillors were thenceforward not chosen by wards, but by guilds, and this simply made legal what had been a *de facto* privilege. Our imaginary old man looking back into the past would have shaken his head in sorrow.

In the first nine years of the century the mayor had invariably been classified in the records as a knight. Until 1346 he had more often than not been called a gentleman. But for the remainder of the century the grocers, the fishmongers, the mercers and the goldsmiths had divided the office between them, with the victualling trades having a slight preponderance. Whenever a mercer or a goldsmith was mayor the price of food went down. When a grocer or a fishmonger was in office it went up.

In a word, it was a never-ending struggle for power, and power meant solely the power to use government for one's own profit. Some, like Brembre, Philpot and de Stodeye, became very rich. Philpot owned a splendid house with a large and lovely garden in Eastcheap. Others left substantial sums to charity so that their fortunes would at least buy them a good reputation. But during the last fifty years of the century only a single mayor stands out for his vigorous sense of justice, his desire to clean out the city's administration, to end the victuallers' monopoly and to put an end to the era of short weight, rotten fish, inflated prices and huge profits that had lasted over a generation. This was John of Northampton.

In his *Historia Anglicana*, Walsingham makes clear that in spite of the man's courage and intelligence he was probably attempting the impossible. He was a member of the Drapers' Company, and the owner of not inconsiderable wealth, but he frequently used power when he acquired it in ways opposed to his own private interests.

He was something of a moral reformer too, yet his opponents who survived him had nothing but ill to say of him. During his mayoralty he conducted campaigns against both licentiousness and the jurisdiction of the ecclesiastical courts, and that is perhaps why Walsingham refers to him as 'inspired by John Wycliffe...to carry out things in censure of the prelates'.[4]

During his two terms as mayor, from 1381–3, he forced through legislation of various sorts. Common harlots, who were not only prostitutes but thieves and 'molls', were ordered to wear hoods of striped cloth so that they could be identified. He took steps to stop poor people being fleeced during the obligatory church ceremonies of baptism, marriage and funeral. The proper charge for a priest's services was a farthing. But priests had often claimed that they could not give change, and poor people had generally been too embarrassed to insist. Thenceforward, if a priest refused to accept the proper fee the poor man was entitled to pay nothing. On the other hand, the rich who paid more than they had to out of ostentation were prohibited from paying more than forty pence on pain of a fine of twenty shillings.

His attack on dishonest fishmongers was even more direct, for he was primarily interested in lowering the price of food. On 5 May 1382 a certain John Welburgham was convicted of selling stinking fish. The mayor ordered him not only to repay what he had received for them, but to be exhibited for a warning in the stocks. On 10 August in the same year a fishmonger called Welford was ordered to reduce the price of his fish by a hundred per cent.

A fortnight later Northampton and his aldermen met 'to enquire as to a certain lot of fish, namely 7,000 herrings and 800 mackerel brought to the said city and exposed for sale, to whom such fish belonged and by what person or persons they were brought to the same city, seeing that the herrings as well as the mackerel aforesaid seemed and appeared to be corrupt and unwholesome for man'.

One Reynald atte Chaumbre was identified as the wholesaler. And here was a very serious matter indeed, for the fish were worth a fortune. 'Wherefore...Reynald was forthwith arrested bodily the same day and brought to the Guildhall before the said Mayor and Aldermen, and questioned as to the matters aforesaid, how he would acquit himself thereof. Upon which he could not deny the falsity and deceit aforesaid, but of his own accord acknowledged all that was imputed to him, and wholly submitted to, and threw himself upon the favour of the Court.'

And 'therefore, by award of the Mayor and Aldermen, it was adjudged that the said Reynald should have the punishment of the pillory for six market days, there to remain for one hour each day; and that the same herring and mackerel should be burnt beneath him'.[5]

The fishmongers were aghast, for they were not normally treated so roughly. Were they not men of standing? On 7 November one John Filiol, fishmonger, was brought before the authorities because he had said that 'John Norhamptone, the Mayor, had falsely and maliciously deprived the fishmongers of their bread'. It is a tale with which we are familiar. In open court Filiol called Northampton 'a false scoundrel or *harlot*' (which epithet, incidentally, had no sexual connotation) and he was sent to prison for defamation.

Slanders against the mayor were frequent, and they became more complicated as his enemies tried to make them stick, perhaps on the principle of no smoke without fire. Early in 1383 we find one William Berham sentenced to the pillory. He had gone to the Chief Justice and accused Northampton of advising a witness at the assizes to tell a lie. For this he was sentenced to stand for six days with a whetstone hung round his neck. All through history, reforming politicians seem to have been more often slandered than conservatives.

When the grocer, Nicholas Brembre, succeeded Northampton in 1383-4, he not only had his predecessor's ordinances annulled (it was not until 1390 under another draper that a man was again prosecuted for selling stinking fish), but began at once looking round for grounds on which he might have Northampton brought to trial on a charge of sedition.

On the day of the former mayor's arrest five hundred men are reported to have marched down Cheapside to guard him from the authorities. There were 'seditious meetings' at the Goldsmiths' Hall, but we can understand the need for meetings when we learn that Brembre had been elected only because on the day of the ballot he had packed the Guildhall with armed men.

In vain Northampton petitioned to have the election declared void. He held meetings and made speeches in St Paul's Churchyard, in St Michael Quern, in the parish of St Mary le Bow and in the Tailors' Hall. It was no use. The victuallers were too strong for him. But his arrest was followed by riots all over the city. A certain John Bere, a haberdasher, even went so far as to compare him to St Thomas of

Canterbury. On Tuesday, 11 February 1384, all the shops in West Cheap and Budge Row were shut in protest.

After a long and terrible commotion he was convicted, sentenced to be hanged and sent to Tintagel. In the end, his enemies obviously realized that they had gone too far, and the sentence was commuted. But he never held office in London again.

Even during his mayoralty he had only been head of a minority government. For between March 1380–81 and March 1383–4, there had been thirty-five aldermen belonging to the non-victualling guilds, but only six of these had been Northampton's supporters. Only while he was mayor did friends of his, More, Carleton, Essex and Norbury, represent the city in Parliament. Two of them must have been agitators of a sort, for Essex, More and Northampton himself had been sent to the Tower in 1371 for disturbing the peace. On another occasion Northampton had been bound over for the same offence. But then, it was a violent time. Brembre had his private army. Northampton had only his tongue.

As I have said, the laws passed against profiteering were rescinded, and Brembre, the grocer, seems to have acted ruthlessly and indeed brutally to render any of his antagonists' friends harmless thereafter. One Joan Payn, for example, joined a crowd outside Brembre's house while Northampton was being held there. So Brembre had her arrested and committed to Ludgate, and she later complained that the keeper, 'desiring to please the said Sir Nicholas, procured and abetted the prisoners there to beat her in her bed and else where so continually and so horribly that her life scarce endured'.[6]

Brembre himself was brought to trial in the February of 1388, accused among other things of 'having used his position at Court to make his own fortune by gifts of land and jewels and issues from the taxes, and of having procured land and jewels and offices for relatives and for those who would give him a commission on the grant'.[7] The trial lasted four days, but before it started, obviously guessing what was in store for him, Brembre transferred all his personal property to a brother-in-law and to certain friends. And he had judged rightly. He was convicted, and on Wednesday, 20 February, he was drawn in a cart to Tyburn and there hanged.

In the twenty-three years before 1387, seven of the Fishmongers' Guild had been elected mayor. In the twenty-three years that followed there was but one. Their power had been broken as the power of Richard II who supported them was eventually broken. But the rising power of the capitalist class suffered no loss at all.

One sad footnote I must add to this much abbreviated, and indeed simplified account of what happened, and it has to do with Thomas Usk, Northampton's secretary, the only man of any literary talent amongst the whole profiteering crew. In July 1384, a month before Northampton's trial, he was arrested and induced to supply evidence against his former friend and employer.

This he agreed to do, for, as he wrote later in extenuation of his betrayal, he had hoped to preserve peace in London. On 18 August he appeared as witness for the prosecution, and after Northampton had been convicted, joined Brembre's party. But three years later, when Richard, the king, was looking for some means of overthrowing Gloucester's power, Brembre and Usk seem to have plotted some illegal act on the king's behalf. They were brought to trial at the same time, and twelve days after Brembre had been hanged, Usk, too, was taken out in the cart, drawn, hanged, but then immediately cut down to have his head severed. It required some thirty strokes of the sword.

Brembre left hardly a trace of himself. At least Usk left his *Testament of Love*. It is a pseudo-allegory in prose, partly autobiographical, but full of both lies about his own part in city politics and plagiarisms from Gower, Chaucer and even Langland. He and Chaucer had worked together in the Customs Office, and Usk refers to him as a noble philosophical poet, and one who 'passeth all other makers in wit and in good reason of sentence'. Skeat, who edited the work, calls it 'vague, shifty and un-satisfactory', but at least it has been found worth reprinting. A few self-revealing touches there are to interest us. He says he had once conspired with others [Northampton] to effect certain changes in govern-ment, for 'me semed them noble and glorious to al the people'.[8] In his youth he had been a follower of Wycliffe too, he adds, but he had aban-doned the Lollards as he had abandoned Northampton, for he had no wish to be 'a stinkinge martyr'. That, no doubt, was honest enough, but it hardly endears him to us any more than it did to his contem-poraries.

So the London of Chaucer's last years was in almost every respect different from the far more simple city he had known in his youth. But in spite of the vast numbers of beggars and swindlers (fifty-five people had been crushed to death in 1322 when alms were being distributed at the gate of Blackfriars monastery), in spite of the deformed, the crippled, the diseased, in spite of large colonies of foreigners, goldsmiths, weavers, dyers who had set up workshops in damp basements, in spite of the fact that many great houses had been turned into tenements and were in a state of disrepair there must have been something exhilarating about the place.

Rascally old Dunbar, who wrote the bawdiest poetry of his time, the scholar, mendicant and minstrel (as Quiller-Couch called him) loved London when he first set eyes on it even a hundred and fifty years afterwards, London with its 106 parish churches jangling with bells. 'Sovereign of cities', he called her,

> *Of high renown, riches and royaltie;*
> *Of lordis, barons, and many goodly knyght;*
> *Of most delectable lusty ladies bright;*
> *Of famous prelatis, in habitis clericall;*
> *Of merchauntis full of substaunce and myght;*
> *London, thou art the flour of Cities all.*

How he sings to those delectable ladies (they broke his heart, but he always came back for more), he who had sung the sad song about death that had devoured even Chaucer, flower of poets. Scotsman he may have been, but London filled him with pride. 'Above all rivers, thy river hath renown', he writes, and describes how the swans swim there and the barges sail and the ships rest under the walls of this 'towne of townes'.

> *Upon thy lusty Brigge of pylers white*
> *Been merchauntis full royall to behold;*
> *Upon thy stretis goes many a semely knyght*
> *All clad in velvet gownes and cheynes of gold.*

> *Strong be thy wallis that about thee standis;*
> *Wise be the people that within thee dwellis;*
> *Fresh is thy ryver with his lusty strandis;*
> *Blith be thy churches, wele sownyng be thy bellis;*
> *Riche be thy merchauntis in substaunce that excellis;*
> *Fair be their wives, right lovesom, white and small;*
> *Clere be thy virgyns, lusty under kellis:* [hoods]
> *London, thou art the flour of Cities all.*

The city walls stretched in a great jagged arc from the Tower in the east to the Fleet Ditch just west of St Paul's, and they enclosed an area a little over a mile long and about half a mile wide, broken by seven gates—from the Postern Gate at the Tower to Ludgate in the west. Round that wall a deep trench or moat had been dug, in some places as much as

200 ft wide. But by the fourteenth century it was so silted up and filled with refuse that it had begun to stink. Not even the fish survived in it. Edward III had it cleaned out in 1354, but twice more before the end of the century it had to be cleaned out again.

Even the walls looked ragged because for decades people had been carting stone away to build new houses or to repair the old. As for the streets and alleys–many of them (ran the old joke) just wide enough for wheelbarrows, made before peasants had become rich enough to buy carts–although the old Roman sewers and cisterns still existed, most householders used their rush-covered ground floors as middens for both rubbish and excreta which, when it became too offensive, was simply swept out into the roadway.

What had originally been a town of little rivers–the Fleet, the Westbourne, the Tybourne, the Holbourn, the Walbrook (covered over during the fifteenth century) all running down into the Thames, became a city of open sewers. A city of pure wells, the Clerkenwell, the Shadwell, the Holywell, St Clement's Well, found that its wells were gradually blocked up with rubbish, and all the filth, from rivers, wells and street kennels, found its way gradually down into the Thames, for the 'rakyers', whose job it was to sweep refuse down out of the courts and kennels, simply raked it down on to the riverbank. In Chaucer's time, when the population had long been about 40,000 but was rapidly increasing (there were 20,397 over the age of fifteen, according to the poll tax records of 1380), there were only twelve refuse carts in all London, one to every four or five thousand of population.

So infectious diseases were far more prevalent than they are today. Cuts, abrasions and small wounds almost invariably turned septic. Running sores, skin diseases and intestinal inflammations were the rule and not the exception. And in Kent Street, across the river in Southwark, lay the hospital for lepers and for other miserable folk with mortal diseases.

Long before the fourteenth century Fitzstephen wrote that upon the river-side, between the wine in ships and the wine to be sold in taverns 'is a common cookerie or cookes row. There dayly for the season of the year, men might have meat, rost, sod or fried, fish, flesh, fowles fit for rich or poore...all viands whatsoever a man desireth...and they which delight in delicatenesse may bee satisfied with as delicate dishes there as may be found elswhere.' In his day Londoners had not yet acquired their passion for oysters, of which many a fourteenth-century citizen made his midday meal.

Most shopping for comestibles was done in the markets, of course, for fish in Fish Street Hill or Old Fish Street or in the Stocks Market (stockfish were dried, imported fish), meat in Eastcheap or Newgate Street, eggs and poultry in Cornhill and Leadenhall, cereals in Grace-church Street or in St Michael le Quern at the west end of Cheap (buyers bought corn and oats and ground them at home). Bread came up daily in carts from Stratford, and it was baked in bigger loaves than London bread. The chapmen or regrators bought loaves at thirteen to the shilling (the baker's dozen) and sold them for a penny apiece. There were herb markets for onions, celery, parsley, fennel, rosemary and thyme.

Down the twisting lanes under the 'solars', upper floors projecting on wooden pillars to catch the sun, came hawkers ('huckster' had originally been the female variety), costermongers (because they sold costard apples), women with little hand-carts, crying bread, beer, fish, eel and meat pies. At the street corners one found *tiplers* who sold drinks to passers-by out of little casks.

Cheapside was the elegant shopping centre (the Bond Street of the day). Between Queen Street and Bow Lane one found the shoemakers, on the corner of Bucklersbury the ironmongers. Soap had been shipped in from Bristol or Spain (which is why it is still sometimes called Castile), ribbons and lace from Milan, and thus called millinery.

There was Smithfield just outside the walls,

a plaine field, both in name and deed, where every fryday, unless it be a solemne bidden holy day, is a notable shew of horses to be solde. Earles, Barons, knights and Citizens repair thither to see or to buy: there may you of pleasure see amblers placing it dilicately: there may you see trotters fit for men of armes: there may you have notable young horses not yet broken: there may you have strong steedes, wel limmed geldings, whom the buiers do specially regard for paces and swiftness: the boyes which ride these horses, sometimes two, sometimes three, doe run races for wagers, with a desire of praise, or hope of victorie. In an other part of that field are to be sold all implements of husbandry, as also fat swine, milch kine, sheepe and oxen: there stand also mares and horses fitte for ploughes and teames with their young colts by them.[9]

Butchers bought their meat live, walked it to the bull ring in each market and there slaughtered it, and their boys swept the blood and offal into the kennels. But it was drink, says Stow, that was the real plague of London. As early as 1309, there had been 1,334 breweries in the city. But he has little to add to what we know about the taverns. Instead, he goes on to describe how not only the victuallers, but every trade–the mercers, the haberdashers, goldsmiths, cooks and even beadmakers and writers of texts–have each a particular section of the city where they have set up stalls.

Lydgate tells in his *London Lackpenny* about being besieged outside Westminster Hall by Flemings crying, 'Master, what will you buy? Fine felt hats? Spectacles?' At Westminster Gate the cooks cried bread and ale and wine and ribs of beef. 'Hot peascods', somebody called, or ripe strawberries, spices, pepper and saffron. In Cheapside he was offered velvet, silk and lawn (linen of Laon) and 'Parys thred, the fynest in the land'. In Candlewick Street it was hot sheep's feet and mackerel. In East Cheap they tried to sell him ribs of beef again and various pies, pewter pots and harps and pipes, all stacked in heaps. He heard street singers too, and when he got to Cornhill he saw piles of stolen goods. It was there a taverner took him by the sleeve and finally sold him a pint of wine for a penny.

There were processions and festivals too–in January 1382, for example, when Richard II married his child bride, Anne of Bohemia–and the gossip went round that 'never was so great a sum paid for so little a scrap of humanity'. Anne first started the custom of women riding in side saddles, and it was she who introduced the fashion of wearing such long toes to the shoes that eventually they had to be tied to the wearer's knees.

In 1391, on the Sunday after the Feast of St Michael, there was a great tournament in Smithfield. As Clerk of the King's Works, Chaucer was in charge of having the scaffolds erected at a cost amounting to £8 12s. 6d.

At the day appoynted, there issued forth of the tower, about the third houre of the day, 60 coursers, apparrelled for the Iusts, and upon every one an Esquier of honour riding a soft pace: then came forth 60 Ladyes of honour mounted upon palfraies, riding on the one side, richly apparrelled, and every Lady led a knight with a chayne of gold. Those knights, being on the Kings party, had their Armour and apparrell garnished with white Hartes and Crownes of gold about the Harts neckes, & so they came riding through the streetes of London to Smithfield, with a great number of trumpets and other instruments of musicke before them.[10]

And it had been only a few years earlier when wages were still a penny a day that Thomas, Earl of Lancaster, had been able to spend £7,957 13s.

4*d.* a year in household expenses, of which over £5,000 was for food. He had bought 184 tuns (each holding 210 gallons) of red wine and a tun of white, 6,800 dried fish, 6 barrels of sturgeon, 1,714 lbs of wax and 2,319 lbs of tallow candles, plus groceries, linen, parchment and food for horses.

Hugh Spencer, before he was banished, owned 59 manors in various parts of the country, 28,000 sheep, 1,000 oxen and steers, 1,200 cows with their calves, 40 mares with their foals, 160 horses for pulling loads, 2,000 pigs, plus armour, plate, jewels and ready money to the value of £10,000—as well as a notable library.

Of such men one can easily believe, as Chaucer wrote of his franklin, that it snowed in their houses of meat and drink. But the rich were not the only ones who enjoyed themselves.

In the moneths of June and July on the Vigiles of festivall dayes, and on the same festivall dayes in the Evenings after the Sunne setting, there were usually made bonefiers in the streetes, every man bestowing wood or labour towards them: the wealthier sort also before their doores neare to the said bonefiers, would set out Tables on the Vigiles, furnished with sweete breade and good drinke, and on the Festivall dayes with meates and drinks plentifully, wherunto they would invite their neighbours. These were called Bonefiers as well of good amitie amongest neighbours that, being before at controversie, were there by the labour of others, reconciled, and made of bitter enemies, loving friends, as also for the vertue that a great fire hath to purge the infection of the ayre.[11]

We are not told at what date this custom was practised, except that it was 'time out of mind until the year 1539', so we may reasonably conclude that it was known in fourteenth-century London.

The London archives printed by Riley are full of stories about how citizens lived and almost what they talked about, what was very probably the current gossip. There we read the regulations laid down in the charters of skinners and dealers in fur. We read about girdlers and fripperers who sold second-hand clothing, or frippery; about furniture salesmen, saddlers and the quarrels they had with the lorimers who made bits, spurs and the metal mounts of their saddles.

We learn about tricksters. John Brid, baker, for example, was accused of stealing dough that people brought him for baking. It seems that he had a hole like a trap door cut in his kneading table, and when he threw dough on to it a confederate seated underneath opened the trap and pulled large amounts of the dough down out of sight, 'frequently collecting large amounts of such dough falsely, wickedly and maliciously …to the great loss of all his neighbours and to the scandal and disgrace of the whole city'.

In 1331 it was ordered that a gallon of best Gascon wine should be sold for no more than fourpence, and a gallon of Rhenish for eight. In February 1337 John le Whyte, skinner, was caught in the act of stealing goods worth a hundred shillings from a mercer's shop. He was ordered to be hanged. In May of the same year Desiderata de Toryntone steals certain silver dishes and salt cellars in Fleet Street 'in the suburb of London', and she too is hanged. Stephen Salle of Canterbury steals a green hood, a russet hood and various other articles of clothing from Wool Wharf. He is hanged. Walter Barry steals a coat and a blanket during the hours of darkness, Adam of Nottingham a cup, Walter Curteys several pieces of velvet. A Florentine steals silver belonging to his master, and each time there follows the sentence of death by hanging. Each time the report ends with the words 'chattels has he none'. In a word, the thieves were destitute.

In 1345 a complaint is made that the king's highway between the stocks and the Conduit is 'so occupied on flesh days by butchers and poulterers with their wares for sale, and on fish days by fishmongers with their wares that persons going that way and returning cannot pass through without great hindrance'. At the same meeting it was shown that Thames water at Dowgate 'has become so corrupted by dung and other filth thrown into the same dock, that the porters who carry water from the Thames at the said dock to different places in the city are no longer able to serve the commonalty'. So five carters are ordered to clear away the dung.

A petition from the gardeners asks that they be allowed to stand as of old by the side of St Paul's churchyard to sell vegetables, but this is disallowed because they make such a racket that it disturbs the people in church. And the mention of vegetables reminds one that there were not only many private gardens; there were even farms in the city. Nearly a hundred and fifty years afterwards there was a large farm just north of the Tower near the Minories, able to support thirty or forty cattle, where Stow in his youth used to fetch milk, three pints for a halfpenny.

In 1346 lepers were forbidden to 'have carnal intercourse with women in stews and other secret places', for it was thought that they had been trying to infect others deliberately. Wheatley's *London* quotes a Scottish Act of Parliament intended, no doubt, to be more merciful. According to the act, rotten pork or salmon offered for sale in the market was to be seized and given to the lepers free of payment.

In 1350, the year after the plague, masons, carpenters and plasterers were ordered not to charge more than 6*d*. a day in summer and 5*d*. in winter, tilers a penny less, and common labourers were not to have more than 3½*d*. and 3*d*. At the same time regulations were made about the cost of transport and building materials. Thus tiles were to be charged for at no more than 5*s*. a thousand, lime for no more than 5*s*. a hundredweight. A carter carrying clay or sand from Aldgate was to charge no more than 5*d*. to the Conduit, and 8½*d*. if he went beyond that point.

Among articles of clothing, a coat and hood might not be priced at more than 10*d*., a woman's gown at more than 2*s*. 6*d*. Leather shoes were to cost no more than 6*d*., and a pair of boots no more than 3*s*. 6*d*. Sheepskin gloves were to cost a penny, and no cook was to ask more than a penny for putting a capon or a rabbit into a pie.

The farriers were to charge no more than before the plague, that is, 1½*d*. for a horseshoe of six nails and 2*d*. for one of eight. Servants who demanded higher wages than before the plague were to pay a fine amounting to double the excess, but the employer who paid more was to be fined treble. Of course this would hardly deter a man who could afford to burn a ton of candles in his house every year.

But how little these regulations were obeyed even by the authorities we can gather from another account of the same year. The Conduit in Cheapside had to be repaired, and the city itself paid men 8*d*. a day to do the work, as well as an extra 4*d*. each for drink at noontime. This was their *nonechenche*, literally a noontime pouring out, a nuncheon. Luncheon, on the other hand, consisted of a *lunchion*, a lump of bread.

In 1351 an ordinance was published prohibiting whores from wearing fur 'like good and noble dames', for of course, then as now, the prostitute was anxious to look genteel. No, they might wear hoods and habits of unlined cloth only so that they could immediately be recognized. Thirty years afterwards the ordinance had to be passed again. In 1386 these same women were said to be going about their trade in what had used to be the garden of St Katherine's Hospital by the Tower, and (like modern London parks) the land had to be enclosed to keep them out.

Over and over again we read about punishments for selling carrion. Henry de Pesselwe, cook, sold two rotten capons baked in a pie, so he was sentenced to the pillory. Richard Quelhogge 'bought a pig that had been lying by the waterside of the Thames, putrid and stinking, of one Richard Stevenache, porter, for fourpence, and from the same had cut two gammons for sale, and had sold part thereof in deceit of the people'.

So he, too, was sentenced to the pillory and the two gammons were burned beneath him.

In 1355 the fosse by Fleet Prison was found to be choked with refuse from eleven separate 'necessary houses' built above it, and the stench was so abominable that prisoners had actually been made ill. In addition, there had been three tanneries established on the banks. So the water had to be cleaned and enquiry made whether latrines ought to have been erected there in the first place.

The wonder is not that the poor were often hungry to the point of turning thieves and scavengers, or that retailers were greedy, or that the rich were making splendid fortunes, but that anything lasting and beautiful was accomplished. Not only did the lovely ladies riding side-saddle on their palfreys lead out knights on golden chains: Chaucer at that very moment was writing his *Book of the Duchess*, his *Troilus* and his *Canterbury Tales*. Langland was composing his tortuous and powerful diatribe against the unununderstandable, and many great builders and sculptors were at work. Music was being sung, so richly polyphonous that it could move men to tears, and there were dreams abroad of such muscular bigness that it must have seemed to the dreamers as if there were only a single step to be taken, and it would open the door out of a sweet and bitter world into a paradise that was actually all around them. And yet, Chaucer asks,

What is this world? what asketh men to have,
Now with his love, now in his colde grave,
Allone, withouten any companye.

The 'trompes loude and clarioun' rise on the air, the poignantly graceful ladies in their low-waisted dresses and pretty fillets, the sweet bells of London's 106 churches, the great colour-washed fronts of the cathedrals, the stately towers, these too were the fourteenth century. So now we shall step up out of the streets and hear what else these people had to say for themselves.

CHAPTER NINE

The LYF SO ShORT, The CRAFT SO LONG TO LERNE

During the Second World War I once spent several days on leave in the hills behind Conway. One night in the inner room of a lonely pub– I never actually saw him until later, only heard him–a young man sprawled on a table with his back to the wall, strumming a guitar. He was singing to himself in Welsh, hesitantly with many pauses, sometimes falling silent between phrases as though in thought, and this interested me. So I asked one of my companions what the song was about, for because I speak no Welsh I could not understand a word of it.

'It is a ballad, look you,' I was told. 'He is singing about how he and his friends drove the Italians west out of Africa last year.'

And I remember thinking even then that the same thing must have happened in many a hall and many a tavern when lads came home from Poitiers with longbows strapped to their backs. So it must have been at Greek campfires when the first footsoldiers came drifting home from Troy, for within a mere handful of years they had already collected a vast body of anecdote, rhythmical and memorable because it had been told to music. Later it had been enlarged, made cohesive and more formal. Then in time Homer had taken this revised and purified material, some of it perhaps already in great rolling hexameters, and by suffusing it not only with red bronze and iron, but with the oblique half-light that casts the most revealing shadows, built it into the most magnificent poem in the world.

The point is, though, that whether after Troy or Roncesvalles or Poitiers, such singers had been the first journalists, the first brief chroniclers, some of them painstakingly truthful, some ignorant, but guessing about the facts, all magnifying. Minstrelsy of course was part of the twelfth, thirteenth and fourteenth centuries as of any others, but it is more to the point to examine what grew out of such medieval reportage and the thing that finally evolved was a quite original idea about human relationships.

We can easily imagine the great hall, the roaring fire, the servants scurrying here and there with food, and after supper the scene when some traveller, some clumsy poet like the old soldier, Minot, stood and sang out his crude and rhythmic bragging.

Whare are ye, skottes of Saint Johnes toune?
The boste of yowre baner es betin [beaten] all doune;
When he bosting will bede, [offer] sir Edward es boune [ready]
For to kindel yow care and crak yowre crowne.

This is as primitive as a crested helmet to give a man height, or the Pict's tattooing to frighten the enemy when he roars into battle. But in the Middle Ages a strange and wonderful thing happened to the old journalistic ballads. They began to be concerned not so much with fighting and bloodshed as with a remarkable new experience called love. Not lust, not passion, but adoration.

It began in France where the ironclad feudal world fastened people into moulds just as it did in England. The soldier, the descendant of Ajax and Agamemnon, was now the knight. But we must immediately put out of our minds any preconceptions we may have about knighthood. The word comes originally from the Anglo-Saxon *cniht,* a boy or a servant, and the knight, like the villein, was a dependent, but one whose function was at the risk of his own life to kill, to plunder and to terrorize on behalf of his feudal lord. The men who did this with the greatest courage and ruthlessness were obviously the most highly valued, the most nobly rewarded. On their entrance into the hall they were treated with the greatest deference, and when the troubadour sang he flattered them with the most fulsome praise.

All such a man did was done on behalf of his lord, to whom he owed an irrevocable loyalty.

Aside from having to fight, therefore, the knight's function was to obey. And the collapse of the Carolingian empire in France made it of fundamental importance that he fulfil this most personal of obligations. He and his lord stood back to back against a dangerous world. But of course times gradually became less uncertain. Slowly, the knight's function changed.

I think I have quoted Shelley before, who said that poets were the unacknowledged legislators, and it is true because great poets have a sense for the way the wind is blowing when the rest of us do not. They are in touch with the tides or with the still inexperienced spirit of an age. They rarely lead. Milton did not lead, or Shelley or Chaucer, but they sang out the road the rest of us were already following unawares.

So in the eleventh and twelfth centuries as the social organism evolved, the Provençal troubadours began singing not only swordplay and terrible, ruthless deeds, but as they sensed the coming of an easier and less brutal world, they began to sing new knightly virtues, generosity, hospitality, bigness of heart, *largesse* (which they hoped to receive), so that to paraphrase Painter,[1] a disregard of caution in the use of money began to be considered the mark of a nobleman.

Largesse came to exist on the battlefield too, for the nobility thought of themselves as members of a superior class. A largehearted man did not attack a helpless enemy. He succoured the weak. He entertained a nobleman he had captured as a guest until the man could be ransomed.

The poets began to praise not only acts of bravery, but of honour, and scrupulous adherence to one's word. Which came first, the song or the deed, makes little difference. King John of France was captured at Poiters and released in exchange for a number of hostages. When one of the hostages broke his parole and escaped, the king returned of his own free will to his captivity in London. Froissart writes of a common soldier who killed the Comte de St Pol in battle. But he boasted of the fact loudly and vulgarly, and his commander ordered him hanged out of hand for having had the effrontery to kill an adversary so much nobler than himself. It was one of the criticisms that the French levied against the English that during the Hundred Years War they had ceased to fight like gentlemen, but employed low-born archers, more interested in looting and murder than in chivalry.

Subtly, gradually, the church too brought its great weight to bear not only upon the times, but on the intellectual climate and on the poets who exemplified it. The *Chanson de Roland,* the *Perceval* of Chrétien de Troyes, even the *Queste del Saint Graal,* which was probably written by a Cistercian monk (and in which Galahad first appears) turned tales of knightly exercises into romance, into propaganda for the employment of courage, *largesse* and the love of fame, not only on behalf of one's sovereign, but–and here was a new thing–on behalf of Christianity. Roland carried his immortal horn into battle not only with his liege lord, but with God, against the infidel. Perceval and Galahad represented the new ecclesiastical chivalry built into a frame of Arthurian myth. It has been neatly pointed out[2] that Galahad (surnamed the chaste) 'divided his time about equally between performing heroic knightly deeds, resisting the advances of lovely ladies and listening to moral discourses in monastic cloisters'. The quest for noble adventure was transformed into a quest for the Grail.

How the idea of courtly love (as opposed to the love of God) first entered the lists is too complex and much argued a story to be entered into here. To describe how women, who had at best been property, married for reasons of policy or financial advantage, the producers of male heirs; at worst, peasant girls who might be toppled onto their backs *modica coactio*, with a sort of gentlemanly compulsion, who might be highborn infidels who crept into the beds of noble knights only to be sternly repulsed, or the wife of one's lord who had to be protected against calumny–to describe how these figures became subjects of adoration, and to make the whole complex story clear would require a book to itself.

It is enough to say that the idea took root, again probably first in Provence. Women might actually be loved (a quite revolutionary thought), and such a love, even if it was unrequited, could act as a spur to knightly prowess. Above all, this love might conceivably end in sexual fruition, but in the beginning, and with very few exceptions, it had nothing whatever to do with marriage and very little to do with sex.

The whole shadow-play that then developed has to be understood in the context of its age. Love was a game. It was a charade played in talk, in the mind, in the courtly imagination, and men and women paced through its dance as though it were some silent and interminable chess match which has neither a beginning nor an end. It had little to do with lust. It was a poignant and delightful emotion that had as much resemblance to reality as a schoolboy crush has to mature human relationships.

For these lovers there was no madness like that of Dido or Medea or even Shakespeare's Cleopatra. The women of the troubadours and of the later love allegory, the innumerable lost damsels and adulterous wives were simply abstractions, and one does not either marry or copulate with an abstraction. One can only give it an arbitrary value and say that the pursuit of it ennobles the pursuer. Carnality would only degrade.

Andreas Capellanus (Andrew the Chaplain) wrote a manual of love, and he makes it very clear that sensual enjoyment may very well be the goal, but that it must be approached through eloquence, honesty, modesty, courage and generosity. Love is a state of mind, and it ends by being a source of goodness in the lover himself.

All ladies, married or not, ought to take courtly lovers, for they too can thus be transmuted into something finer than they have been before. Indeed, true love began to be thought possible for a married woman only in adultery. Sex in marriage had something tawdry about it; it contained an element of duty, of a desire for procreation, of the banal. In fact, sexual union in marriage was the real adultery, for it had nothing to do with the honour, the *probitas*, the excitement to moral virtue, the pure and delightful danger of true love. True love was a mixture of the divine love one might feel for the Virgin, or pursuit of the Grail, and of knightly honour itself.

In a word, the courtly lover gradually made an amalgam in his mind between the pure love of God and the pleasurable pursuit of women. And slowly this new erotic religion became a parody and a rival of the old. Cupid became, if only in jest, the new God. In him was heaven. His ladies were God's saints and the rules of courtly love, God's commandments. 'If', says C. S. Lewis, 'you picture the lover praying, sinning, repenting and finally admitted to bliss, you will find yourself in the precarious world of medieval love poetry.'[3] It was another example of the medieval world trying to put a rational gloss on what was essentially–like religion itself–an emotional experience.

Suddenly, love lyrics became all the vogue. Their conventions had never existed before, but their notions of courtesy, of deference and of a sexuality essentially romantic have influenced our attitude to women ever since. And the curious thing is that all this was the invention of an age essentially barbarous, but one which, feeling the first stirring of renaissance, and having just rediscovered classical poetry, was trying to emulate a Roman society which it could read about but scarcely understand.

Ovid's *Ars Amatoria* was the new Bible, and the *Ars Amatoria* is simply a long didactic poem about certain well-tried methods of seduction. It was no more a philosophy of love than a drinking song is a study in alcoholism. To Ovid a woman had been a toy, a pleasure, a plaything that gave delight. One took her seriously only in so far as she disturbed one's senses, the way a dog takes fleas seriously that give him a chance to scratch. The serious things were books, politics, civic virtue, science and the nature of the gods. What had the little Lesbias, the Cynthias, the Delias and Bibulas to do with truth and goodness?

But to the Middle Ages this made no difference at all. The troubadours were looking for classical models, for a classical methodology they could apply to their resurgent society. It is the scholarly fashion to say that they misinterpreted Ovid. I think it likely that they read him at least as clearly as we do, but that, because he answered to the spirit of the time, they evolved through him their new sexual morality. It is as if, knowing that both marriage and loveless copulation were a bore, they had invented an upper-class literary game which, cleverly played, could be made more pleasant than either.

No contemporary, not even the Black Prince or Bertrand du Guesclin, lived or loved or thought about women like Lancelot or Gawain or any one of a hundred other invented lovers. Instead, it was the poets who sang, who wrote, who created immortal ladies with narrow waists and eyes that haunted one at night. The soldiers simply listened and daydreamed about the impossible.

Fetys [trim] she was, and smal to see;
No windred [plucked] browës haddë she,
Ne poppëd hir, [nor tricked herself out] for it neded nought
To windre hir, or to peynte hir ought.
Hir tresses yelowe, and longë straughten,
Unto hir heles doun they raughten:
Hir nose, hir mouth, and eye and cheke
Wel wrought, and al the remenaunt eke.
A ful gret savour and a swote [sweet]
Me thinketh in myn hertë rote, [root]
As helpe me god, whan I remembre
Of the fasoun [shape] of every membre!
In world is noon so fair a wight;
For yong she was, and hewed bright,
Wys, plesant and fetys [graceful] withalle,
Gente [exquisite] and in hir middel smalle.[4]

Here is the ideal, and one can see her in a hundred medieval drawings.

But the Latin poets had never described their women so much as they recounted what they said and did. The little honey-mouthed bitches were kind or unkind. They were vulgar; they betrayed. They took rich lovers, or any lovers they pleased. They pissed in public. They quarrelled and got drunk and padded about the room *en déshabillé*. They were chatterboxes, spendthrifts, flirts. They painted themselves outrageously. One can actually smell them. But the fair ladies of the Middle Ages are like the Holy Grail itself, whom only the perfect knight can hope to win. The Romans strike one as flesh and blood, the Provençal as heroines in Victorian (and some modern) fiction. They are like Edmund

Wilson's *Princess with the Golden Hair*, as impervious to the touch of reality as any lovely ghost.

The important thing for our purpose is that the convention I have been describing was invented in France. And during the fourteenth century the flood of the renaissance which had begun to swell in Italy crept northwards, and by way of the peripatetic Englishman who saw and heard about the beautiful new world abroad, began here and there to be rumoured even in the brackish backwater of England.

In the north they were still trudging from shrine to shrine to kiss the relics of dead saints. In Padua, doctors and students from the University were carrying candles to the house of the poet Musattus, greeting him with trumpets and bringing him Christmas gifts. They carried Petrarch to the house in Arezzo where he had been born and informed him that the city had passed an ordinance ensuring that nothing should ever be done to disturb it. Arquà, where he died, became a place of pilgrimage, and he was revered there much as the English hundreds of miles to the north revered St Cuthbert. The Florentines, as Burckhardt reminds us,[5] planned to turn their cathedral into a Pantheon for the bones of Accorso, Dante, Petrarch and Boccaccio. Meanwhile, Dante lay amid the saints of San Francesco in Ravenna. One night the candles were taken from the high altar and placed round his grave instead, for the unnamed heretic who moved them thought him more worthy of candles than Christ.

The tomb of Virgil in Naples became a holy shrine, for his beautiful, pitiable and mortal Dido had become the romantic heroine of the age.* The two Plinys were carved on the front of Como Cathedral, and men complained in anguish that Ovid could not be brought home, for he had been buried in exile on the shores of the Black Sea. In a word, fourteenth-century Italy had begun to break away from the dead drifting of theological speculation and to rediscover the beauty and majesty of the human spirit, particularly as it was exemplified in the poets and painters among them.

---

* Helen Waddell wrote that 'They could not read the lines in Homer where the old men on the wall hushed their swallows' chattering as Helen passed by; they knew her only in Dictys, sweet-natured, long-limbed and golden-haired, or in the amazing flashlight vision of Virgil, crouching on the steps of the Temple of Vesta in the light of the fires, "Erynnis to her father's house and Troy". But Dido they took to their hearts…St Augustine broke his heart for her; and the schoolboy Alcuin, waking at night and watching the devils nip the toes of the other monks in the dormitory, called anxiously to mind that he had scamped the Psalms to read the *Aeneid.*' *The Wandering Scholars*, p. xxvi.

The English pilgrim travelling south and east across Europe would have been stunned by the sheer brilliance of colour in the church of San Francesco in Assisi, or the lightness, the insubstantiality of the Doges' Palace in Mantua, or the enchanting little church of Santa Maria della Spina in Pisa with its delicate sugarcake turrets and its walls in two shining tones of marble. What could London, built on Thames shingle, old wattle-and-daub London with its houses of warped timber, offer comparable to the glowing half-circle of splendid houses on projecting arches that fronted the sunlit sea of Genoa?

Almost wherever he went–Germany, Italy, Spain, France, Flanders–the English traveller felt himself expanding under the brilliant blue of the continental sky. In the south there were oranges, lemons, great hillsides green and purple with grapes. Even in the north he found almost everywhere a man-made colour and invention, an almost incredible profusion of fresco and mosaic.

So when Chaucer, who may very well at least once in his life have sat and talked to Petrarch, who certainly read his Boccaccio as well as he read English, who said of himself that he owned a library of sixty books, when Chaucer undertook to translate the *Roman de la Rose* of Guillaume de Lorris and Jean de Meung, he broke clear away from the didactic, from the recounting of bloody deeds, from the self-importance of so many of his predecessors, and did a thing no English poet had ever done before. He wrote something amusing.

He sings, not paradise or a battlefield, but a garden, a veritable island of the Hesperides, and there everything is brightness, sunlight, beauty as clear and fresh as water. This is no Minot chanting war, no penitential lament, no praise of Christ's mother. Instead, it is a poem full of birds that sing blissful, sweet and piteous songs. It is full of enchanting ladies. He says of the portress who opens the gate to him that

Hir heer was as yelowe of hewe
As any basin scourëd newe.[6]

He tells us about her large grey eyes, her little mouth, the cleft in her chin.

Fro Ierusalem unto Burgoyne
Ther nis a fairer nekke y-wis,
To fele how smothe and softe it is.
Hir throte, al-so whyt of hewe
As snow on braunche snowëd newe.[7]

Everyone he meets in the garden is alive with the same joyous youth and beauty. He says of Mirth,

> *As round as appel was his face,*
> *Ful rody and whyt in every place.*
> *Fetys he was and wel beseye, [trim and fair to see]*
> *With metely mouth and yën greye.*[8]

The personifications of Mirth and Gladness dance, he with the face like an apple. In fact,

> *Bothe were they faire and brighte of hewe;*
> *She semedë lyk a rosë newe*
> *Of colour, and hir flesh so tendre,*
> *That with a brerë [briar] smale and slendre*
> *Men mighte it cleve, I dar wel sayn.*
> *Hir forheed, frouncëles [unwrinkled] al playn.*
> *Bentë were hir browës two,*
> *Hir yën greye, and gladde also,*
> *That laughëde ay in hir semblaunt,*
> *First or [before] the mouth, by covenaunt...*
> *Hir heer was yelowe, and cleer shyning,*
> *I wot no lady so lyking.*[9]

The author meets Beauty herself, and again the shining face, the newness of everything about her. Her eyes laughed too, very likely, before her mouth did.

> *Ne was she derk ne broun, but bright,*
> *As cleer as is the monë-light,*
> *Ageyn whom alle the sterres semen*
> *But smale candels as we demen.*[10]

Light, he writes, sprang even out of the stone. It shone from the bodies themselves, and one could perceive it through their very clothing.

> *For through hir smokkë, wrought with silk,*
> *The flesh was seen, as whyt as milk.*[11]

or again,

> *She was not broun ne dun of hewe,*
> *But whyt as snowe y-fallen newe.*[12]

above A lady and gentleman obviously on friendly terms, bathing in wooden tubs. (Radio Times Hulton Picture Library)

below Fishing with nets. (The British Library Board)

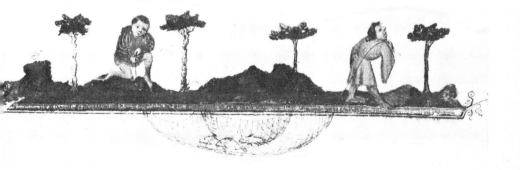

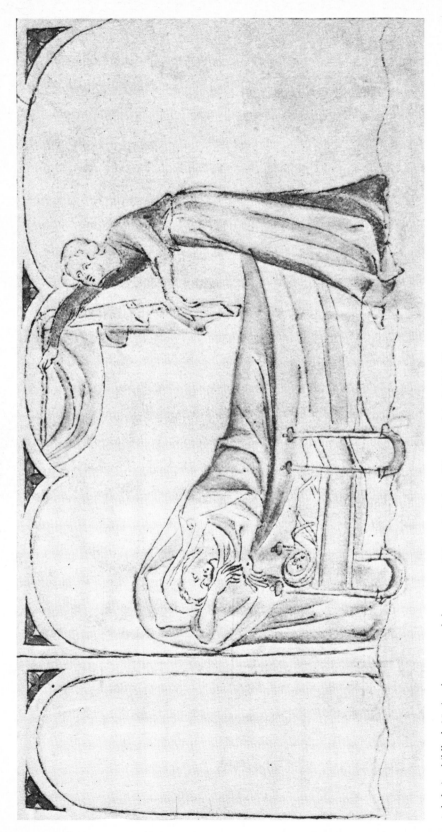

A lady in childbed. Notice the grace, and the pure proficiency in design. (Trustees of the British Museum)

Brightness falls from the air, we think to ourselves, and the newness, the freshness permeate all visible things. The glad eyes, the ears, the sense of touch are all employed. The flowers are positively incandescent.

And by the stremës over al elles
Sprang up the gras, as thikke y-set
And softe as any veluët,
On which men mighte his lemman leye,
As on a fetherbed to pleye.[13]

This is not Chaucer, you will say. This is Guillaume de Lorris. And so it is, although Chaucer makes many subtle changes to sharpen the picture for English eyes. In fact, it is more than either. It is sunlight. It is the two thousand year old Mediterranean world rippling north like laughter into the cold Atlantic. It is the shining Madonnas or the sun-struck Ducal Palace of Mantua beginning to haunt the rat-riddled tenements of London. It is the first glow of the Renaissance rising from far away into the rickety feudal world of the north.

First from above, first in the halls of the splendid berry-bearded king, then permeating slowly downwards, the change came. Early in the reign of Edward III the clothing–as it has always done–changed to fit the temper of the times. Before then, gowns for both men and women had been loose and flowing, never held to the body by more than a belt. Suddenly, as though Englishmen had been turned into Spaniards or Italians, the garment began to fit the figure. Hoods, mantles, tunics and hose appeared in brilliant colours, or else were parti-coloured left and right, or in quarters. The man's cote-hardie, or jacket with buttons from neck to hem, reached halfway down the thigh and was secured at the hip with a broad, jewelled belt. But all during the century it rose until by 1380 the hemline was on the hips and the men had to wear codpieces. Sleeves were cut in jagged edges that grew longer until by the time of Richard II they actually trailed on the ground. Men wore no shoes indoors, but soles were added to the tights and wooden pattens strapped to the feet with leather thongs for going out. And, as I have said, the toes of one's stocking-shoes curled up more and more until, after the new queen added her spendour to the court, they had to be fastened with little gold chains to the knees.

Fur, fur linings, jewelled embroideries, heraldic motifs in bright colours were all the rage until, like Chaucer's squire,

> *Embrouded was he, as it were a mede,*
> *Al ful of fresshe flourës, whyte and rede.*[14]

As for the ladies, their gowns began to be fitted closely to the body too. Tiny corsets came in to accentuate the waist–and lasted without a break until little more than a generation ago. And while it was considered indelicate for a woman to show her arms (she invariably wore sleeves to the wrist), the dress itself was worn décolleté to expose the collar bones and sometimes even the shoulders. Poets from Chaucer to Wyatt almost two hundred years afterwards seem more aware of long and slender arms than we are.

In the early part of the century women had been swathed in coifs and robes, and might almost–except for the colours–have been taken for nuns. By the time of Richard II the clothing had changed to make them look as graceful and slender, as flower-like as any of the little figures in the chivalric love stories or in Chaucer's garden. Like Criseyde or May or Alisoun, they have come stepping down out of the magic wood where Lancelot rides, demure, slim-waisted and lecherous, their small mouths sweet with lies and their grey eyes laughing for sheer delight at being taken in adultery.

Padua, Florence and at least eight or ten other cities in France, Germany and the low countries were grander and more poignantly beautiful than London. But in Chaucer's time the great spire of St Paul's stood with its weathercock 489 feet above the street, far higher than anything built in the city until the twentieth century, and a man up beside the high cross would have seen the great shaft of Cornhill, the maypole near St Andrew Undershaft, and then the White Tower standing what looked a mere stone's-throw below him. He could have looked across to Southwark, green with trees, to large private houses and gardens and out to the Kentish marshes.

Westwards he would have seen the Temple, John of Gaunt's great palace of the Savoy near the village of Charing, then the towers of Westminster Abbey, a blaze of colour now washed away, and beyond them, the wooded wilds of Knightsbridge and the low hills that hid the roads to Oxford and St Albans. Almost at his feet, a maze of crooked alleys rose noticeably from the river, and a conglomeration of tall wooden houses with sharply sloping roofs, mostly of red tile.

Down behind the high altar of St Paul's lay Erkenwald, eighth-century Bishop of London, and Ethelred, ninth-century king of the West

Saxons, as well as many others in elegant and sometimes gilded tombs. Outside the north gate in Paternoster Row and up in Ave Mary Lane the text writers lived who wrote books to order. They were the first stationers, from *statio*, a position, a place of work. The parchment skins on which they wrote cost three-halfpence apiece, but lately much cheaper paper had been coming from Bordeaux and a careful workman could turn out a cheap paper Bible for about forty shillings.

Then there were the beadmakers who turned beads for devotions. Just beyond them the bowyers, or bow-makers lived, and then the great square convent of the Black Friars facing on to Ludgate from where the road ran down to Fleet Bridge and thence westwards out past Fickett's field into the country.

The Savoy, a little over half a mile off, was probably the finest house in the kingdom, and it had just been rebuilt at a cost of about £35,000, or close to £5,000,000 in modern money. But the building of great churches had more or less come to an end. Only the 'imager' or sculptor was still hard at work. He had used simply to be a talented master mason who erected figures on the façades and along the inner walls. But now, like the poets, he had begun to be inspired by his own particular facet of the Renaissance visible all over Europe.

Even fifty years earlier he had never made any attempt to create likenesses of the dead or to individualize his subjects. Purbeck marblers had even shipped out tombs and effigies to order, ready carved. But gradually men like William of Ireland up in Northampton or William Torel in London had begun trying to do more graceful work, to capture–in stone or bronze, or even in wood–the figure living and in movement, for the old-fashioned columnar draperies had begun to seem primitive.

In the York Chapter House, for example, a Madonna in curls and with her cloak falling in folds over her feet stood as though about to step out of her niche. Carvings of women began to have narrow, sloping shoulders. They raised their arms and turned their heads, smiling at the observer. In Rochester a reading monk leaned forward over his book with deeply set eyes and furrowed brow. In Canterbury carved monks sat talking at mealtime. In Winchester a female figure rested its weight on one leg and seemed to be swaying, and the drapery that covered her was so thin, so nearly transparent that it showed the bones and the surface of the flesh 'as whyt as milk' beneath it.

Carved dresses became tighter, and faces began to display an astonishing variety of mood and expression. As vaults became more complicated, their bosses too were carved more gracefully and with unexpected elaborations. To be sure, England never produced anything remotely of the quality of a Pisano or the Naumburg master, for she was not a nation of sculptors. There never would be an English Giotto or Michelangelo or Leinberger or Rodin, and the thought of an English Leonardo is simply ludicrous.

Nevertheless, the wind had blown up out of the south, and they did what their talents allowed. At Alnwick in Northumberland there stands a lady with a wimple under her chin, and her veil falls gracefully in thin folds over her shoulders. Her lips are parted, her hands joined in prayer. At Ledbury an exceedingly beautiful lady's train is actually draped over the edge of her tomb chest.

In London are two magnificent bronze effigies–of Henry III and Queen Eleanor–cast by William Torel, and although they are probably not from the life (even though the king had approved the pattern), they are not stylized either, but realistic representations of a thoughtful man and woman. At Chew Magna in Somerset a knight lies leaning on one elbow, head resting on his hand, the left leg stretched out, the right bent at the knee as though he were lying where he had fallen in the field.

And as we look at the figures I have mentioned, or at a pensive king at Exeter with one leg crossed over the other, an old man running his fingers through his beard, they begin to seem familiar. Middle and late-fourteenth-century sculpture begins to resemble the figures in middle and late-fourteenth-century poetry, for both have ceased to be artificial and taken on mortal dimensions.

The lady at Alnwick might well be Chaucer's 'Emelye clothed al in grene', the dying knight at Chew Magna with his right knee bent, Arcite, for whom 'the sore encreaseth at his herte more and more'. In a word, they have come alive, and if they lack grandeur, they have become recognizable human beings. They have grown as the age has grown and acquired the mortal anguish we find in the greatest of the poetry.

Over and over again in drawings and illuminations we meet the same figures, the lithe ladies with their graceful fingers, the clerks that could their 'legges casten to and fro', the young wives, slender and demure, but with plucked brows and lecherous eyes. Always, unless they are peasants, priests or charlatans, it is the grace that strikes us first of all. The delicate and fastidious bodies bend; they gesture with their arms and look sidewards out of oval faces, or stand watching, timelessly silent, with the tips of their fingers at their mouths. They could be figures out of a dream, and that is in fact what they are. They are Emilye and Alisoun, twelve-year-old Virginia of the *Physician's Tale*, or May, whom 'to biholde it seemed fayerye', or the Lady Meed of Langland, or even the beautiful Criseyde, who in the beginning stood all still (as Chaucer says) like a bright star under a black cloud.

She was not the smallest of creatures, he writes, but all her limbs were so well suited to womanhood that there was never anyone who seemed less mannish. But then, unlike the figures in sculpture, she and perhaps the fair lady of the Gawain poet are the products of genius, and particularly do we realize how true this is when we understand the convention out of which she grew. Like some of the great ghosts in the *Iliad*, she had long been foreshadowed in the sometimes clumsy and stereotyped *chansons* of the previous three hundred years.

Her predecessors had exhibited nothing but the most superficial contradictions in human behaviour, so they had never been tragic figures. But we feel our almost unbearable pain and joy in Criseyde because she is. She senses time passing with a more than mortal intensity. Even when she was happiest, a hand on her warm cheek would have felt her trembling. She is so fallible amid the raillery, the practicalities, so easily made hopeful, so easily broken, for all her straight back, she is so intrinsically feminine, trustful and physically weak, uncertain, yet willing to be bold, frightened, yet eager to find a way past her own limitations that in the end she becomes one of the most moving creatures in all English poetry. And when those limitations have finally destroyed her and she says, 'To Diomede algate [at least] I wol be trewe', she can move us to the brink of tears. Not Juliet or Hardy's Tess or Shaw's St Joan or even regal Cleopatra can do this to the same degree.

In a mere handful of years Chaucer had made a great leap forward, not only from the songs of Minot he might have heard in his youth, but from the simplistic two-dimensional figures of the medieval love poem. He had acquired a conception both of drama and of character that can stand comparison with everything that has been written since. 'The lyf so short, the craft so long to lerne', he had written at the start of his *Parlement of Foules*. In all modesty he had added,

> *And out of oldë bokës, in good feith,*
> *Cometh al this newë science that men lere.*[15]

But it was not true. And the proof is that not one of his contemporaries learned the same things. Not for two hundred years was any English poet to learn anywhere near as much.

CHAPTER TEN

Now with his love, now in his colde grave

By science Chaucer simply meant knowledge, of course, and that which came out of 'olde bokes', out of the classic poets, was more than anything else a knowledge, or at least a renewed understanding of human motivations. Science as we understand it had not yet arrived. The cast of the medieval mind worked against it. I have talked about Bradwardine's geometry at Merton, or Wycliffe's study of optics or of the fact that Roger Bacon could have built a telescope if he had known how to grind lenses. But he probably never tried.

These men were not interested in classifying or finding out the why of things. Instead, they wanted to make God's purposes clear, for anything from the flight of comets to the illness of a child was looked at teleologically. It was part of a mysterious plan which all serious students, all theologians and moral philosophers, were at one in trying to unravel. A Bradwardine, a William Rede or even a Wycliffe would have been aghast at the notion that such a divine plan did not exist, for if phenomena were to be ascribed to ascertainable material causes, then what had become of the God whose world moved only to make plain his moral purpose? To postulate a physical universe, governed by laws that neither man nor God could alter, to postulate human ailments brought about by chemical imbalances or by the presence of micro-organisms would have been to turn one's back on a thousand years of theological science which by now rested on foundations, they would have thought impossible to be destroyed.

Medieval truth did not make free. It bound one into the cosmos, and was capable of filling the investigator with wonder and delight as he began gradually, after thousands of hours, to understand the nature of the divine. Therein lies the difference between them and us, that they had been taught in their schools, not to investigate what could be found out, but to learn what was already known. They possessed a body of teleological wisdom that required enormous application before it could be ingested. We, on the other hand, have been taught to discard the inessential, and to accept at any given time only what controlled experiment or the new and highly complex physics and mathematics are not yet able to contradict.

In the non-Christian world, there had, to be sure, been slow advances in what we should call scientific methodology. Galen had dissected animals in the interests of a physiological study of disease and in a desire to learn curing by contrarieties. The great Persian, Rhazes, had practised medicine in Baghdad and become the first man accurately to describe measles and smallpox. Over a period of several centuries there had been some three hundred Arabic and Jewish writers on medicine.

But in medieval Europe these writings were either unknown or disregarded. In France Guy de Chauliac, whom I have already mentioned in connection with the plague, seems to have been a surgeon of real ability. His English contemporary, John of Gaddesden–another Merton graduate–was physician to the court, but his writings, such as they are, seem utterly lacking in originality. They are nothing but commentaries on Galen, Hippocrates and Avicenna, commentaries on the learning that had authority behind it. His *Rosa Medicinae*, by which he is best remembered, lacks even evidence that he had eyes to observe.

John Arderne of Newark was another notable physician, and he seems to have gone up to London when Gaddesden died and taken over a good part of the older man's practice. But like all his contemporaries, he lacked any sense for physiology and, in spite of the many drawings he has left, any real knowledge of anatomy. He seems to have been a first-rate obstetrician and a simple and practical surgeon, but for the rest, medicine was a matter of providing palliatives. Thus he alleviated the pain of stone in the kidney by applying a hot plaster of pigeon's dung and honey.[1] On the other hand, he invented an operation for fistula which was in use a generation ago and which, for all I know, may even be used today.

It was he who diagnosed a prolapse of the rectum in Henry IV, and he treated it with steam. But for a cough he recommended holding the breath; it warmed the lungs. For epilepsy he prescribed that the names Jasper, Melchior and Balthazar be written in blood taken from the little finger, that gold, frankincense and myrrh be put into a box. Three paternosters and three aves were then to be said every day for a month on behalf of the souls of the three kings, and peony juice had to be drunk daily also, mixed with beer or wine. 'Slime of gold' mixed with both perforated and unperforated pearls he calls a very sure method to alleviate heart attacks, and while this, like his other remedies, may very well have done good psychosomatically, and thus actually have cured large numbers of his patients, it did not, as he no doubt thought it did, increase the sum of human understanding.

So not only did the investigative mind not exist, the temper of the time was opposed to it. At the universities one might learn geometry, theology, logic, rhetoric, law, perhaps alchemy, but these led nowhere except into the past. And for those who were not primarily students, the process of learning was even more casual.

It was the custom for noblemen's sons to be sent at the age of seven or eight to the houses of other noblemen, there to be trained with an impartiality of which parents themselves did not feel capable. And the custom was as old as anyone could remember, for the Teutonic knights had done the same.

By the middle of the fourteenth century certain abbots and other literate gentlemen had started schools of a sort. Warton writes of the Abbot of Glastonbury, 'whose apartment in the abbey was a kind of well-disciplined court, where the sons of noblemen and young gentlemen were wont to be sent for virtuous education, who returned thence home excellently accomplished'.[2] At Bury St Edmunds, Lydgate did the same. 'For after studying at Oxford, Paris and Padua, and after mastering with special delight the writings of such poets as Dante, Boccaccio and Alain Chartier, Lydgate opened...a school of rhetoric in which he taught young nobles literature and the art of versifying.'[3] Oxford and Cambridge were mainly for scholars, sons of poor fathers as I mentioned earlier, boys who would have to make their way in the world, and although the Black Prince and Henry V are said to have been students at Queen's College, Oxford, such students were more the exception than the rule.

Learning by rote was the usual way of learning anything at all, for books were scarce and expensive. So naturally one got by heart whatever seemed really important—if one were poor, the psalms, the ave and credo, the paternoster, if one were rich, the principles of good behaviour. And even as late as the eighteenth and nineteenth centuries, although the subjects studied may have changed, the method of learning them had not. A young man in Johnson's England who had not a hundred Latin tags in his memory could hardly call himself literate at all.

After the time of the plague, when there was a shortage of labour, girls too were sent off to learn certain fundamentals, for if they lacked reason, it had to be confessed that they probably possessed souls. So the daughters of good families were delivered into the hands of nuns, among whom they might hope to learn decency, modesty, good house-keeping and the elements of religion.

Daughters of tradesmen and small landowners were 'placed' in other families, first to be given instruction and then gradually to be taken into service. Marriage may have been the goal, as it generally has been for most women, but their chances were smaller than they are in the twentieth century. Not only was a vast proportion of eligible husbands locked up in holy orders, but in the competition for those that remained a girl had to be able to offer hard, practical advantages: money, unusual beauty or sheer competence at household management.

What gently born boys had chiefly to learn was manners. This one did by profiting from the example of one's elders and betters, by waiting on them at table, by serving them in the bedchamber, by copying their speech, their dress, and even by washing up for them in the kitchen.

So John Russell, usher and marshal to Humphrey, Duke of Glouces-ter, who was patron to both Hoccleve and Lydgate, set down early in the fifteenth century his *Book of Nurture*, which was a manual of etiquette and good sense for anyone who wished to manage a great household. Or there is the *Book of Curteisie*.[4] Don't stare, the author says, or look at the ground when you are spoken to. Keep your nails and hands clean. Don't speak loudly. Don't stuff your mouth with food. Don't dirty the table linen or pick your teeth with your knife. Don't take salt with your fingers or blow in your cup to cool it.

The writer of *The Italian Relation of England* a generation or so after-wards, says that

The want of affection in the English is strongly manifested towards their children; for after having kept them at home till they arrive at the age of seven or nine years at the utmost, they put them out, both males and females, to hard service in the houses of other people, binding them generally for another seven or nine years. And these are called appren-tices, and during that time they perform all the most menial offices; and few are born who are exempted from this fate, for everyone, however rich he may be, sends away his children into the houses of others, whilst he, in return, receives those of strangers into his own. And on enquiring the reason for this severity, they answered that they did it in order that their children might learn better manners. But I, for my part, believe that they do it because they like to enjoy all their comforts themselves, and that they are better served by strangers than they would be by their own children.[5]

If it is part of a fourteenth-century social history to record that it was considered bad manners to pick one's teeth with a knife, it is equally important to add that men and women went naked to bed, kings and commoners both, and that even among the gentry soap was used only for washing clothes. As much as a hundred and more years afterwards in the court of Henry VIII it was ordered that cooks and scullions 'shall not goe naked...nor lie in the nights and dayes in the kitchens or [on the] ground by the fireside'.[6] So Chaucer's Alisoun may never have used soap, and she had certainly never heard of toothbrushes. But these things are more matters of custom than they are imperative, for her mouth tasted as sweet as apples laid in hay.

But before my long digression we were talking about 'the lyf so short, the craft so long to lerne in Chaucer's *Parlement of Foules*. The craft, of course, is love. He has read until the daylight fails, he says, and 'berafte me my book for lakke of light'. Then, being full of the new science, the new understanding, he falls asleep and dreams afresh what he has been reading. But in his dream he transforms it and in so doing slips from the Middle Ages into the Renaissance. He had been the poet of courtly love, of an imaginary world, an arbitrarily invented world, all grace, a conspiracy between author and reader to invent a pageant that moved by laws of its own.

The *Book of the Duchess* is another such story of an encounter in a dream, an encounter in an unreal world, and it is full of a poignancy all the more immediate because, although the wound is tangible, it is timeless, because the stranger met in a wood, though his unhappiness and sorrow are explained to us in terms of the real world, has about him something more nearly unalterable than reality. Unlike a living man, he can no longer either be hurt or comforted. Nothing will ever evolve. Nothing will change any more than will a figure in a tapestry.

But already Chaucer is moving forwards. He humanizes and gradually the figures in the tapestry acquire a power to make us afraid. The dreamer walks through a forest. Suddenly a dog comes up and fawns on him.

Hit com and creep to me as lowe,
Right as hit haddë me y-knowe,
Hild doun his heed and Ioyned his eres,

And leyde al smothë doun his heres.
I wolde han caught hit, and anoon
Hit fledde, and was fro me goon.[7]

And the dog, though a dog in a tapestry, is real. Then presently,

I was war of a man in blak,
That sat and had y-turned his bak
To an oke, an hugë tree.
'Lord,' thoghte I, 'who may that be?'...
And ther I stood as stille as ought,
That, sooth to saye, he saw me nought.[8]

So the dreamer, Chaucer, the living man becomes part of the pageant. We look at and listen to insubstantiality through his living eyes and ears, and because it is thus made real the poem acquires a fearful power to move us and make us uneasy.

Now two things have to be said, first that this capture of the elusive moment was in the fourteenth century peculiarly un-English. It was Machaut and Guillaume de Lorris and Jean de Meung. Secondly, the audience for whom Chaucer wrote was a nobility that often thought in French, that had been taught in French, but had nevertheless become used to speaking with an English tongue. It cannot too strongly be repeated that with very few exceptions (men like Blake and Hopkins come to mind) no English poet has ever written well except as he was moved by the spirit of his time, except as he spoke to an audience with whom he shared a large measure of common ground.

In the fourteenth century there were only two potential audiences, the nobility and the church. And without a patron to support him, as Lydgate had the church, as the Gawain poet had a west-country nobility, as Gower had Richard II (who asked him to write the *Confessio Amantis*) as Chaucer had John of Gaunt, who paid both him and his wife an annuity–without an audience, any one of these would have had to live like Rutebeuf who wrote, 'I have no food, and long have had none; none is offered me, none given. I cough with cold; I gag out of an empty maw... I bed down in straw that is no bed, and in mine there is nowt but straw.'[9]

In a word, to be known (as even Chaucer and Gower were known) brought no financial reward except for the *largesse* of one's master. There might be three hundred manuscripts of *The Romaunt of the Rose*, or forty-five of *Piers Plowman* (at least those are the numbers that have survived), but the only man who got a penny profit out of them was the copyist.

So Chaucer wrote *The Book of the Duchess* for his patron whose beloved wife had just died. John of Gaunt is 'the man in blak' who leans against a tree in the forest, and Chaucer has immortalized the moment of deep grief. If the patron had taste and the poet talent, matters went well. And the patron whose linguistic upbringing had been French felt most at ease with work in the new fashion and formed on French models. We may take it that that was why Chaucer was given pensions and controllerships in the port of London and why Langland starved. For leaving aside their comparative merits, Langland set his mind to the sociological and theological problems of his day, and Chaucer reflected with urbanity and wit the cosmopolitan life of those who paid the piper. In so doing, he became the literary idol of the literate and the most honoured poet among his contemporaries.

The plague? Chaucer mentions it in passing, though his uncle and grandfather very likely died of it. Langland tells us vividly what changes it made in the life of the peasant. The Statute of Labourers? Chaucer might very well never have heard of it; at least, he never mentions it. Langland moralizes about it at some length. Wat Tyler's rebellion? Although Chaucer lived above Aldgate and the mob streamed out to its Mile End meeting with the king under his very windows, there is in all his work only a single mention of Jack Straw and a reference in one line to 'the cherles rebelling'. Although Langland does not mention the rebellion either, except obliquely (probably through fear of the consequences), Piers Plowman's name was used in a rallying cry by the mobs that swarmed up out of Kent. As for the boy king, whose weakness and stubbornness dominated the last quarter of the century, while Langland comments at length, Chaucer again has not a word to say. For the poet who wanted to encompass Petrarch and Boccaccio, it would have been to labour the commonplace.

There are records aplenty, not only of where Chaucer lived, but of his childhood in the Vintry, who his parents and grandparents had been, what public work he did, whom he married, where and when he travelled and of his wide acquaintanceship with the prominent men of the world. He had dealings at various times not only with Nicholas Brembre, who was helpful, with Philpot who captured pirates, with John of Gaunt and Sir William Walworth, but with some of the greatest noblemen in Italy. Even little Thomas Hoccleve, clerk at the Privy Seal, who seems to have been with him on his deathbed, knew and loved him.

Of whom Langland knew or who knew him we have no record. We cannot tell with any certainty even where he was born or when he died. In all the multitude of fourteenth-century papers that have been examined his name is never once mentioned, not even to say that he rented such and such a place, or owed some anonymous benefactor money or was sued for such and such a sum. We know only what he tells us.

So Chaucer, who travelled widely and read widely in several languages, who knew and conversed with lovely ladies, who was at ease in the noblest company, who had been on embassies abroad, who had gone to the wars and even been ransomed by the king, this Chaucer, a man of great energy and genius, could dare to experiment, could learn, could look at the society in which he moved with the perceptiveness of a man of the world and with a tolerance possible only to those who feel at ease.

Langland, well read, but less well educated, peripatetic, but untravelled, a man unknown who struggled all his life for a peace of mind he probably never found, a man who had nothing original to propose, who wrote in what was by then an old and hackneyed form (Chaucer called it 'rum, ram, ruf'), this Langland reflected an entirely different milieu because it was what nourished him. But if he lacks Chaucer's subtlety and acuity, he does now and then rise to a sublimity that his more urbane contemporary could never achieve.

All his life a hireling, yet he could sing 'the sea and the sun and the sand after', could dream tormented dreams of an ultimate mercy and righteousness, then wake to hear the Easter bells and be filled with such bliss that he called Kit and Nicolette, his daughter, and bade them come to church, to crawl on their knees to the cross and kiss it because it had borne God's blessed body.

There are moments in Langland so splendid that we see clearly what an intensity of power could possess him. Edmund Gosse thought his 'harrowing of hell' unsurpassed until Milton, and this is probably true. He stumbles through his long, endlessly revised and complicated vision, and seems now and then to grow with it towards some ultimate terror and fulfilment. We have to imagine him in his room at night, the tall, gaunt man (for so he describes himself). Nine-tenths of London is asleep; only a few of the stragglers still flown with insolence, still racketing along the alleys, the voices dying, somebody somewhere calling 'Be stille', off in one of the tenements, a baby crying. And the merely articulate grows under his hand into magnificence as he writes how

Kynde huyrde tho Conscience . and cam out of the planetes,
And sente forth his foreyours . feuers and fluxes,
Couhes and cardiacles . crampes and toth-aches,
Reumes and radegoundes . and roynouse scabbes,
Bules and bocches . and brennyng aguwes;
Frenesyes and foule vueles . these foragers of kynde,
Hadden pryked and preyed . polles of people;
Largeliche a legion . lees the lyf sone.
Ther was—'harow and help! . her cometh Kynde,
With Deth that is dredful . to vn-do ous alle!'
The lord that lyuede after lust . tho aloud criede
After Comfort, a knyght . to come and bere hus baner.
*'Alarme! alarme!' quath that lorde . 'eche lyf kepe hus owene!'**

It is saddening to think that these tremendous rhythms are lost on anyone who cannot read them in Middle English, for they are like a trumpet call in the midst of music, a clenching of the heart when we are happiest, death in the midst of laughter.

And Chaucer? I have quoted these lines once before.

What is this world, what asketh men to have?
Now with his love, now in his colde grave,
Allone, with-outen any companye.[10]

In the juxtaposition of those two passages one has the two men. For Langland, there is no comfort, only a cry, 'To arms! To arms!' For Chaucer who perceived no less the mutability of things, there is simply a poignant awareness of our common mortality.

Reading had only lately become a silent or even a private activity. It was noted with astonishment of St Ambrose that he read without speaking, without even moving his lips. So very little was composed merely to be read to oneself. Some of us who have never been taught to read music would think it unusual to 'listen' to a tune by 'reading' it on paper. Music is meant to be heard. In the same way a poem is meant to be sung or

---

* Then nature hired awareness and came out of the planets, and sent forth his foragers, fevers and fluxes, coughs, heart spasms, cramps and toothaches, rheums and running sores, foul scabs, boils, tumours and the burning agues. Frenzies, filthy evils, these messengers of nature rode hard and preyed on us, on the heads of the people. Most of a legion were about to lose their lives. There was harrow and help, here cometh nature, with death that is dreadful to undo us all. The lord that lived as he pleased then cried aloud for comfort, a knight to bear his banner. 'To arms, to arms,' quoth that lord, 'now it is each man for himself.' *Piers Plowman*, C. XXIII, 80–92.

recited, an adventure to be recounted by a story-teller to an audience. So
The Book of the Duchess or *Troilus and Criseyde* are meant to be heard,
The Canterbury Tales to be told.

Of course this makes a great difference in the manner of one's exposi-
tion. Rhythms have to become more emphatic. One has to use words
that are more simple and direct. The tone has to be conversational, and
the similes and metaphors almost casual in their familiarity. We need
only look at the prologue to *The Canterbury Tales* to see the method in
operation.

Of Northfolk was this reve, of which I telle.[11]

Of the pardoner Chaucer says,

No berd hadde he, ne never sholde have,
As smothe it was as it were late y-shave;
I trowe he were a gelding or a mare.[12]

Always the personal, the narrative touch, the comment suitable to one
who speaks. Of the clerk, he says,

As lene was his hors as is a rake,
And he nas nat right fat, I undertake;[13]

Langland wrote like a preacher to a congregation prepared, perhaps for
an hour or two, to hear a man work through the tortuosities of his argument. Chaucer read to perhaps fifteen or twenty, watching their eyes as
he progressed from line to line, ready to stop whenever it looked as though
he might be losing their attention. And because attention wanders, he
had to say much in little. Unlike a dramatist, he had no actors to vary
the rhythms for him, to break a monotonous section with a bit of business, no action to help carry the words along. He could rely on nothing
but his voice. The story had to be vivid; it had to speak for itself.

So because no later writer of any importance was bound by the same
restrictions, no later writer was really like him in style. In all of later
literature, only figures like Falstaff or Micawber bear any resemblance to
the Chaucerian. Falstaff's boasting, his transparent lies, his self-knowledge
in the midst of frivolity and 'Thou owest God a death', or 'Patch up
thine old body for heaven', these might very well have come from Chaucer, who was to two hundred years of Englishmen what Shakespeare
has been to us ever since. And it is the deceptively simple things in

Shakespeare, Macduff's 'He has no children', or Caliban's 'When I waked I cried to dream again', it is these that chiefly recall the Chaucer who had the art of saying much in little.

Like Shakespeare, Chaucer is all fullness, but unlike Shakespeare he pretends to be so delighted with the surface of life that he never looks into the depths. No grumbling for him in the heart of the sea. But therein lay one of his subtleties. Unlike Langland or Wycliffe who dug into the devil's hide to frighten us with what they found, Chaucer was wise enough to know that the truly serious sicknesses cannot ever be cured. All he can do is be precise, and rouse in us pity and fear–pity, laughter (he and Shakespeare are our two greatest masters of comedy) and a deep sadness at the passing of time. And this he does.

It is a truism but the greatest poetry, like the greatest music or the greatest mathematics, for that matter, is the one that comes nearest to slipping the infinite off the back of the wrist, saying the allusive and evocative thing with such economy that the listener can hardly see how it has been done. This Chaucer could do in so matter-of-fact a way that for the first time in English poetry he made living bone and pain (to paraphrase Yeats) out of a mouthful of air.

And I have not said a word about his bawdiness, his variety, his irony, his wisdom, his laughter that could 'set the table on a roar'. But I have said enough. After his death he was revered and imitated by a whole host of 'Chaucerians', though with one or two exceptions they were hollow men. Anyway, the times had changed. His radiant world had died with him and his successors had nothing to put in its place.

So in spite of being called the father of English poetry he left no literary descendants. There could be–indeed, there have been–lesser Miltons, lesser Wordsworths, Popes, Herberts. There is no lesser Chaucer. Hoccleve, who imitated him and knew him well, the just and upright Gower who said of himself that he wanted to work in the middle ground, Lydgate who revered him more than most, even Henryson, the greatest of his successors–none of them came anywhere near the Chaucerian high plateau. His time and the circumstances that made such a man possible no longer existed.

I said Hoccleve knew him well. Little Thomas Hoccleve seems to have been born about 1362 and to have lived half-way through the century that followed. He failed to get the benefice he hoped for, so he worked as a clerk in the Privy Seal office, and like many a modern young solicitor or city spark he may have had to stoop and 'stare upon the shepes

Above A woodcarver at work, very probably a self-portrait. From a church misericord. (Radio Times Hulton Picture Library)

Below Wood carving in Ludlow Parish Church, *c.* 1388. The woman warms her hands in front of the fire. (Radio Times Hulton Picture Library)

Two examples of the humanism of Renaissance European sculpture which influenced English artists of the fourteenth century:

Above The so-called Roettgen Pieta, *c.* 1300. (Rheinisches Landesmuseum, Bonn)

Ekkehardt and his wife Uta, in the West Choir of Naumburg Cathedral, he a martial man, but barefooted, she a paragon of cold elegance and beauty. (Bildarchiv Foto Marburg)

Above Medieval medicine. Trepanning of a skull, two stages in the operation. (Radio Times Hulton Picture Library)

Below The portrait of Chaucer painted in green and purple for Thomas Hoccleve. Part of the text beside it reads: Although his life be quenched, his likeness hath in my mind so fresh a liveliness that to put other men in remembrance of his person, I have here had his picture made, to this end, in truth, that they who have let slip the thought of him and the memory may in this painting find him again. (The British Library Board) skyn' by day, but he tried to be a man of the world by night. 'There never yet strode wyse man on my fete,' he said of himself.

In the end he is old and in need of spectacles, but too vain to wear them. In his youth he had been wild, he writes, but now it is four and twenty years that he has drunk too much and had a greedy mouth. He had used to be generous with his money when he had it, so cooks and taverners had always been glad to see him. Sometimes on a summer's day when he should have gone back to his desk he had gone wandering instead in his fashionable wide-sleeved cloak, walked down to the river perhaps, and hired a boat. And because he had always tipped so well the boatmen had called him master, and that had made him feel like a made man.

No one at the office had sat up as late as he, or drunk so much or been so loath to rise in the morning. His fellow clerks, Prentys and Arundel, had got drunk, and sometimes they had lain in bed till nine. But they had kept their health, and never been given a dressing down. Unlike him, they had been witty, and this had amused their masters.

Now he is ill. He has a wife who actually beats him. Yet he remembers days at the Paul's Head Tavern near the cathedral when there were lovely, lusty girls to be talked to and cajoled. So full of laughter they were, so trimly dressed that in spite of his poverty he had not been able to keep from buying them wafers and sweet wine. For all that, it had never gone as far as it might have done.

> *Had I a kus [kiss] I was content ful weel,*
> *Bettre than I woldë han be with the deed:*[14]

In fact, if men but speak of 'the deed', he turns quite red with shame.

In spite of the lad's silly foolishness, Chaucer must have thought his innocence appealing, for Hoccleve has left ample record of their friendship and of the fact that Chaucer tried to help him polish his verses. 'My dear master,' he writes, 'God his soulë quyte!'

> *And fadir Chaucer fayn wolde han me taght,*
> *But I was dul, and lerned lite or naght.*[15]

He seems to have been at Chaucer's bedside when he died, for he complains that not even as he lay dying could Chaucer bequeath him his 'excellent prudence'.

One last service Hoccleve did perform. Chaucer's face is still quite clear in his memory, he says, but it may not be so for others. So he has had a likeness made. And there in the margin of his *De Regimine Principum* it stands. The manuscript is in the British Museum, and, as Skeat remarks, the likeness is the only one of all the many that can be accepted as authentic.

Except in Gavin Douglas, there are no sunsets in medieval literature. The writers, the poets, the sermonists may have expressed pain, laughter, a terrible sense of time passing, but they never knew when it was twilight. Up to the very end, the loud day seemed to be going on. And after Chaucer's death the age may have limped on for a little while, but it was really over.

Only Hoccleve spoke a lament for the warmth of the living past, for his teacher and friend. 'Oh, master,' he wrote,

O maister, maister, God thy soulë reste!

CHAPTER ELEVEN

KING RICHARD AND THE TRUE COMMONS

When rebellion finally came, the roads the villages and even the towns had been loud with disaffection for almost forty years. Men had been fined; men had been imprisoned; it made no difference. The employer paid or his crops rotted, and still the migration off the land continued.

In London too the labourer found himself at a disadvantage. Masters of most trades had used to have small organizations that had enrolled two or three apprentices, each of whom might in time hope to become a master himself. But gradually the little factories had been forced to the wall by capitalists in the various guilds, and these men employed hundreds who could never hope for advancement and who could rarely expect even a living wage.

To be sure, they still had apprentices, but any apprentice who hoped to start in business for himself was faced with enormous difficulties. A dozen or more hurdles, some technical, some deliberately obstructive, were put in his way. So he remained an apprentice and, being grossly dissatisfied, formed unions and societies just like those of his agricultural fellow countrymen. Over seventy years earlier there had actually been a union of shoemakers, but it had been suppressed as being opposed to the public interest.

In 1350 there had been similar troubles among the clothmakers, who had insisted that no workman be allowed to serve his master until they had come to an agreement about wages, for 'heretofore, if there was any dispute between a master...and his workman, such man has been wont to go to all the men within the City of the same trade, and then by coven and conspiracy between them made, they would order that no one among them should work...by reason whereof, the masters...have been in great trouble and the people left unserved'.[1]

So men who struck were ordered to be fined. But three folios further on in the record, masters complain that workmen who had formerly been paid 3*d*. or 4*d*. a day, depending on the season, were demanding piece rates instead, 'and do so greatly hurry over the same that they do great damage to the folk to whom such cloth belongs'. Even so, journeymen were better off than the unskilled whose numbers were constantly being augmented by new arrivals from the country. These never found anything but casual labour, so they lived on the brink of starvation, crowded into cellars and unheated attics.

Meanwhile villeins in the country began speaking out more and more boldly, not only about wages, but about the injustice of heriot, merchet and the other innumerable fines and restrictions. They looked askance at the intrusion of sheep on to what had been arable land, for sheep restricted their ability to grow the crops on which they could see a profit. The old customs were dying. Even among those who stayed at home there was a growing and gradually more voluble awareness of how unjustly they were being treated.

The landowner too had difficulties, and only the great landowning abbeys were still unaffected. They had capital, they could weather a rise in wages. But they, too, saw their villeins becoming recalcitrant. At Bury St Edmunds, for example, the vast eleventh-century Benedictine establishment owned enormous tracts of farmland as well as much of the town itself. In the previous fifty years the townspeople had risen against the abbots on four or five occasions.

In 1327 they had demanded and been granted a charter, but the sheriff had stormed in, hanged a few of the ringleaders and seen to it that the charter was rescinded. A few years afterwards some men kidnapped the abbot and carried him off to Brabant. So the town was fined 2,000 marks. Now there was a silent civil war going on, for the pope had chosen one abbot and the monks another, and while the pope's choice, Edmund Brounfield, lay in prison for importing the papal bull, the abbey itself was in the charge of John Cambridge, the prior, and Cambridge was cordially hated by the townsfolk of whom he was the nominal master.

In Winchester the small tradesmen were at odds with an oligarchy of mayors and aldermen. In Norwich a large body of indigent labourers complained of grievances not unlike those in London. In Lincolnshire there seems to have been a consciously revolutionary movement that called itself the Great Society. In Cambridge the municipal authorities had for several generations been intermittently at war with the university. At St Albans the struggle was one between abbot and townsmen, just as at Bury.

On every side, therefore, was a sense of being wronged, and everyone knew precisely who in his particular case was to blame. Not only that. On every side the evil was compounded by a shortage of cash. The landowner had trouble meeting his commitments, the labourer in paying for his food, the merchant in finding money for expansion. And for this two causes, two scapegoats had been established in the popular mind.

One was the foreigners, the Flemings, the Lombards, the Hanseatic merchants in London. For years the king, anxious to establish English industries, had been inviting these men into the country, the Flemings because they were skilled craftsmen, the Lombards because the money of northern Italy facilitated trade.

Xenophobia has existed in most ages. Edward I had expelled the Jews. Now many of them had come back, calling themselves Lombards (which perhaps they were), but Lombards 'trade their chaff for our corn', says Gower, and 'in their hearts plan to pillage us of gold and silver'.[2] They turn up dressed as menials, but after a year in London are able to dress as well as any burgess.

To the city labourer the careful and assiduous Fleming was not only a foreigner. He not only took the bread out of English mouths. He actually exported his wages, either to support some alien family or to be used in manufacture in Flanders. He was therefore an exploiter and a man who lived on sweated labour. But he was also visibly foreign in dress and speech. And he was a moral evil, for were not half the whores in London Flemish girls? Did he not keep himself apart, just as the Jews had done? On this most workmen were agreed. Like alien friars, alien priests and bishops, the Flemings kept good Englishmen poor.

But the second great cause of their poverty was the war. For almost fifty years the English armies, men pressed into service from every village in the land, had been fighting and dying during interminable forays into France. France was a symbol; it was the Somme, the Ypres, the Gallipoli of the fourteenth century.

In the early days there had been victories, but for years now there had been nothing but one debacle after another. In spite of all the blood and pain–could one not see the cripples in the streets?–now the old enemy was actually making raids against England, burning and looting on the coasts. And since the crown could borrow nowhere else to pay for the catastrophe, there had been a tax imposed twice in the past four years against common men. All the money in the kingdom, said the authorities, was going into the hands of workmen. So workmen had to be made to pay. But when there had been booty back in the good days, that had gone to the knights and the great lords. Half the castles in England were lined with French tapestries. The rich ate off gold and silver pillaged out of France. But common soldiers had never earned anything but blood and broken bones.

In brief, almost every part of the nation had lost confidence in itself; it was suffering a *mal du pays*. So in November 1380 Parliament assembled in Northampton to decide on a course of action. Why Northampton instead of London? Because a Genoese envoy had lately been negotiating permission to establish a staple at Southampton for Mediterranean goods. Eleven years earlier Chaucer had actually been sent abroad to discuss with certain citizens of Genoa the choice of some English port where the Genoese might establish a commercial base, another link, so to speak, in a common market. Now a certain John Kirkeby, leader of a group of London traders, had murdered the envoy, and in spite of a good deal of sympathy in London for the murderer, he was about to be tried. Parliament simply had no wish to be disturbed by the marches and counter-marches that would inevitably follow. So Parliament moved to Northampton.

It was a wet, cold winter. Northampton offered too little housing for the members. Indeed, there had been so many floods that many arrived late, and when they did finally reach the city, they found a great lack of food and forage. But on the fifth of the month that miserable session was convened by Simon Sudbury, Chancellor, Prime Minister and Archbishop of Canterbury. Ironically enough, Parliament had pleaded ten years earlier that none but laymen henceforth be made 'chancellor, treasurer...or other great officers of the realm'.

Sudbury had nothing but unhappy news to impart, for the financial outlook was all but desperate. The Earl of Buckingham's recent expeditions to France had emptied the Treasury. Whatever grants had been made to pay for a continuation of the war had proved inadequate. Customs duties had brought in less than expected. There had been trouble in Flanders, so exports of wool were down. The king's jewels had been for two years in pawn to the mayor and commonalty of the City of London as surety for a loan of £5,000. Even so, there was three months' wages due the garrisons of Brest, Cherbourg and Calais, and nothing to pay them with. In the face of this, the king needed the vast sum of £160,000 if he was to continue the war.

This was almost a fifth of the gross national income, and Parliament heard Sudbury and the Lord Treasurer, Bishop Brantingham of Exeter, almost in consternation. But since there could be no thought of breaking off the war, it set about deliberating how to raise the money. And the members were advised that only three ways existed by which this could be done.

First, they might exact a poundage or sales tax to be paid by the seller on all mercantile transactions. Second, they might impose a wealth tax like the old tenths and fifteenths on property. Or they might levy a poll tax which would have to amount to a shilling–three groats–a head on all persons over the age of fifteen.

It was probably only to be expected that after long deliberation they would choose the last, for poundage would have to be paid by merchants, the tenths and fifteenths by landowners, but, as they said, the poll tax would have to be paid by everyone. So they voted to raise £100,000 by this means–by an impost on every adult–if the church, by far the richest body in the country, would raise the rest. And this, in the main, the church agreed to do. The convocations would raise 50,000 marks, or two-thirds of the sum demanded.

One proviso was made which would alleviate the burden on the poorest. In each district the rich would pay up to six groats per man and wife (a groat was fourpence), so the tax would fall less heavily on others. Even so, it was the heaviest charge that had ever been imposed. In 1377 the labourer had been required to pay only a third as much. In 1379 the workman had paid his groat, and the rich had paid more, each according to his rank. Thus the Duke of Lancaster had paid £6 13s. 4d. and earls, countesses and the Mayor of London £4. But now the tax on the poorest was to be trebled, the tax on the rich to be reduced, and the only people to be excepted were beggars. When the decision had been reached the Lord Treasurer quite obviously foresaw what was in the wind, for he resigned, and Sir Robert Hales, Prior of the Knights Hospitaller, was appointed in his place.

'All great revolutions,' Trevelyan wrote, 'have in them a mysterious element.'[3] And often this is true. But the revolution that was about to break, that was to provide one of the most dramatic and terrible weeks in a thousand years of English history, had nothing mysterious about it at all. Trevelyan thinks also that the upheaval had been planned. I do not know, nor I think does anyone else. The best one can do is to set down the facts so far as they can be ascertained, and let them speak for themselves.

During the winter, the wet and miserable winter of 1380-1 that followed, the tax collectors rode out on their business, and in most towns and villages the money was paid, *non sine diris maledictionibus*, as it was said, not without hearty curses on the part of the peasants who had to do the paying. Haystacks lay flooded in the fields and the roads were here and there almost impassable. Gradually, as the returns began to be examined in London, it became apparent that something had gone very wrong. There had been falsifications all over the country. In 1377, excluding figures from Durham and Chester which have been lost, the adult population had numbered 1,355,201. Now, without any visible reason, the number had fallen to 896,481, or by more than a third.

Of course large numbers had disappeared in the meantime, had taken to the roads or become outlaws. But surely not a third of the country, and surely not a preponderance of women. For there turned out to be an astonishing shortage of widowed mothers in the returns, of aunts, sisters and unmarried girls. Barring wives, women seemed all but to have vanished, and in the poorer counties the disparity was greater than any-where else.

In Westmorland, for example, the population was presumably half what it had been four years previously. In Devon some 45,000 had paid a tax in 1377. Now there were only 20,000. In Somerset barely half as many paid as had paid four years earlier. So it was in Worcestershire, in Wiltshire and in Essex. In Colchester, for example, there had been 2,955 taxpayers in 1377, but only 1,609 in 1381.

Running one's eye down the lists, one sees the same thing over and over again. It is Johannes Hankyn *et uxor eius*, Walterus Taylor *et uxor eius*. In a word, entry after entry is of payment by a man and his wife. Other members of the family do not exist; they have vanished into thin air. So when the returns began to be examined they were greeted with open anger.

On 16 March, and at the instigation (so it was said) of John Legge, one of the king's sergeants-at-arms, new commissioners were appointed to travel out into the provinces, to compare the lists with the actual populations in each hundred, to compel the tax evaders to pay, and to arrest and imprison whoever tried to obstruct them in the performance of their duty. Almost at once 600 defaulters were found in Norwich alone, and some 13,000 in Suffolk. The evasion had simply been too widespread to have any chance of success.

Whether or not the rebellion had been planned one can judge only on the basis of the evidence. At any rate, when the spark was struck it flared up and spread with quite remarkable speed. The government had undertaken to call almost half a million people to account, perhaps one in four of the population. It is as though the modern Inland Revenue were to start proceedings against twelve or thirteen million citizens at once.

On 30 May one Thomas Bampton, steward to a certain Essex landowner, rode out to Brentwood to root out the local defaulters. He was certainly not expecting trouble, for he had brought with him only three clerks and two sergeants-at-arms. But when he reached Brentwood he was met not only by the local citizens, but by others from the tiny fishing village of Fobbing. These had already consulted with their neighbours from Stanford and Corringham, and when Bampton sat down to go over the lists, a hundred or more men from the three villages announced to him in a body that they would pay no more.

There was a violent argument. When the steward tried to assert his authority he was shouted down, so he sent his sergeants into the crowd to arrest the ringleaders. At this the peasants turned savage and began flinging stones, and after a few minutes the commissioner, his sergeants and clerks scrambled back into their saddles, forced a way through the now violent mob and fled back up the road to London.

As for the villagers, they were either terrified at what they had done or else now openly planning rebellion, for they took to the woods. Whatever their reasons, this immediate flight had certainly not been planned for they had not even thought to provide themselves with food. Nevertheless, during the next day or so, very hungry by now and in a state of some confusion, they sent messengers out 'from place to place', says the *Anonimalle Chronicle*, 'to stir up other people to rise against the lords and great folk of the country'.

They would not have seemed strangers to us, those rebels. They were the same little leather-necked Englishmen who today, six hundred years afterwards, drink in rural public houses, the sometimes shabby, but generally practical men who can carry a young steer on their shoulders if they have to, the men with bailer twine tied round their jackets at the waist, the men with broken nails and ragged hats who have more sense for the state of the midden or the hayrick than they sometimes have for ideas, the slow, chaffing men who hang together because no one else can possibly understand them, no one except the boys they knew in their 'hurling days', the men who in monosyllabic communion do the same work day after day and every morning pull on the same sweaty clothes they took off the night before.

Three days after the quarrel in Brentwood a certain Abel Ker was leading a little band of rebels down in Kent where the orchards had just finished blooming. They broke into a monastery and demanded confusedly that the abbot support them. Then they found some boats to ferry them over the Thames estuary and held a meeting with their friends in Essex. Other Kentishmen tramped in a body into Dartford, and in what must have looked remarkably like an act of cohesive planning, 'traitorously moved the men of that town to insurrection'. From then on the riot grew by what it fed on. They must have felt that they had burned their bridges behind them, for Robert Cave, a baker and the first leader who was not a mere peasant labourer, led a mob towards Rochester.

But already the government had reacted. Robert Belknap, Chief Justice of the Common Pleas, was sent down to Brentwood to arrest the rioters. But the authorities seem not even yet to have understood what was afoot, for they sent him down without any sort of guard. It was Belknap, therefore, not any rioter, who was seized. His 'evidence' was burned. He was accused, probably to his horror and astonishment, of treason against the king, forced to swear on oath that he would never go on such an expedition again, and then let go. But three of the local jurors who had undertaken to identify the ringleaders were beaten to death with clubs and beheaded. So were three of Belknap's clerks. The heads were stuck on to poles, and marched round the neighbouring villages to be shown.

This was on Sunday, 2 June, and now with murder having been committed the die was cast. 'The churl, like the willow,' one remembers, 'sprouts the better for being cropped', and the government would no doubt exact a terrible revenge. All during that weekend messengers travelled out round southern Essex and even across the river into Kent to drum up cohorts ready to fetch out their billhooks and forks.

On Whit Monday, the 3rd, Sir Simon Burley (an old campaigner who was to be hanged seven years afterwards) rode into Gravesend with two armed men and seized a villein of his called Belling who had escaped some time before.* But Belling had friends in the town, and in the course of a violent altercation these made a formal proposal that they be allowed to buy him free. But the knight was not an old soldier for nothing. Even the sympathetic chronicler calls him an irritable and angry man. He had fought his way back and forth across France, been in many a bloody skirmish, and a few savage peasants in Gravesend were no match for him. If they wanted to buy the man, he said, the price was £300, and when this ridiculous figure was met with cries of

---

* So the *Anonimalle Chronicle* reports, but Simon Burley is elsewhere reported to have been in Bohemia at the time. So it may have been his brother, John, who came to Gravesend. Both men were Kentish landowners.

anger he hauled Belling up on to the crupper of his horse and with his companions fought a way through the press and galloped off towards Rochester.

At the same time the government sent a Justice down into Kent, carrying indictments against a large number of defaulters. With him went John Legge, the king's sergeant-at-arms. But when they tried to ride into Canterbury they found a great mob already in possession of the town, and like Belknap hurried back to London. All over the south-east, alarm grew as men realized how swiftly the rebellion had spread.

Noblemen and landowners began hurriedly packing their families and such possessions as they could carry, and galloping off towards the safety of the city, for almost every hour new uprisings and manifold depredations were being reported.

And there was method in the violence. In Dartford and Strood the mobs seized and burned great masses of official documents. Here and there they broke into a manor house and carried away court rolls and lists of villeins, records, deeds–whatever, in short, had any bearing on the status of local peasants. At North Cray they burned down the manor house and drove off cattle to be used in furnishing a rebel larder. They seized hostages, some of them prominent country gentlemen, made them swear loyalty to 'King Richard and the true commons', and marched them off to be used for what purpose nobody quite knew. They invested Rochester Castle, took it without even a struggle, freed Burley's serf who had been carried off out of Greenwich, and carried away Sir John Newton and his family. Newton was later used to take messages to the king.

And here one has to make clear a curious point about the uprising. For some reason the rebels everywhere spoke of themselves as allies of the king. It was not Richard who had impoverished the nation, levied taxes, allowed a few lords or merchants to grow rich, or imposed the terrible conditions under which they lived. It was the half-anonymous 'traitors', as though Lenin had come to the Finland Station in Petersburg to attack the autocracy but to support the Tsar.

People remembered the proceedings of the Good Parliament only five years earlier, and now, they said, it was the Duke of Lancaster who had caused their present miseries. Indeed, one of their watchwords was, 'We'll have no king called John.' It was the great extortioners who were to blame, men like Richard Lyons, traitors like Latimer or Lord Treasurer Hales, or Chancellor Sudbury (though the two latter were actually innocent) who for years were said to have stuffed the nation's wealth into their private pockets.

Even the king seems to have suspected that many of his tax collectors had abetted the making of false returns. Had not the men of Fobbing claimed that they had already paid, that they had Bampton's receipt for the money? Yet the commissioners were still riding out all over the country, demanding more. No, the young king was innocent, and if he and his commons could make common cause, if they could only make the truth be known and lop a few heads, their troubles would be in a fair way to being solved.

Within a mere forty-eight hours, bands from all over Kent were already marching to join the main body at Maidstone, and during those first few days a good deal of damage was done in the surrounding countryside. Lawyers and adherents of John of Gaunt were attacked whenever they could be found, unpopular landlords were driven out of their houses, food and money were seized for the campaign that looked to be in progress, and of course records were burned, for these were diabolic signs on paper which few of them could read, but which they knew had been used for generations to their disadvantage.

It was not until Friday, the 7th, at least so far as the chroniclers were aware, that the powerful, very possibly the charismatic figure of Wat Tyler first appeared. Who he was, how he seized command, what his history had been not even his contemporaries seem to have known. One document calls him Walter Tyler of Colchester. The Rolls of Parliament refer to him as Walter Tyler *del countée de Kent*, but juries in Faversham mention one *Walterum Tyler de Essex*. There is a legend, according to which he was an artisan of Dartford whose daughter had been molested by a tax collector, but this story first appeared in the sixteenth century and is probably an invention. Froissart said that he had fought in the French wars under Richard Lyons. Grafton's Chronicle reported that Lyons 'once had Tyler living with him and at a tyme did beate him', in London, and at the famous meeting in Smithfield one of the king's attendants claimed to recognize the man as a famous highwayman.

It makes no real difference. What does matter is that when he took charge of or was chosen to command that heterogeneous mob in Maidstone on 7 June he gave almost immediate proof of no mean military talent. The angry, but hitherto disorganized peasants who were said by then to have numbered almost fifty thousand, began to be told off into companies. Attempts were made to organize a commissariat and to collect weapons, and on the 10th, after only three days in power, Tyler marched the main body of his army to Canterbury.

Possibly they were under the impression that the hated Archbishop

Sudbury would be there. In any case, they entered the city without meeting any opposition (in fact a good number of the citizens joined them), sacked the Archbishop's palace, and even swarmed into the cathedral in the midst of a service. But to the relief of the terrified monks, they did no harm, only shouted from the nave that the congregation had better start electing a new archbishop, for Sudbury had been sentenced to death and was going to be executed.

Then they tracked down Sir William Septvans, the sheriff, jostled and frightened him considerably, seized all his official records, and burned them in the street. 'Have you traitors here?' they shouted, roaming the city in bands. 'Show us your traitors. Bring out your traitors.' Three men were named as enemies of the villein, dragged out of their houses and beheaded. Mayor and bailiffs were forced publicly to take oaths to support 'King Richard and the true commons'. More manorial rolls were destroyed, more houses sacked, more weapons and food collected.

Meanwhile, so well had Tyler organized his men that on both sides of the road back towards London there were forays organized to collect the old bows, the swords, the billhooks, the staves and axes with which the mob was to be armed, to herd the cattle and sheep that were to feed them. More recruits arrived to be marshalled and given orders. John Ball was rescued out of the archbishop's prison in Maidstone, and at once he became the rebel *Pasionaria*, was carried on their shoulders and sang out his famous rhymed, monosyllabic calls to action, advising, exhorting, preaching over and over again that now they had to take matters into their own hands, that all men had to be made free.

'Right and might,' he cried, 'will and skill. Now God haste you in every thing.' How long had they not been drowning the throne of heaven with their tears, how long deafening Jesus and Mary with their petitions? But at last the time for action had come. 'Now God haste you in every thing. Time it is that Our Lady help you with Jesus her Son, and the Son with the Father, to make in the name of the Holy Trinity a good end to what has been begun. Amen, Amen, for charity, Amen!'

For twenty years, having been priest in York and then in Colchester, John Ball had been tramping the roads, dusty, oftener than not hungry or wet with rain. He had walked through blizzards to carry his message; the summer sun had made him lean as a rake, this mad priest, as his enemies called him, for he had been an agitator longer than Wycliffe. He too had preached against the pluralists and the political churchmen. He too had preached evangelical poverty–and practised it. He too had thumped the wood of his pulpit as he thundered against the deadly sins of gluttony, lechery, pride and covetousness in high places. And at last, in June 1381, 'God give us aid,' he cried, 'for now is the time. Amen!'

The weakness of legitimacy in a perpetually changing world is that it more often tries to perpetuate itself than to ask the necessary questions. It breeds monuments. Revolution, on the other hand, throws everything open to question and breeds prophets. But prophets are never legitimate until they are dead. Establishments have no patience with them when they are alive.

John Ball was not the only one, simply the most fervent. All over the country little unknown parsons from poor parishes came leading groups of their cottagers, men who had no weapons except their hoes, old rustics who had fought at Crécy and Poitiers, young men tough and seamy-faced from thousands of hours in the fields and many an alehouse brawl.

But now, 'John Ball hath rungen your bell', they heard, and the old Saxon words rang out like bells indeed. News came that up in Essex the commons were marching too. After three hundred years of political repression, they were rising almost spontaneously against their alien masters.

On Tuesday, 11 June, Tyler turned north-west and began moving his ragged army up to join the Essex men outside London. If one remembers that he had been only four days in command, if one imagines the difficulties, the complexity of organization, if one learns (as we shall in a moment) just how he planned to take his sprawling horde of red ants and use it to swarm into the walled and moated city where his enemies were already gathering, one has to look at him with a good deal of respect.

CHAPTER TWELVE

When Adam Delved and Eve Span

Tyler left Canterbury on the morning of the 11th, and in just thirty-six hours he travelled a little over seventy miles. For on the night of the 12th he and his army trailed into Blackheath, and all that afternoon watchers in the Tower must have been able to see the dust of that army drawing nearer over the low hills. On that same night the Essex men arrived at Mile End outside Aldgate, another 50,000 strong, and they too had travelled with great speed. In less than a week there were over 100,000 peasants in the field.

Both armies must have marched at least part of the previous night, here a man carrying two or three hens with their legs tied, another with a slaughtered sheep over his shoulders, and everywhere the whores and camp-following girls like flies round a cow's dugs. Men who would have winced to see a cat in a snare told bloody tales as though they had been dealing in bloodshed all their lives.

They had few horses, and what few they had must have been used to drag the waggons of the commissariat. Now, 50,000 men, even if they march in military formation eight abreast, will be strung out along a road for several miles. But untrained men do not march in military style. They are more like a horde, like chaff in the wind. They spread out across the fields. The mass is too wide for the bridges, so hundreds at a time ford little brooks. A patrol comes to an empty manor house, detaches itself from the main body, knocks down the door and goes through the rooms, smashing chairs and tables. Here a man picks up a lady's dress and stuffs it into his wallet. Somebody crouches amid laughter and defecates on the bed. Others are pulling down hangings from the walls. Then there is a cry that they are taking too long, and they tumble out again like a body of bees hurrying to catch the rest of the swarm.

This is the time when John Gower fled, as he tells in the *Vox*

Clamantis, and hid in the woods. But he was at least partly apprehensive without reason. Tyler's army were not murderers, not during that march through Kent. A few lawyers were killed, but even conservative Langland hated lawyers, and Lydgate said they never opened their mouths before they had been paid cash down. But landowners generally suffered no more than the loss of property.

No, it was what they called a 'hurling time', a time of shouting and contention, of tramping feet when at night the torches might have been seen for miles on end, the campfires burning under the spitted oxen and the songs roared out, the pipers piping whatever men liked to march to, their laughter raucous and echoing under the Kentish oaks.

'With whom hold you?' they shouted at strangers, and heard the answer they expected: 'With King Richard and the true commons.' True commons as opposed to the so-called commons in Parliament, who were not men with faces, but a class, landowners, merchants and knights of the shire, men who, as Langland said, walked about 'in countenance of clothing'.

Some of John Ball's phrases sound like catches or refrains. 'John the Miller hath ground small, small, small', he sang out, as if this great body were parts of the mills of God and he the turning stone.

On the same day that Tyler arrived at Blackheath, the priest John Wrawe, leading a detachment of Essex rebels, sacked the manor of Overhall owned by the great merchant, Richard Lyons. But, like Sudbury, Lyons was in London and not so easily to be caught. He still had two days to live. Then, late on the afternoon of the 12th, Wrawe's men and the other armies led by Thomas Farringdon (himself a London man), Henry Baker of Manningtree and two other captains, Adam Michel and John Starling, came swarming down the long flat lands to make camp at Mile End outside the city walls.

And London had no army to defend it. The king's uncle, the Duke of Lancaster, was in Scotland. Thomas of Woodstock was in the Welsh marches. Edmund of Cambridge was in Plymouth, about to set sail with an army bound for Portugal. Messengers were sent down to stop him, but Edmund had no stomach for mixing it with a mob of his own countrymen, so he actually hurried aboard ship and left harbour in the face of a contrary wind. The king, who had been at Windsor, hurried to London and retired into the all but impregnable Tower.

With him were Lord Treasurer Hales, Chancellor Sudbury (who now offered his resignation–a matter of too little and too late) and the old

Earl of Salisbury who had fought beside the Black Prince at Poitiers twenty-five years before. Henry Bolingbroke was there, a boy of fifteen, who was eventually to have Richard locked up in Pontefract. The king's half-brothers were there, the Earl of Kent and Sir John Holland. And that night the king's mother, the once-beautiful Joan of Kent, came clattering over the bridge on her way home from Canterbury, where she had gone to visit her husband's tomb. She had driven through the heart of Tyler's army, but the rebels had done her no harm, only peered in at the windows, seen who it was, and with a loud joke or two given orders that she be allowed to proceed.

She was almost the last traveller to reach London from the south. The drawbridge was raised. Cattle were driven in from the fields as they always were at sunset and the gates were closed. In the Tower the council sat in almost continuous session. And it had to face the fact that the only fighting force at hand was the king's guard of 600 archers and men-at-arms. The aldermen of the various wards considered arming the citizens, but then rejected the idea as too dangerous. There were thousands of malcontents in the city who might make common cause with the invaders.

So, since there was no other initiative that could be taken, William Walworth, the mayor, sent out three aldermen, John Fresch, John Horne and Adam Carlyll, to make contact with Tyler and hand him the king's order that he forthwith disperse his rebel army to their homes. The first two men conveyed the government's message, fatuous though it might have been. But Horne, a fishmonger, managed to secure a private meeting with the Kentish leader. The whole of London, he said, was ready to rise. If Tyler would make a determined assault on the bridge, he could guarantee helpers to open it from the city side.

What he stood to gain one cannot really imagine, unless there was actually a plan to overturn the government and form a new administration composed of common men. In such an administration men like Horne–and his coadjutors, of whom we shall hear more in a moment–might have been given places. In any case, he took three of Tyler's lieutenants back with him into London and lodged them that night in his house.

Then late in the evening the rebels moved six miles forward out of Blackheath. The tower sentries saw a procession of torches coming up past the lepers' hostel in Kentish Street south of the river as Tyler's men began occupying the suburb of Southwark. There they gutted Lambeth Palace, crying 'A revel! A revel!', broke into the Marshalsea Prison, let

G

out the prisoners and lighted their watchfires full in view, not only of the guards on the bridge, but of king and council in the Tower itself.

In the city that same night, apprentices and rootless workmen roamed the streets and drank in the taverns almost until dawn. Down on the wharves, the rattle of winches as goods were swung up out of ships to be stored under lock and key in the warehouses. Blacksmiths worked through the dark hours, forging weapons.

> '*Tik tak! hic hac,*' *the poet said about blacksmiths,* '*tiket, taket, tyk, tak!*
> *Lus bus! lus das! Such a life they lead,*
> *Those horse dressers: Christ give them sorrow.*
> *May no man at night for these water burners have any rest.*

Cautious householders had been laying in stocks of food all during the previous day. Jewellers in Goldsmith's Row were busy far into the dark, carrying gold and precious stones down into the vaults under their houses. Few slept. For Tyler was coming in; no question about that, Tyler with his barelegged, bare-arsed barbarians, his wild and howling vandals, so tatterdemalion a crew that you could see dirty skin through the rents in their clothing. Across the water one could hear the voices, the shouts and laughter. They had probably liberated the Flemish whores.

But in fact, this was no Jacquerie, though gentlemen must have been remembering with considerable foreboding what that Jacquerie had done twenty-three years earlier. They had gutted *chateaux* all up and down the Oise. They had murdered the landowners, sometimes after terrible tortures. They had raped the wives and daughters and cut their throats to stop the screaming. 'I dare not set down what unbelievable horrors they perpetuated,' Froissart had written.

These Kentish peasants were recognizably different, however. They did not molest women. What murders they committed were of specific individuals whom they considered, sometimes rightly, to be their enemies. They had marched out to achieve certain goals, in the name of what we would consider justice, and what they, if they had known the words, would have called social democracy. Like the Puritans some two hundred and fifty years later, they were dimly aware that since the Norman Conquest they, the free Anglo-Saxons, had been ruled by alien conquerors. Whether they recognized the fact or not, whether or not they even formulated the thought, they were revolting against the Norman oligarchy that oppressed them. They were the first Roundheads.

'My nation', Milton wrote almost three hundred years afterwards, 'my nation was subjected to your lords. It was the force of conquest: force with force is well ejected when the conquered can.'[1] And Christopher Hill says of Milton (the parallel is remarkable) that 'He rejected a state church and the tithes that went to pay its hireling ministers; he approved of mechanic preachers and disapproved of University-trained parsons; he disliked any distinction between clergy and laity. He rejected all forms of ecclesiastical jurisdiction.'[2]

That Milton was a republican and hated lawyers, that he rejected the House of Lords, that he was a defender of regicide in the name of the conflicting rights of the commons, this we knew. But it has not always been so clear that in these and many other doctrines he simply exemplified for his generation the spirit, the diverse yet similar spirits, perhaps, that moved men like Wycliffe and John Ball and caused so many poor parsons actually to take up arms.

Here was where it began, for from the fourteenth century onwards there has been a stream in English thought of what has been called apocalyptic millenarianism. And it is this, accompanied by a sense that, whatever may befall, the English are still God's chosen people, which separates England from all the nations in Europe. The revolt of the English peasantry in 1381 is as much as Cromwell a part of the history of Puritanism; as much as Keir Hardie or Aneurin Bevan, a part of the history of British labour. The Jacquerie had been driven wild by the same sense of injustice a generation before, but all it had wanted was revenge; it had had no social programme. So in fact it is true that they order these matters differently in France.

On the morning of Thursday, the 13th, the traitor Horne rode out across the bridge again, this time carrying a royal standard to which he was not entitled, but which lent him a spurious authority. Again he had a meeting with Tyler, and apparently told him that the bridge would be opened as soon as rebels inside the city had moved forward and taken possession of the city end. It was on this same morning that John Ball, standing on a stump, or perhaps from the back of a horse, preached the sermon for which he is most vividly remembered.

'In the beginning all men were created equal,' he said, 'but slavery was introduced unjustly because of the greed of wicked individuals.' If God had intended some to have lordship and others to be villeins, he would have made that distinction at the start. But this God had not done. According to the *Chronicon Angliae*, which has left us the fullest report, the preacher stressed that Englishmen now had the chance, if they only dared to take it, of breaking the shackles that had chained them for so long, and acquiring the simple freedom that had always been their right.

Therefore they must now take courage–and it is noticeable how often the word *now* occurs in his reported speech–and not only carry their harvest into the barn, but go back afterwards into the fields and burn the tares that had all but choked the grain. The tares were the oppressive rulers, the greedy landlords, the judges that cared nothing for justice and lawyers that cared for nothing but the letter of the law. The tares were unscrupulous bishops, the archbishop who was Chancellor, the robber who was Lord Treasurer. When these had been uprooted, then there would be peace and plenty for all.

But above all he emphasized, as he had done so often in the past, that it was the true commons, the sheep, who stood to inherit what had been so long denied them. He too was 'John Schep, some time Saint Mary's priest of York'. And he greeted them as fellows, parts of the great, anonymous deprived. 'John Nameless', they were, and 'John the Miller and John Carter'. They must beware of the guile, he said, the snares of those in the town, for their enemies were clever men. 'Stand together in God's name,' he had cried earlier, 'and bid Piers Plowman go to his work.[3] Chastise well Hob, the robber, and take with you John Trueman and all his fellows *and no more*.' And on that morning of the 13th he ended with the great, unanswerable chant which was (as I have said) not even his own, but which encapsulated the argument for even the meanest understanding.

> *When Adam dalf and Eve span,*
> *Who was then a gentilman?*

The mob, it is said, shouted to him when he had done that they would make him chancellor and archbishop, for Sudbury was going to the block. 'Small, small, small', they chanted.

Jack Miller asketh help to turn his milne aright. He hath grounden small, small, small. The King's son of heaven, he shall pay for all. Look thy milne go aright with the four sails, and the post stand in steadfastness. With right and with might, with will and with skill, let us help right, and skill go before will, and right before might, then goeth our milne aright.[4]

It was probably while this last sermon was being preached that word arrived that the king had decided to meet them. He was coming across the river, for they had claimed they were his loyal subjects and wished only to list their grievances. So he intended to land on the shore below Blackheath and listen to what they had to say.

Obviously, the government hoped that if he gave them a reasonable hearing and perhaps made certain promises he could induce them to disperse and return to their villages. According to contemporary reports, Sudbury and Hales had stressed the danger of leaving the Tower. But military counsels like those of Warwick, Oxford and Salisbury had prevailed.

So about mid-morning the royal barge was observed to pull out from the Tower and, accompanied by four smaller boats, to be making its way downstream across the tide towards the Greenwich shore. By now that shore was alive with a crowd of almost 10,000 men. Tall and wavering in their midst were about forty pennons and two great banners covered with the cross of St George.

Suddenly, when the barge was still forty or fifty yards offshore there was a shouted order. The oarsmen plunged in their blades and began backing against the current to hold the craft still, and the king's voice sang out, calling to ask what his subjects wanted.

According to Froissart it was Salisbury who had counselled against landing. For they were not meeting a disciplined army. It was a mob, 'madmen without reason', writes one chronicler, and to disembark in their midst–voices could be heard shouting for the heads of Sudbury and Hales–would have been to take a ridiculous chance.

But to the king's question what they wanted, all that could be heard were cries for him to land. How could they possibly carry on a shouted conversation across the water? So after a minute or so Salisbury decided to break off the parley and gave the order to row back upstream. At once the uproar on the bank increased. There were shouts of 'Treason!' But not a bow was bent, and although the party must have expected at any moment to be shot at, they got safely away, and within a very few minutes were back out of range on the city side.

The later report of the London sheriffs states that after this fiasco there was actually talk among the rebels of going home. They had collected enough stores to feed themselves on the march up from Canterbury. But now a good many were beginning to be hungry, and Southwark could not provide half enough provisions to feed 50,000 men.

But Alderman Horne had been right. They had friends in high places. That very morning Walter Sybyle (or Sibley), Alderman of Billingsgate, had marched on to the bridge with a body of armed men, ostensibly to hold it. Walworth had offered reinforcements, but Sybyle had turned them down. The bridge was his responsibility, he said (because it lay in his ward), and he did not intend to be deprived of his prerogatives.

Then–and it had obviously been agreed beforehand–as soon as the peasants moved up towards the southern piers Sybyle gave orders to have the drawbridge lowered, for, as he later explained, it would have been impossible to defend it. So without an arrow having been loosed the peasants moved across the white pillars up into London. 'In companies of two and three hundred they marched,' Froissart wrote, 'and by twenties and thirties, according to the populations of the places they had come from, and by villages as they entered, so by villages they found lodgings in taverns and tenements.' At almost exactly the same time Alderman William Tonge opened Aldgate to the men of Essex, and by late that morning or early afternoon London, which only twenty-four hours earlier had looked invulnerable, had been occupied by 100,000 men.

Some merchants, seeing how peacefully the villeins behaved, and hoping perhaps to curry favour, rolled hogsheads of Rhenish and Burgundy out into the streets, and ragged, awestruck fellows who had never tasted anything in their lives better than brown ale, drank, stood about, and gaped out over the many red-tiled roofs upon wonders neither they nor their fathers and grandfathers had ever beheld.

It was not only the bustle and colour that delighted them. There were dark, winding lanes and flower gardens. There were white churches and wharves with ships drawn up from places they had never heard of– Genoa and Cadiz, Africa and the Muslim east. There were brown and yellow men, men with scarlet turbans, men with rings in their ears. For the first time in their lives they heard the voices of their own alien countrymen–brisk, sour-tongued Londoners, men out of the midlands with words that tumbled like cartwheels out of their mouths, men from Devon and Dorset who for all they could understand might just as well have been foreigners.

The government was of course back in the Tower. From every part of the city one could see its tall perpendicular battlements with St Catherine's Hill behind them and the royal standard fluttering overhead in the bright sun.

Whether the first violence was led by Londoners or by the peasants out of Kent and Essex no one knows, but that afternoon a mob began streaming westwards out through Ludgate, past little villas with gardens and orchards towards John of Gaunt's great palace of the Savoy. There they broke down the gates, stormed up into the lavishly furnished rooms and destroyed whatever they could lay hands on. Jewels, rubies and emeralds were crushed with hammers. Tapestries, beds, chairs and oak tables were heaved out of the windows into the Thames. But they were not thieves. One man who tried to steal a silver cup is said to have been executed on the spot by his fellows.

Down in the vaults they found hogsheads of wine, and after an hour or two when the greater part of the crowd drifted back out on to the road, having set the place afire, they heard drunken singing from the cellars where large numbers of others still did not know they had been trapped. Suddenly three barrels of gunpowder which the finders had thought filled with gold and silver went up with a roar. The roof collapsed on whoever was left indoors, and all one could hear afterwards was the crackling of flames.

Another body of rioters under the leadership of Thomas Farringdon headed out past Aldersgate and attacked the Priory of St John, Clerken-well, for it was one of the residences of Sir Robert Hales, the hated Lord Treasurer. In the church they found seven Flemings who had fled there for sanctuary, and with cries of joy dragged the poor wretches out and cut off their heads. The Fleet prison and Newgate were opened and the prisoners released. At the Temple they swarmed into the muniment rooms and threw all the legal documents they could find into the street to be burned, and as for the lawyers, according to the chronicle they 'scrambled away like rats'.

When darkness fell some of the rebels were still busy in the city, but a vast number wandered out to Tower Hill and St Catherine's wharf and made camp there under the Tower walls. All night the beleaguered government could see their cooking fires and hear their laughter and the occasional shouted speeches. Once the king sent out two knights who delivered a letter asking the peasants to set down their demands in writing and then go off to their villages. One of the knights clambered on to a chair to read out the king's command by torchlight. But he was greeted with laughter and shouted at until he had to withdraw.

Meanwhile, according to Froissart, the council in the Tower 'sat silent with awful eye'. If they had ever imagined that the mob would get into London so easily, king and government could have ridden off west or north and managed in time to gather an army with which to fight their way back into town. But now they were trapped, and it was difficult to decide what could safely–or even reasonably–be done. Once or twice during the evening Richard climbed up on to the walls himself to look out over the many heads. The whole sky was red, for the Savoy, the Temple, the Inns of Court, the Priory of St John and Hales's great house in Highbury were all in flames.

Mayor Walworth was all for making a sortie out into the crowd. He was certain they would be joined by six or seven thousand armed citizens, the wealthier sort with their bodies of retainers. Sir Robert Knolles, for example, was still in the city with a garrison of 120 troops guarding his house, and the rebels, half of them drunk, half unarmed and without any real leaders, would never be able to make a stand against disciplined soldiers.

But Salisbury, the most experienced campaigner there, was against it. Such a sally might start well, he said. But if it degenerated into street fighting in a dozen scattered places and if the Londoners themselves joined Tyler's army, no one could foretell the result. 'If we begin what we cannot carry out,' Froissart quotes him as saying, 'we shall never be able to put things right again. It would be all over with us and with our heirs, and England would be a desert.'

So since the proclamation read out to the mob had failed to achieve anything, there was only one more remedy to be tried, there was only one more thing to be done, and it would be dangerous in the extreme. The king would send out an invitation to the rebels for a conference at Mile End outside the city walls in the morning. He might very well be killed or taken prisoner, but the position would hardly be worse than it was at present, for those locked in the Tower were as helpless as dead men anyway. If, on the other hand, he could promise whatever they liked and induce them to go home, he would have achieved a personal victory of no mean order. The only alternative was to hold out where they were until a rescuing army could be brought in from Scotland or Wales. But if one looked out over the burning houses, it was clear that long before help could arrive London might very well be levelled to the ground.

Meanwhile Tyler and his friends were busy at their own conference at Farringdon's house in the city, and it must have been late that night when a messenger arrived, carrying the king's offer. It was certainly well after midnight when the man came back with their answer. The invitation had been accepted.

But before that meeting, Hales and the old archbishop had if possible to be got away, and there was very little time, for in mid-June the sun comes up over London at about a quarter to four in the morning. So

ove A gentleman is dressed by his servants in front of the fire. (The British Library Board)

low Fourteenth-century belt chapes, or buckles. (London Museum)

bove Froissart's version of the happenings at Smithfield. Tyler is struck down while the king looks ...ignly on; on the right Richard is pictured addressing the rebels. (Radio Times Hulton Picture Library)

...posite above The king's ride across the Thames to address the rebels in Southwark; after Froissart's *...ronicles*. (Mary Evans Picture Library)

...posite below John Ball – as illustrated in Froissart – addressing the multitude. Since the unnaturally ...l-dressed peasants are carrying royal standards we have to presume that Ball's speech was being made ...r the Mile End meeting. (The Mansell Collection)

The white hart, emblem of Richard II, in Westminster Abbey. (By courtesy of the Dean and Chapter of Westminster. Photo by A. F. Brown)

while it was still dark a small skiff was brought round to the water gate
and the two men were bundled into it. But immediately afterwards, as
soon as the craft drew out into the river, someone on St Catherine's
wharf saw it and raised the alarm, and the boatmen had to pull hurriedly
back under the shelter of the walls.

It was then that Sudbury and Hales probably realized they were
doomed, so they retired to the Chapel of St John in the White Tower.
Now there was nothing to do except wait. At last the dawn began
brightening. The mob could be seen beginning to move up past the
Convent of the Crutched Friars, so the gate was opened, the drawbridge
was lowered and at a little before seven o'clock the king's cavalcade rode
slowly out into the midst of the rebel army. Joan, his mother, was still in
her bed, and the garrison stayed behind too. It was probably assumed
that out in the open they would have been no match for the peasants
anyway, but that at least the Tower could be kept secure.

But the drawbridge was not raised again after the king's departure, and
this fact has never been satisfactorily explained. It may have been left
lowered in token of good faith. Salisbury may have been anxious
to leave the way clear if it should prove necessary for the little troop to
fight its way back from Tower Hill.

There was a danger that at any moment the mob moving along on
every side might have got out of control. Once Thomas Farringdon
pressed forward, actually seized the king's bridle and began crying out
that he wanted justice. He wanted revenge on the traitor, Hales. Richard
answered that all men would be given justice. Then a man called
Trueman stopped Brembre, the late mayor, and began shouting insults
at him. Nevertheless, slowly and with little interruptions, the troop
with the king at its centre rode on through Whitechapel and Stepney.
Somewhere after they had reached open fields the king's half-brothers,
the Earl of Kent and Sir John Holland, put their heads to their horses'
necks and galloped off to safety. But no one tried to stop them; no one
followed, and at last the main body reached Mile End fields and Tyler
and the fourteen-year-old Richard finally came face to face.

The commons were carrying banners and many tiny pennons, and they
all knelt, says the *Anonimalle Chronicle*. Then, before anything else,
Tyler made his first demand, that they be allowed to seize the men who
had been traitors to both king and peasant. The conference proper
seems to have been loud and long. Here and there scuffles arose, for we
know that a certain John French was killed, though we do not know
who he was.

In the Tower during the previous night it had been agreed that the government had only two alternatives, to fight or to make peace. To fight was impossible, so without putting up any real argument, without even haggling for different terms, Richard one by one gave in to Tyler's demands. Serfdom was to be abolished and all feudal services were to be remitted. Villeins were to become free tenants and pay 4*d.* an acre for the land they tilled. (That would have been about half the equitable price.) Market monopolies were to be abolished, and there was to be a general amnesty for crimes committed during the uprising.

All this having been agreed, the rebels were drawn up in ranks, and the representatives of each district were given a royal banner to indicate that from now on they marched as loyal subjects of the king. At the same time–there in Mile End fields–thirty clerks were set to writing out charters of freedom and amnesty. And it strikes one that if the royal party came provided with banners, clerks, pens and parchment, they must already have decided precisely what course the conference would take.

There remained only the matter of punishment for those the commons had designated traitors, and on this point Tyler was particularly insistent. He wanted permission for himself and his men to seize the people and try them. It seems, however, that Richard replied evasively. All traitors would be arrested, he said, and dealt with according to law.

Perhaps Tyler misunderstood him. Perhaps he too, had arrived at Mile End with a preconceived plan. Perhaps, having now gained everything he had demanded, he decided that he could with impunity do whatever else he pleased. Or perhaps at this juncture, when he first understood the extent of his power, the ideas began to turn in his mind that everyone else first heard of in Jack Straw's confession on the following day. Whatever the reason, he now suddenly left the meeting, and with the clerks still writing out charters, collected a few of his followers and rode hurriedly back into London. Some of his men had already started home, carrying the documents that made them free.

It cannot have taken Tyler more than half an hour to get back to Tower Hill. There the drawbridge was still down, the portcullis still open. So when a band of about 400 men suddenly swarmed in, the captain of the guard had to make up his mind instantly whether or not to resist. If he did, it might very well mean the death of the king. Whatever the reason, he hesitated too long; he did nothing, and the rebels ran baying like hounds at a kill across the green and up into the White Tower.

One group broke into the king's private chamber; another invaded the bedroom of the Princess of Wales, his mother. She is said to have fainted, and attendants carried her into a boat and rowed her away unmolested up to Baynard's Castle, between the river and St Paul's.

As for Sudbury and Hales, ever since the king had left for Mile End they had lain buried, as it were, in the now silent Tower, hearing mass in the small chapel of St John. There, amid the thick pillars and the Norman arches (the whole chapel hardly larger than a tomb) Sudbury, according to the *Anonimalle Chronicle*, 'shrived the Prior of the Hospital-lers and others, and then heard two masses or three, and chanted the *Commendacione* and the *Dirige* [which were parts of the office for the dead], and the seven psalms and a litany, and when he was at the words *Omnes sancti, orate pro nobis*, the commons burst in and dragged him out of the chapel of the Tower and struck and handled him rudely, as they did also the others that were with him, and dragged them to Tower Hill'.

'They paid no reverence even to the Lord's Body,' says Walsingham, 'which the priest held up before them, but worse than demons... dragged him by the arms, by his hands, by different parts of the body towards their fellow rioters...and when they arrived there, a most horrible shout arose, not like men's shouts, but worse beyond all comparison than any human cries, and more like to the yelling of devils in hell.'

Walsingham writes that at Mile End Richard had agreed that the then in the Tower were to be delivered over to the mob. Tyler's cohorts, men and afterwards, certainly spoke and acted as if they thought this to be true. It may be, on the other hand, that the Tower guard had simply never been given orders to resist. No record exists to establish the truth. At any rate, the fact is that Sudbury, Hales, John Legge, the Sergeant-at-arms, and Sir William Appleby, a lawyer and surgeon who seems to have been an adherent to John of Gaunt, were one by one dragged to a block and decapitated.

From all accounts, Sudbury had been an honest, a kindly and a pious man, but a weak archbishop and chancellor. He possibly had no real idea why he was so hated. As head of the government, he had had fifteen days since the first riots in Brentwood to take some effective action. He had taken none. Even Walsingham says of him that he ought to have punished heretics more firmly. At the end he obviously knew that his death was inevitable, for when the time came, he seems to have died well.

Hales, once Admiral of the Fleet, was no more guilty than the archbishop of putting the country into the terrible state which almost thirty years of error, of peculation and downright blindness had finally brought about. But he had been treasurer for the past seven months, and that was enough.

The executions of the four (some chroniclers say seven or eight) cannot have taken more than five or ten minutes. When they were over, the heads of Hales and Sudbury were fixed on to poles, marched in triumph to Westminster and back, and at last placed over the gatehouse leading to London Bridge.

At the same time it seems an order went out that anybody who wanted to kill Flemings was now free to do so. The mob coursed down to the Church of St Martin in the Vintry, dragged thirty-five screaming and struggling immigrants out into the street and there beheaded them. Many of the headless bodies were simply piled like logs in the kennels. When in the *Nonne Preestes Tale* of Chaucer the fox carried Chaunte-cleer off on his back into the wood, everyone in the barnyard ran off in pursuit, yelling like fiends in hell.

> *Certes, he Iakke Straw and his meynee,*
> *Ne madë never shoutës half so shrille,*
> *Whan that they wolden any Fleming kille,*
> *As thilke day was maad upon the fox.*[5]

Some time during that day they tracked down and beheaded another of their great prizes, Richard Lyons, in Cheapside. In fact, according to Riley's *Memorials,* there was hardly a street in the city in which there were not bodies to be seen of those who had been decapitated. Some 150 foreigners were killed before nightfall. It is said that whenever the mob had run down a suspect they would ask him to say the words 'bread and cheese'. Those who answered 'brod und käs' were dragged off to be executed. Other passers-by heard the shout, 'With whom hold you?' And unless the prompt answer came, 'With King Richard and the true commons', they too were seized and dragged to a block. No one was killed except by what the rebels considered due process of law–that is, with an axe.

The king did not return to the Tower, but rode with his companions back to the unfortified Baynard's Castle to join his mother. That Friday night, the city, with no one to defend it, lay utterly at the mercy of the crowds. Sir Robert Knolles, who had accompanied the king to Mile End, was back in his house with the armed men he had collected there. But Mayor Walworth made no attempt to call together any supporters.

The authorities seem to have been stunned, as though each were waiting for one of the others to act. Nicholas Brembre, the ex-mayor at whom William Trueman had shouted insults that morning, even opened his door after dark had fallen to find the same man threatening him with a group of rebels at his back. So he finally gave them £3 10s. od. to go away.

All this time the clerks were still writing out charters and, as the chronicler remarks, on this occasion they did not demand fines or fees for the sealing. But the mob spent most of the night working out its revenge. With cries of triumph they broke into Lombard houses and robbed them of whatever valuables they could find, for by now, of course, there were not only peasants in the crowds, but hundreds of released prisoners. In many parts of the city houses were set on fire. One group went out to the suburb of Knightsbridge and burned down the house of John Butterwick, under-sheriff of Middlesex.

That evening Alderman John Horne is said to have marched from place to place with a mob scrabbling along behind him, shouting out that if any man wanted justice he need only ask for it. He levied fines on some who were accused of usury, tore up bonds to free debtors of their debts and even forced people to vacate houses that others claimed they had occupied illegally.

In a word, on that Friday night of 14 June, Wat Tyler and his rebels controlled London more completely than even they could have imagined possible. To be sure, some of the more peaceable–or perhaps the more in-nocent–were already on the way home. But in all directions, and par-ticularly to the north and east, messengers were also going out to tell those who had not yet marched how easy and how crushing the victory had been.

In their simplicity or self-delusion many of them went further. For they took the king's surrender at face value. Richard had come to the rescue of his beloved commons. Whatever they did was henceforward done in his name. Serfdom was dead. Traitors were being hunted down and punished, manor rolls were being destroyed, great abbeys being made to deal justly. They were the king's army. They marched under the royal standard, for Mile End had entitled them to carry it. Had not John Ball promised them the new and green Jerusalem? Tomorrow, or the next day it would be theirs.

CHAPTER THIRTEEN

VAE TERRAE UBI PUER REX EST

If I were to set down all that happened more or less at the same time in various other counties to the north, my story would be all but interminable. The rebellion is very well documented indeed.

But there were certain fundamental differences between what happened in Kent and Essex and what happened elsewhere. In the three counties of Norfolk, Suffolk and Cambridgeshire the rebels never marched under a single leader as they did in the south. They made no effort to join the main army in London, and, what is perhaps most interesting, they were led in various places by country parsons and even by landed gentlemen.

Towns like Ipswich, Norwich and Yarmouth had large commercial establishments, and even the villages were populated almost as much by small artisans as by peasants. But there was great diversity between the degrees of freedom enjoyed by different boroughs. Norwich lived under a splendid charter while Bury St Edmunds was gripped in the dead hand of the church. On some manors there were more freemen than serfs. On others, masters still demanded all the work days and the fines that would have been demanded a hundred years before.

So in one place–Bury St Edmunds, for example–it was the church that was attacked, in another a harsh landlord, in a third a little municipal oligarchy. Even poor parsons joined in the fighting. One detachment was led by a certain Sir Thomas Cornard, and there were members of great families like Thomas de Gyssyng, whose father had sat in the parliament of 1380 as member for Norfolk, like John Talmache or Richard Talemache de Bentley or Thomas de Monchesey who led other disparate groups. So it was not merely a rebellion of the poor against the rich, but one in which men of all classes acted with great violence and in unison against what they considered intolerable grievances.

These people had had to suffer not only the injustices visited on Kentishmen and Londoners, but the incursions of foreign armies. The Scots had so frequently devastated the north that one county, Northumberland, seems to have been unable to pay any tax at all. In East Anglia there had been French attacks that had damaged trade and commerce extensively. To be taxed for the continuation of a war that brought them nothing but suffering must have seemed an even greater burden than it was elsewhere.

As in London, there was no force raised for counter-attack, so in the beginning, at least, the rebellion was practically unopposed. In every hundred there was a strong body of archers that might have been mobilized. But nothing was done. Most of the action in East Anglia came after the conference at Mile End, when word had spread that they had the king's authority to hunt down 'traitors', so a great deal of the possible opposition was stifled before it had a chance to be formed. Even so, the outbreak was never centred in any one place. It was bloodier than that in the south. It was like a fire that eddied and ran with the wind. Sometimes it leapt half a county and left intervening towns and villages quite untouched.

Powell thought the rebel claim that Richard supported them far from improbable.[1] This would explain the universal loathing that rebels felt for the Duke of Lancaster, and the events of 15 June (which we still have to consider) when the Kentish mob openly accepted the king as their new leader. It would also, he feels, explain the actions of some of the country gentry who supported the insurrection.

But it would leave unexplained the fact that John Gower (an ardent royalist) and hundreds of other intensely loyal gentlemen were forced to flee for their lives, that men of great power and prominence–Sudbury, Hales, Lyons, Imworth, Legge–were wantonly sacrificed, and it would leave utterly inexplicable the ability of a fourteen-year-old boy to communicate with rebels who must have seemed at best unreasonable, and at worst contemptible opponents of all privilege and order. He would have had to do this, moreover, without the knowledge of his council, his army commanders and of various members of his own family. Perhaps most important of all, it would have destroyed the hegemony of crown and mercantile oligarchy which alone had made the English style of government possible.

In East Anglia as in the south, manorial rolls were burned, lawyers and Flemings were attacked. But here the great landowning abbeys were attacked too, and attacked with a savagery seen nowhere else in the country. In Norfolk, although bands of rebels had been gathering for days, there was no real action before the 17th, three days after the Mile End meeting. On that Monday Geoffrey Litster and Sir Roger Bacon assembled a vast crowd on Mushold Heath, just outside Norwich. Sir Robert Salle, who was in command of the city, began arming the citizens to repel what looked like an imminent assault. But when a demand came from the rebels that he ride out to confer with them, he rode out at once and alone to hear what they had to say.

To his astonishment the peasants wanted him to join them as their leader. He turned the offer down, and he must have done so with a certain anger and contempt, for as he started to climb back into the saddle he missed the stirrup—the horse seems to have been frightened by all the shouting and commotion—and a cry went up to attack him and finish him off. At once he slapped his horse to drive it off and give himself room, and drew his sword. The mob leapt at him, but he flashed his blade, sweeping it from side to side, *'que c'estoit grand beauté de le veoir'*,[2] and managed to wound or kill twelve of his attackers before he was himself brought down by sheer weight of numbers. With their leader dead, the Norwich citizens lost all stomach for the fight—or perhaps there were too many traitors among them—for they opened the gates, and the rebels, says the record, marched in, armed and with pennons flying.[3]

Here, as in London, there was a massacre of Flemings and lawyers. The Justice of the Peace was captured, dragged to an improvised block and beheaded. Sir Robert Salle's house was gutted and £200 worth of his goods were carried off. The archdeacon's house and that of the tax collector were also plundered.

Over in Cambridgeshire a certain John Greyston, having witnessed the executions of Hales and Sudbury in London, rode north and rallied his countrymen to join him, claiming that he had the king's authority to put down traitors. A man called John Stannford was making the same claim, and by 15 June violence broke out all over the county. As in Norfolk, landlords and unpopular ecclesiastics, judges and retainers of the Duke of Lancaster were attacked and saw their property either destroyed or confiscated. The Bishop of Ely's court rolls were burned and his gaol emptied of prisoners. Between the 15th and the 17th the rioters seem to have been in complete control of Cambridge itself, where Town and Gown had been at war for generations.

Only two months previously the townsmen had broken into the University Treasury and made off with certain charters which they had burned. On the night of the 15th they broke into the house of the university *Bedel*, and during the next day or two, documents, jewels and 'utensilia' were stolen from various churches and from the Carmelite monastery which stood where Queen's College now stands. These documents and the university muniments were burned in the market-place. Even six hundred years afterwards one cringes to read of an illiterate harridan called Margaret Starre, who kicked and stamped on the ashes, on the medieval records of Cambridge University, while she kept shouting, 'Away with the learning of clerks!'

In Hertfordshire rebels actually marched under the king's banner given them at Mile End. In all the counties to the east and in most of those to the north the revolt was practically everywhere successful. And if the rebels had had a commander of any ability to lead them they might very well have changed the history of England. But they had not. In any case, when Salle was being butchered in Norwich and the mob running rampant through the streets of Cambridge it was already too late. For John Ball was in flight and Wat Tyler lay dead in Smithfield. An act of cool and deliberate courage had crushed the rebellion in the course of a single hour. The young king–like his father before him–had won his spurs and given promise of a golden future which was never to come to pass.

All the night of the 14th Tyler's men had killed, burned, beaten, bullied and swaggered round London. Crowds of thugs like modern football rowdies had pounded on people's doors and chanted slogans, overturned carts and threatened passers-by into giving up their purses. Here and there, no doubt, some servant girl was chased up an alleyway by a band of drunks and raped, and here and there, men with power in their hands for the first time in their lives carried out revenges and cancelled private wrongs.

As for Tyler and his confederates, while we do not know if they were drunk or dry that night, they must by now have been turning over in their minds where next to go, how best to consolidate their advantage. For it was clear that only through continued pressure would they be able to gain permanently what they had thus far achieved so quickly and easily.

They had no understanding of the powers of Parliament, so they had made no effort to secure the franchise. To have done so successfully would have altered the course of English history. Ever since the Model Parliament in 1295 the great merchants had had political representation, and by means of it they had formed an alliance with the crown that had been

H

hugely advantageous to both sides. For the oligarchs possessed a financial strength that made them independent of the monarch. Parliament, their lever and their forum, thus increased in importance as it did in no other European nation. And through Parliament the great mercantile families had been able to ensure that the expansion they desired into other European markets had powerful political support, so that in the end the fragmented German and Italian states became quite unable to compete.

The crown, on the other hand, was not only perpetually in need of money that only members of the oligarchy could supply. It needed the mercantile representation in Parliament to ensure the passage of whatever bills were required to maintain its own stability. In time even the peerage, the knights of the shire and the landed gentlemen came to support these twin pillars of the state, for they acquired common interests. On the Continent, merchant and nobleman were members of mutually exclusive classes. But a certain elasticity in the English character, a certain pragmatism and love of cold cash allowed them to intermarry, so that eventually commerce and coronets worked towards the same purposes. Even five hundred years afterwards, many a nineteenth century barony was built, not on land, but on mustard pots and the exports of Lancashire.

When Edward III imported Flemish weavers he was trying consciously to build trade in England that would make him independent of foreign bankers. He wanted to put fiscal power into English hands, for how could he conduct a foreign policy based on Lombard money that might at any time be cut off? And the sturdy independence he thus brought about not only gave England power. English currency, minted only in London, provided far harder coin than the thaler or florin minted haphazardly by German and Italian princelings in a score or more of city states. It was this hardheaded English policy of the fourteenth century which was slowly and inexorably to turn England into the strongest mercantile power in the world. In 1350 most foreign trade in London was still in foreign hands. But change was already in the wind. Two hundred years afterwards the last of the foreign merchants had either been expelled or absorbed, and English power under Elizabeth was ready for the vast political and mercantile expansion that came after. If Wat Tyler's rebels had secured the franchise they would have changed the rules of the game.

So the insurgents were at cross-purposes with a political current that had just begun strongly to move. They had neither arms in sufficient quantities, nor adequate military leaders. They were bound to be crushed by any one of the distant armies as soon as it could be recalled. Even if this had not been so, they lacked any practical experience of government. They lacked the necessary discipline, the necessary cohesion, the necessary education and perhaps the necessary intelligence.

According to the *Anonimalle Chronicle*, they were now demanding that the church be disendowed, that the woods on private estates be opened for the use of peasant tenants, that the laws of outlawry no longer operate, and that lawyers and justices who had enforced the Statute of Labourers be deprived of their powers. It was a mixture of half-understood Wycliffism, half-formulated Socialism, hatred of a judicial system that seemed never to work to their advantage and, on the lowest level, a desire on the part of those who could not read to have all books and records abolished.

John Ball and Tyler, Farringdon, Sybyle, Horne, Jack Straw, they were all men with some inkling of the limits of practical politics, and they must have spent many hours in argument about what ought next to be done. I believe on the basis of probabilities that Jack Straw's later confession came somewhere near the truth.

It is getting a little ahead of our story to discuss this point, but it has a great bearing on our being able to understand what the rebels had in mind on the last day of the revolt. According to the *Chronicon Angliae*, when Straw had been condemned on the day of Tyler's death (or possibly the day after), Mayor Walworth offered to have masses said for his soul if he would now confess just what the rebel plan had been. Most writers on the subject have come to the hesitant conclusion that Straw's answer owed more to braggadocio than to fact. But if one puts oneself into Tyler's position, if one tries to imagine what actual alternatives he had, it looks more and more likely that Straw was telling the simple truth.

If the saying of masses for his soul was important enough to induce him to confess, it would have been madness to lie, for a lie in the hour of death might very well have cancelled out the virtue of the mass. And we have to remember, as I have already pointed out, that rebels and government were both aware that within a week or ten days the king would be able to collect such a large and disciplined force that if the rebellion had not spread in the meantime it would inevitably have been crushed.

The only alternative to further action would have been to collect the Mile End charters and go home. But, as we have seen, that was something Tyler was unwilling to do. It was only after Mile End that he actually set about the business of slaughtering the commons' enemies.

Only then were emissaries sent into East Anglia to foment further rebellion. And within thirty hours he was actually in conference with the king again, this time at Smithfield, and here he laid down further demands.

At Blackheath they had talked of making John Ball Archbishop of Canterbury. 'Shape you to one head', the priest had cried. But was that head Tyler, or was it the king? Did a man of Ball's intelligence really believe that the Mile End meeting had abolished serfdom? Or would they have to go on and extirpate–or in some way make powerless–the forces that would eventually be levied against them before they could feel safe in having accomplished what they had set out to do?

It seems to me that the answer admits of little doubt. And if this is so, how to make those forces powerless? Jack Straw's confession provides the only possible answer. For he reported that Tyler had intended to take the king hostage as so many Kentish gentlemen had already been taken hostage. It was to be 'King Richard and the true commons' indeed. And with that one stroke, with the legitimate and divinely ordained power in their hands–not as their captive, but as their putative leader– they would at once have divided any opposition that might arise.

Tyler, he said, intended to take the king with them round the shires. In the king's name he would have arrested and executed whatever individuals had been traitors to the commons in the past or could be expected to serve as the heads of any resistance in the future.

They would have seized church property. And this, incidentally, would have brought them support from many who believed like Wycliffe that it had been a sin for the church to acquire property in the first place. They would have thrown down all bishops, all abbots, all rectors, and left no clergy except the mendicant friars. In the end (according to Straw) they would have had to kill the king himself, 'and when there was no one left with greater power or more learning than we, we would have been able to make whatever laws seemed to us right'.

The whole rigmarole sounds like the grand, half-logical formulation of men inexperienced in larger affairs, the same that we heard when the Lincolnshire rebels called themselves members of a great society, or that we heard in the plan to make John Ball an archbishop, presumably without benefit of papal authority, or that we saw in the plan to make laws that could only be enforced after the lawyers had been killed. It was really nothing but a half-savage and pathetic protest against what had become intolerable conditions of servitude, a desire for sovereignty by one-eyed men in a country wherein everybody else had first to be made blind.

For the young king who awoke that morning of the 15th in Baynard's Castle, to bells ringing out from all the 106 church steeples in London (if there were bells that morning) it was a desperate situation. He had gone as far as it was possible to go, acceded to every demand, sacrificed archbishop and treasurer, even put himself at the mob's mercy by riding out of the Tower to meet them. But now the city was actually more nearly anarchic than it had been the day before.

It is tempting to imagine what was likely to have been in his mind, the mind of an adolescent boy, raised in luxury, the only son of an heroic father and the favoured child of a notoriously beautiful mother, a boy who was uneasily aware that his uncles coveted the crown, a crown his by right of primogeniture, a boy who as later events made plain was subject to fits of petulance and temper, to vanities in dress and behaviour that made him a by-word among his contemporaries. He was certainly aware that one of the catch phrases of the time was *Vae terrae ubi puer rex est*, woe to the land where a child is king.

He was that child, handsome, tall beyond his years, taught since he had first been able to prattle to revere a father of whom he was the only earthly representative. And this morning, 15 June, was not only the Feast of Corpus Christi; it was his father's birthday. And perhaps for the only time in his life he acted that day with a calm and resolute courage that his father would have thought suitable for a king.

He might have fled with his entourage to Windsor and there waited for a rescuing army. Instead he sent Tyler a message asking for a second meeting, this time at Smithfield, just outside the city walls to the north.

Houses were still being sacked. John Imworth, the warden and 'pitiless tormenter' of the Marshalsea Prison in Southwark–the rebels had already gutted it–was seen trying to make his escape out of London. His enemies, led by a Kentish priest, commandeered a few horses and went galloping after him. Near Westminster they were already hot on his heels, so he tumbled down out of his saddle and ran into the abbey for sanctuary. But the rebels followed, yelling through the great portal, tore him away from a pillar he was embracing at the shrine of Edward the Confessor, dragged him back to Cheapside and there cut off his head.

Walsingham wrote that Tyler had become so confident of success that he was openly bragging of his intention to march at the head of 20,000 men and shave the beards of any who stood in his way. In four days, he said, there would be no laws in England except those that came out of his own mouth. In a word, with so many of his innocent followers already on the way home, he was thinking in terms of a smaller and more manageable army made up of men who had waded in blood all week.

Meanwhile the king, his council and a few armed men acting as guards climbed into their saddles and rode out through Ludgate to the west, past the many quiet gardens, past the Savoy, still smouldering forty-eight hours after the fire and explosion. Outside the abbey they were met by a file of monks carrying a crucifix. The king dismounted and kissed it, and it is recorded that some of his companions, exhausted by the events of the past few days, actually burst into tears.

Then they entered the church and knelt for a while in prayer. Afterwards Richard withdrew in the company of an anchorite, confessed his sins and remained with the man for a long time, deep in conversation. Finally he and his companions rode off again with a jangling of harness to perform what Trevelyan calls 'the act of sober courage which, in spite of all the follies of his manhood, half redeems his memory'.

By all accounts it was a hot June day. Several times during the previous generation there had been complaints about Smithfield, the cattle market, for it was perpetually foetid with the stench of blood and offal. We may reasonably doubt whether the usual Friday horse market had been held there the day before.

Imagine a great flat field with the Church of St Bartholemew to the east (where it still stands), the hospital to the south, planks, awnings and trestles piled where they had been last dismantled, and to the north and west a fair number of houses. A gap at the north-west corner led to Clerkenwell fields.

When Richard and some 200 companions with chain mail under their robes rode on to the field in front of the church at about the hour of vespers, they found facing them to the west—with their backs to the sun—about 6,000 men drawn up in military formation, armed with pikes and bows, each company carrying banners, many of them the royal standards granted only the day before at Mile End.

After a moment they made out Tyler riding towards them on a little brown nag, behind him a 'squire', also mounted and carrying a banner. In front of the king Tyler swung himself to the ground, bowed, then took the boy's hand and shook it vigorously, telling him to 'be of good cheer', for within the next fortnight he would have earned even more thanks of the commons than he had earned so far.

In reply, Richard seems to have asked the obvious question, why the rebels had not started home, since everything they had asked at Mile End had already been granted.

No one of the chroniclers who reported the conversation agrees with any other. There were, it seems, several points that Tyler still wanted to raise. He demanded the abolition of outlawry (though this had already been granted). He wanted the church to be disendowed. There was to be 'no law save that of Winchester', and by this he meant the Statute of Winchester promulgated under Edward I, whereby missing labourers and criminal outlaws were distinguished. He demanded that all bishoprics be abolished. He wanted, in fact, all social distinctions abolished between one man and another, except for the person of the king himself, and as one historian has pointed out,[4] unlike the previous demands made at Mile End, he was now asking for fundamental changes in the structure of church and society, changes which would require not only discussion, but serious thought by the king's council and by Parliament. They could not possibly be granted on the spur of the moment, and by this means Tyler was making an excuse not only to keep his army in being, but to remain in London and to be treated as a negotiator among equals.

Perhaps he hoped to provoke a hostile reaction, for that would give him reason to have the king seized. And in a manner he succeeded, for according to one chronicler, no one at first answered with so much as a word, 'for no councillor dared open his mouth or make any answer, matters being as they were'. Only Richard replied, and in the same equivocal terms as at Mile End, that the commons should have all he could legally grant, except for the regalities of the crown.

At this point Tyler did a strange thing, for he probably felt himself completely master of the situation. He shouted back to his men for a flagon of ale, and when it came, rinsed his mouth, spat and then drained the flagon in one long draught. A moment later as he was climbing back on to his horse, one of the men behind the king was heard to remark that he knew the rebel's face. He was a notorious highwayman and thief. Tyler wagged his head at the man, beckoning him to come out, and when the fellow refused, Tyler turned to his companion who was carrying the banner and shouted at him to draw his sword and cut the traitor down.

The king's retainer cried out that he had done nothing but speak the truth. At this, Tyler drew his dagger out of its sheath (he had been playing with it all during the meeting) and pushed forwards himself. But at once Walworth drew his own sword and offered to put Tyler under arrest for drawing a weapon in front of the king. There seems to have been a short struggle. Walworth managed to get in a slashing blow that struck Tyler on the shoulder. The man almost fell out of his saddle. Then a certain Ralph Standyche, a squire, ran him through the body. Barely able to control his horse, Tyler turned and began riding back to his men, shouting 'Treason!' Then he slipped to the ground.

It is reported that some of his followers, not being able to see clearly what was going on, said 'They are knighting him.' But then, with Tyler's fall, everything became clear. A roar went up. Those in the front rank began fitting arrows to their bows. But at that moment Richard did the only thing that could possibly have saved them. He spurred his horse forwards and galloped towards the mob, holding his hand high to gesture them back. Nobody was later clear what he shouted at them, but it was something like 'Hold, I am your king. *I* am your leader.' Then he cantered straight into the rebel ranks. He was seen pointing towards Clerkenwell fields just outside the market, and the last his followers could make out was the king, still high in the saddle, walking his horse with the rebel horde streaming round him out to the open fields.

Some of the retainers fled for their lives. But Walworth galloped back into the city to raise help. It was his day as much as the king's. It took almost three-quarters of an hour to rout out a band of armed men and muster them in Westcheap. Horne and Sybyle, the traitor aldermen, were riding too, shouting that the king was dead; they had seen him fall. But it was no use. Sir Robert Knolles's men gathered. Men appeared with bills and bows from wards all the way down to the river. Troops were called out from the Tower.

What happened meanwhile out at 'White Well Beech' in Clerkenwell fields no one ever recorded, but when at last the armed loyalists poured out through Aldersgate and across Smithfield, they saw the king still mounted, talking with the rebels who surrounded him. Knolles split his forces in two and swung down the sides of the field to take the peasants on both flanks. A company of lancers rode straight into the throng to take up positions beside the king, and as the chronicler has it, all across that long, flat ground, the rebels sank to their knees, there in the trampled wheat.

Froissart reported that the military leaders were intent on slaughter, but that Richard held them back. 'Three-quarters were only brought here by fear and threats', he said. Turning to the peasants, he called out simply that he gave them leave to go home.

Meanwhile Walworth had been hunting the badly wounded Tyler. He found him in St Bartholomew's Hospital hard by, where some of his followers had carried him. So the mayor sent in a small troop to fetch him, had him dragged out on to the grass and there cut off his head.

Already the Essex men were swarming off to the north-east, but the Kentishmen had the city between them and the bridge. So with a file of knights for escort they were marched through London and sent off across the river they had first crossed in triumph only two afternoons before.

In East Anglia, where almost every town and village had been ablaze, a bishop had suddenly turned fighting man and in a matter of days done what none of the professional soldiers had even attempted. Bishop Henry Despenser of Norwich was obviously more a soldier than an ecclesiastic. Two years after the uprising he was to command the troops of Pope Urban VI in Flanders, defeat the army of the anti-pope at Dunkirk, raise the siege of Ypres and later still, with a helmet instead of a mitre on his head, fight to repel a French invasion of Scotland. Wycliffe had no use for him; he, in his turn, had no use for Lollards.

When the rebellion broke out in June he happened to be in Rutland, and of course he would have heard nothing at first except that there was peasant disaffection in Essex and Kent. Then came news that Suffolk and Cambridgeshire were in ferment too. By the 16th or 17th Geoffrey Litster, who called himself king of the commons, was ravaging Norfolk, and the good bishop decided it was time he returned to his diocese.

According to the *Historia Anglicana*, he had with him only eight lances and a few archers. But no matter. When he reached Peterborough he learned that the abbey tenants there had also risen in revolt. So he sent riders out to collect a few of the local gentry, and as soon as his troop was assembled, galloped headlong into the town. According to Knighton, he arrived just in time to surprise the rebels swarming into the abbey. Some he cut down outdoors, some even at the altar itself. Those who could, fled. Others, we read, were given their absolution by the bishop's sword.

Spenser stayed only long enough in Peterborough to hang a few of the ringleaders. Then he rode on to Ramsey (his little company grown more numerous with volunteers). Here, too, he attacked just when the rebels were entering the monastery, took the whole band prisoner and rode on again.

Storming into Cambridge on the 19th, he routed a small army of rebels for the third time. A country squire who had joined them, a certain John Hanchach, was beheaded in the market-place, and two days after he had entered the town, the bishop rode on once more. Now as his victories began to be noised abroad, loyalists came trooping to join him, for as the *Chronicon Angliae* says, 'when the knights and gentlemen saw their bishop in helmet and cuirass, armed with his two-edged sword', they came out of hiding at last. So by the time Spenser arrived at the gates of Norwich on the 24th of the month, he was in command of a considerable force.

Geoffrey Litster had already evacuated the town. Norwichmen were not his friends, and no doubt he preferred to fight on more favourable ground. So he collected his force at North Walsham, and from there sent out messages in all directions, calling for reinforcements. Meanwhile, he fortified his camp with a ditch and a line of spiked stakes, and behind and to both sides he had waggons piled, chained wheel to wheel. There he took his stand, the first peasant leader in all that month to offer resistance to armed men.

But the reinforcements did not come, for word had got round that Tyler was dead and the revolt crushed in the south. When the bishop arrived, he did not even bother to have archers start a preliminary attack as was the custom. Instead he galloped in with his cavalry like one of the old French warriors at Crécy, jumping the ditch at the head of his men. Although Litster put up a brief resistance, the rebels were cut down in very short order. Litster himself was captured, sentenced to be half hanged and then decapitated and quartered.

Curiously enough, the bishop seems to have felt a certain respect for him, or else suddenly remembered that he had been a priest before he was a soldier. For he took time to hear the man's confession himself, absolved him, gave him the last sacraments and then walked beside the cart as it was drawn to the gallows, holding the prisoner's head up to prevent its being knocked on the stones of the road.

As I have said, after the king's victory at Smithfield, the peasants tramped home with their precious charters. Richard gave Mayor Walworth not only a knighthood on the field, but what amounted to dictatorial powers to seize and punish rebels by any means he chose, and that same night there were arrests all over London. Some of the malefactors were caught still in the act of plundering.

Jack Straw and John Kirkeby were decapitated. So was a certain John Starling, an Essex man, who had gone marching up and down all day with a sword hanging round his neck, shouting to whoever would listen that it was he who had killed Archbishop Sudbury, and that now he wanted his reward. He made the same happy boast to Walworth in the minutes before he was hanged.

Five days afterwards orders went out for the pacification of Kent, and the Earl of Suffolk was sent with 500 men to put down the remnants of revolt in East Anglia. On the 22nd the king himself set out at the head of an army to seize any rebels who could be tracked down in Essex. In Waltham he was met by a deputation who asked that the promises made at Mile End be ratified. But all promises made under duress, he told them, were void. 'Serfs you are,' he said, 'and serfs you shall remain.'

So a last unhappy attempt was made to raise a rebel army and revive the now hopeless cause. And an army of sorts did gather just south of Chelmsford. Like Litster's men before them, they entrenched themselves and chained as many carts as they could find behind them. But they too were overrun, and some 500 killed before the survivors fled into the forest. Eight hundred of their horses were found to have been left in the camp.

John Ball was caught in Coventry and taken down to St Albans to be tried before the Chief Justice, Tressilian. On 13 July he was brought into court, admitted his part in the rebellion, denied that he had been in any way to blame, and at the end refused proudly to ask for the king's pardon. On the 15th, having at the request of Bishop Courtney of London been given two days to devote to prayer and the preparation of his soul, he was taken out into the public square and there hanged, drawn and quartered.

Mayor Walworth died rich and full of honours in 1385. Sir Simon Burley and Nicholas Brembre, as I have already said, were executed three years after that. Sir John Holland, the half-brother who fled at Mile End, lived long enough to be executed by Henry IV. Sir Robert Knolles, the old warrior, old enough to have fought under the Black Prince, survived until 1407. Horne and Sybyle, the traitor aldermen, were brought to trial on a charge of having aided the rebels. But they were actually acquitted, probably as a gesture to please the mob. And Richard himself, grew into a spiteful and irrational manhood, twice, for dynastic reasons, married young girls, was finally deposed to the regret of hardly any, and died a prisoner at Pontefract just after his thirty-third birthday.

The terrible errors of his last nineteen years do not concern us here, for I have been trying to draw only the lights and shadows, the picture of an age, and not to become more than cursorily involved in its politics.

On 15 June 1381 Richard had already lived his finest hour and acquired a moral stature that for a short while, at least, gave him greater power than even his father had had before him. But there was nowhere else for him to go. Not only can power not remain static, but experience teaches that for some strange, human reason, it has to be limited, even in the interests of whoever holds it. If it is not checked somewhere, it becomes vulnerable, perhaps at first only on the periphery. So to hold power successfully is to control a balance, to control in the end a whole system of balances. And for Richard, the fulfilment of his wishes simply baffled him. He was destroyed by having been allowed to succeed.

England had simply not yet come of age. The foundations of future greatness were already there. London was built of wood, while Paris, twice its size, was largely of stone. Florence, Bologna, Pisa, Milan, were already centres of great learning. Pavia had had a university for six hundred years. The German towns were rich and solid almost beyond English understanding.

France, Germany and Flanders contained the most prosperous commercial centres in the medieval world. In Italy a new classical spring had flowered that excited English visitors more than anything they had seen or felt at home. But even in bare, ramshackle, unpopulous England the first flowers had bloomed. Chaucer, Wycliffe and a host of others had proved themselves equal to any of the great talents in the south.

England was to suffer a hundred years of chaos, poverty, brutality and civil war before stable government could once again offer her an opportunity to reassert her real nature. Perhaps it can be said in a single phrase. By the end of the fourteenth century, with the possible exception of Chaucer, Englishmen were not yet of the renaissance. They may have begun to mistrust heaven, but they had not yet discovered man.

NOTES

CHAPTER ONE

1 *Select Pleas of the Crown*, ed. F. W. Maitland, Selden Society, 1888.
2 *Piers Plowman*, C. X. 223 and 264.
3 A.D. 1388. 12° Rich. II, Cap. 5.
4 *Court Baron*, p. 142.
5 *Under the Greenwood Tree*.
6 Hall, Joseph, *The Complete Poems*, ed. A. B. Grosart, Manchester, 1879.
7 *Description of England*, Bk. II, Chap. xii.
8 *Ibid.*, Bk. II, Chap. xxii.
9 *Arch. Journal*, III. 65.
10 *The Medieval Village*, p. 103.
11 *The Eclogues of Alexander Barclay*, ed. Beatrice White, Early English Text Society, 1928.
   V. 62–73.
12 *Life on the English Manor*.
13 *Six Centuries of Work and Wages*.
14 *New Light on Piers Plowman*.
15 *Piers Plowman*, C. VI. 35ff.
16 *Op. cit.* B. X. 300–305.
17 *Piers Plowman*, A. Prol. 40ff.
18 Skelton, John, *Poetical Works*, ed. Alexander Dyce. London, 1843.
19 *Essai sur la civilisation flammande*, Louvain, 1898.
20 Migne, Jacques Paul, *Patrologiae*, vol. 144, col. 228.
21 *Ecloques*, V. 355–6, 365–72.
22 *Pierce the Plowman's Crede*, 420–42. The author is unknown, but the poem was written in
   about 1394. Vivid as the lines are, they lose comparatively little in translation, so I
   offer them here in modern English.

CHAPTER TWO

1 Stubbes, Philip, *The Anatomie of Abuses*, London, 1585.
2 Elyot, Thomas, *Miracles of King Henry VI*, ed. Knox and Leslie, 1923.
3 Strutt, *Sports and Pastimes*, p. 167.

[4] Somerset Rec. Soc. V. 244–5, 259.

[5] Stow, *Survey*, I., 96.

[6] *Canterbury Tales*, F. 1252–5.

[7] *Life on the English Manor*, p. 262.

[8] *Dives and Pauper*, com. III, c. 6.

[9] Wilkins, *Concilia*, I. 581.

[10] *Villainage in England*, p. 318.

[11] *Canterbury Tales*, A. 589ff.

[12] *Life on the English Manor*, p. 159.

[13] Pollock and Maitland, *The History of English Law before the Time of Edward I*. Cambridge, 1898.

[14] Morris, J. E., *The Welsh Wars of Edward I*. Oxford, 1901.

[15] *Henry V*, iv. i. 136ff.

CHAPTER THREE

[1] Amyat, T., *Population of English Cities temp. Edw. III. (Archaeologica)*, vol. xx., pp. 524–31.

[2] Rolls Series, iii. 213.

[3] Rymer, *Foedera*, v. p. 655.

[4] Brook, Lambert, *London*, i. 241.

[5] *South Wales and the March*, p. 259.

[6] *Piers Plowman*, B. Prol. 83–6.

[7] According to Bede, there had been outbreaks of pestilence in England in 664, 672, 679 and 683.

[8] MS. Cotton Domit. A. viii, fol. 124.

[9] MS. Add. 41321, fol. 13.

[10] MS. Harl. 2398, fol. 93b.

[11] *Piers Plowman*, C. VI. 114–16.

[12] *Piers Plowman*, A. X. 185–7.

[13] *Piers Plowman*, C. IX. 304–7.

[14] Riley, *Memorials*, p. 312.

[15] It was Trevelyan who first called attention to this particular case (Anc. Ind. no. 92) in his *England in the Age of Wycliffe*, p. 188.

[16] *Op. cit.*, p. 191.

CHAPTER FOUR

[1] *Euphues and his England*, in vol. II, p. 192 of Lyly's *Collected Works*, London, 1902.

[2] *English Wayfaring Life*.

[3] From Speght's introduction to his edition of Chaucer, printed 1598.

[4] *Canterbury Tales*, A. 750–51.

[5] *Liber Albus*, ed. Riley, intro., p. lviii.

[6] *Registrum Palatinum Dunelmense*, ed. T. D. Hardy (Rolls Series), 1873–8, vol. iii, p. 325.

[7] Matthew Paris, *Historia Anglorum*, ed. Sir F. Madden, London, 1886, vol. ii, p. 60.

[8] *Canterbury Tales*, C. 329–34.

[9] *Canterbury Tales*, C. 398–406.

[10] Rymer's *Foedera*, edit. 1704–35, vol. iv, p. 20.

[11] *Wayfaring Life*, p. 358.

12 *Historical Papers from the Northern Regiments,* ed. Raine, p. 425.

13 *The Itineraries of William Wey,* ed. G. Williams. Roxburgh Club, 1857.

CHAPTER FIVE

1 *Canterbury Tales,* A. 496–500.

2 Richardson, H. G., *The Parish Clergy of the Thirteenth and Fourteenth Centuries,* tr. Roy. Hist. Soc., 3rd Series, vol. vi.

3 Bede, *Historia Ecclesiastica,* ed. J. E. B. Mayor and J. R. Lumby, Cambridge, 1881, iii. 26.

4 Brit. Mus. Nero D. vii.

5 Sir John and Sir Geoffrey wear a girdle of silver, and a baselard or a long knife with gilded studs on the haft. *Piers Plowman,* B. XV. 120–21.

6 *The Chester Plays,* ed. Dr Hermann Deimling, 2 vols., EETS, 1892.

7 *Op. cit.,* iv. 263–4 and 297–8.

8 Greg, W. W., *Bibliographical and Textual Problems of English Miracle Cycles,* 1914.

9 Quoted in Owst, *Literature and Pulpit,* p. 483.

CHAPTER SIX

1 Myrc's *Duties of a Parish Priest,* ed. E. Peacock, EETS, 1886.

2 MS. Roy. 18b, xxiii, fol. 141.

3 MS. Lansd. 393, fol. 63b et seq.

4 *Ibid.,* fol. 128.

5 Ed. J. T. Walter, Paris, 1914. This was a compilation made about 1280, probably by Franciscan friar.

6 Owst, *op. cit.,* p. 301.

7 MS. Harl. fol. 146. Owst, 304.

8 *Gesta Romanorum,* ed. S. J. Herrtage, EETS, 1879.

9 MS. Add. 41321, fol. 19. Owst, 320.

10 MS. Harl. 2398, fol. 9b.

11 MS. Bodl. 95.

12 MS. Roy. 18b, fol. 133. Owst, p. 383.

13 M.S. Harl. 2398, fol. 36b.

14 MS. Add. 41321, fol. 97b.

15 *The Canterbury Tales,* B. 3094–7.

CHAPTER SEVEN

1 *The Canterbury Tales,* A. 269–70.

2 *Ibid.,* A. 243–52.

3 Brooke, Stopford, *English Literature,* 1896.

4 *The Canterbury Tales,* A. 223–32.

5 *Ibid.,* A. 169–71.

6 *Ibid.,* A. 175–8.

7 *England in the Age of Wycliffe,* p. 175.

8 *Chaucer in the Fifteenth Century.*

[9] Workman, *John Wyclif*.

[10] Both in the fourteenth century and today the name Lollard has been confused with loller, an idler. But it meant nothing of the sort. A Lollard had originally described a wandering singer, from the Old Dutch *lollen* or *lullen*, to sing.

[11] MS. Add. 41321, fol. 114b. Owst, 136.

[12] *Chronicles*, I. 249.

CHAPTER EIGHT

[1] *Medieval Cities*.

[2] *Survey*, ii. 166–9. Stow writes that Brembre was beheaded. In fact, he was hanged.

[3] Riley, *Memorials*, 415.

[4] *Hist. Angl.* ii. 65.

[5] Riley, *Memorials*, 471–2.

[6] Thomas, A. H. (ed.), *Calendar of Plea and Memoranda Rolls, 1381–1412*.

[7] Bird, *The Turbulent London of Richard II*, p. 93.

[8] *Testament of Love*, ed. Skeat, I. vi. 57.

[9] Fitzstephen's *Descriptio Londoniae* as quoted in Stow, *Survey*, I. 79–80.

[10] Stow, *op. cit.*, ii. 30.

[11] *Op. cit.*, I. 101. It has generally been understood that a bonfire was a fire of bones, thus of those dead in the plague. Skeat says as much in his *Etymological Dictionary*, but even he describes a bonfire as one used to celebrate festivals. It is not impossible that *bon* and *bone* were both intended, but with different meanings at different times as Stow here suggests.

CHAPTER NINE

[1] *French Chivalry*, p. 32.

[2] Painter, *op. cit.*

[3] Lewis, *The Allegory of Love*.

[4] *The Romaunt of the Rose*, 1016–32.

[5] *Civilization of the Renaissance in Italy*.

[6] *Romaunt of the Rose*, 539–40.

[7] *Ibid.*, 554–8.

[8] *Ibid.*, 819–22.

[9] *Ibid.*, 855–64, 867–8.

[10] *Ibid.*, 1009–12.

[11] *Ibid.*, 1195–6.

[12] *Ibid.*, 1213–14.

[13] *Ibid.*, 1418–22.

[14] *The Canterbury Tales*, A. 89–90.

[15] *Parlement of Foules*, 24–5.

CHAPTER TEN

[1] Arderne's *De Arte Phisicali et de Cirurgia*.

[2] Warton, Thomas, *The History of English Poetry*, 3 vols., 1840.

[3] Morley, Henry, *English Writers*, 11 vols., 1887–95.

[4] Lambeth MS. 853, reprinted by Furnivall in his *Early English Meals and Manners*.

[5] Furnivall, *op. cit.*, p. xiv.

[6] Furnivall, *op. cit.*, p. lxvi.

[7] *The Book of the Duchesse*, 391–6.

[8] *Ibid.*, 445–8, 459–60.

[9] *La Povretei Rutebeuf.*

[10] *The Canterbury Tales*, A. 2777–9.

[11] *The Canterbury Tales*, A. 619.

[12] *Op. cit.*, 689–91.

[13] *Ibid.*, A. 287–8.

[14] *La Male Regle*, 155–6.

[15] MS. Harl. 4866, 1f. 37.

CHAPTER ELEVEN

[1] Riley, *Memorials*, 248–9.

[2] *Mirour*, 25. 439–40.

[3] *England in the Age of Wycliffe*, p. 195.

CHAPTER TWELVE

[1] *Samson Agonistes*, 1205–7.

[2] *Times Literary Supplement*, 29 November 1974.

[3] If Langland makes no reference to the rebellion, the rebels, at any rate here, make reference to him. His figure of the good ploughman who in the end becomes synonymous with Christ was perhaps more widely known than any other figure in contemporary literature.

[4] Knighton, II. 139.

[5] *The Canterbury Tales*, B. 4584–7.

CHAPTER THIRTEEN

[1] *The Rising in East Anglia.*

[2] Froissart, iv. 77.

[3] Coram Rege Roll 483, Rex 19.

[4] Oman, *The Great Revolt*, p. 74.

BIBLIOGRAPHY

Arderne, John, *De Arte Phisicali et de Cirurgia*, tr. Sir D'Arcy Power, London, 1922.

Barnie, John, *War in Medieval Society*, London, 1974.

Bennet, H. S., *Chaucer and the Fifteenth Century*, Oxford, 1948; *Life on the English Manor*, Cambridge, 1948; *The Pastons and their England*, Cambridge, 1932.

Bird, Ruth, *The Turbulent London of Richard II*, London, 1947.

Brewer, D. S., *Chaucer*, London, 1953; *Chaucer in his Time*, London, 1963; (ed.), *Chaucer and Chaucerians*, Edinburgh, 1966.

Bright, Allan H., *New Light on Piers Plowman*, Oxford, 1948.

Britton, C. E., *Meteorological Chronicle to 1450* (Met. Off. Geoph.), Mem. 8, No. 70.1937.

Cawley, A. C. (ed.), *Chaucer's Mind and Art*, Edinburgh, 1969.

Chadwick, Dorothy, *Social Life in the Days of Piers Plowman*, Cambridge, 1922.

Chaucer, Geoffrey, *The Complete Works*, ed. W. W. Skeat, 7 vols., Oxford, 1894–7.

Chesterton, G. K., *Chaucer*, London, 1932.

Cook, G. H. *Medieval Chantries and Chantry Chapels*, London, 1947.

Coulton, G. G., *Chaucer and his England*, London, 1921; *The Medieval Village*, Cambridge, 1925.

Crow, M. M., and Olson, C. C., *Chaucer Life-Records*, Oxford, 1966.

Cutts, E. L., *Parish Priests and their People*, London, 1914.

Deimling, Hermann and Matthews (eds), *The Chester Plays*, 2 vols, EETS, 1892 and 1916.

Donaldson, E. Talbot, *Piers Plowman, The C-Text and its Poet*, Yale, 1949.

Fairholt, F. W., *Costume in England*, 2 vols., London, 1885.

Froissart, Jean, *Chronicles*, tr. Bourchier, ed. W. P. Ker, 8 vols., Oxford, 1927–8.

Furnivall, Frederick J. (ed.), *Child-Marriages, Divorces and Ratifications*, EETS, 1897; *Early English Meals and Manners*, EETS, 1869; (ed.), *Political, Religious and Love Poems*, EETS, 1866.

Gairdner, J., *Lollardy and the Reformation in England*, 4 vols., 1908–13.

Galbraith, V. H. (ed.), *The Anonimalle Chronicle*, Manchester, 1927.

Gardiner, Dorothy, *English Girlhood at School*, Oxford, 1929.

Gardner, Arthur, *Medieval Sculpture*, Cambridge, 1951.

Gasquet, F. A., *The Black Death*, London, 1908; *English Monastic Life*, London, 1924.

Gesta Abbatum (793–1411), 3 vols., Rolls Series, 1867–9.

Gollancz, Israel (ed.), *The Parlement of the Thre Ages,* London, 1897.

Gordon, E. V. (ed.), *Pearl,* Oxford, 1953.

Gordon, E. V., and Tolkien, J. R. R. (eds), *Sir Gawain and the Green Knight,* Oxford, 1930.

Gower, John, *The Complete Works,* ed. G. C. Macawley, 4 vols., Oxford, 1899–1902.

Harrison, William, *Description of England,* ed. F. J. Furnivall, 2 vols., London, 1877.

Hearne, Thomas (ed.), *Historia vitae et Regni Ricardi II,* Oxford, 1729.

Hecker, I. F. C., *The Epidemics of the Middle Ages,* tr. B. G. Babington, London, 1835.

Hoccleve, Thomas, *The Minor Poems,* ed. F. J. Furnivall, EETS, 1892.

Jusserand, J. J., *English Wayfaring Life in the Middle Ages,* tr. Lucy Toulmin Smith, London, 1891; *Piers Plowman,* tr. 'M.E.R.', London, 1894.

Knighton, Henrici, *Chronicon,* ed. J. R. Lumby, Rolls Series, 2 vols., 1889.

Knoll, K., *London im Mittelalter,* Vienna, 1932.

Knoop, Douglas, and Jones, G. P., *The Medieval Mason,* Manchester, 1967.

Langland, William, *Piers Plowman,* ed. W. W. Skeat, 2 vols., Oxford, 1924.

Leach, A. F., *The Schools of Medieval England,* London, 1915.

Lechler, Gotthard, *John Wycliffe and his English Precursors,* London, 1878.

Lewis, C. S., *The Allegory of Love,* Oxford, 1938.

Longman, W., *The Life and Times of Edward III,* 2 vols., London, 1869.

Lydgate, John, *The Minor Poems,* ed. H. N. MacCracken, EETS, 1934; *A Selection from the Minor Poems,* ed. J. O. Halliwell, London, 1840.

Manly, J. M., *Some New Light on Chaucer,* New York, 1926.

Oman, Charles, *The Great Revolt of 1381,* Oxford, 1906.

Owst, G. R., *Preaching in England,* Cambridge, 1926; *Literature and Pulpit in Medieval England,* Oxford, 1966.

Painter, Sidney, *French Chivalry,* Baltimore, 1940.

Pendrill, Charles, *Old Parish Life in London,* Oxford, 1937.

Pirenne, Henri, *Medieval Cities,* tr. Frank D. Halsey, Princeton, 1939.

Powell, Edgar, *The Rising in East Anglia,* Cambridge, 1896.

Powell, Edgar, and Trevelyan, G. M., *The Peasants' Rising and the Lollards,* London, 1899.

Putnam, Bertha Haven, 'The Enforcement of the Statute of Labourers', in vol. xxxii of *Studies in History, Economics & Public Law,* London, 1908.

Ramsay, L. H., *The Genesis of Lancaster,* Oxford, 1915.

Rees, William, *South Wales and the March, 1284–1415,* Oxford, 1924.

Riley, Henry Thomas (ed.), *Memorials of London and London Life, 1276–1419,* London, 1868.

Rogers, J. E. T., *A History of Agriculture and Prices,* 7 vols., Oxford, 1866–1902.

Rörig, Fritz, *The Medieval Town,* tr. Don Bryant, London, 1967.

Rymer, Thomas, *Foedera,* 20 vols., 1704–35.

Sisam, Kenneth (ed.), *Fourteenth Century Verse and Prose,* Oxford, 1946.

Skeat, Walter W. (ed.), *Pierce the Ploughman's Crede,* EETS, 1867.

Smith, H. Armitage, *John of Gaunt,* London, 1904.

Stow, John, *A Survey of London,* ed. Kingsford, Oxford, 1908.

Strutt, Joseph, *Sports and Pastimes of the People of England,* London, 1876.

Thompson, J. W., *The Medieval Library,* New York, 1957.

Trevelyan, G. M., *England in the Age of Wycliffe,* London, 1920.

Vignoradoff, Sir Paul, *Villainage in England*, Oxford, 1892.

Waddell, Helen, *The Wandering Scholars*, London, 1949.

Walsingham, Thomas, *Chronicon Angliæ*, ed. E. M. Thompson, 1874; *Historia Anglicana*, 2 vols. Rolls Series, 1863.

Wilson, R. M. (ed.), *Ancrene Riwle*, EETS, 1954.

Workman, Herbert B., *John Wyclif*, 2 vols., Oxford, 1926.

Wright, Thomas (ed.), *The Book of the Knight of La Tour-Landry*, EETS, 1868.

INDEX